BEHIND SACRED WALLS

The True Story of My Abuse by Catholic Priests

Michael Roberts

Addicus Books
Omaha, Nebraska

An Addicus Nonfiction Book

ISBN: 978-1-950091-53-9

Typography by Jack Kusler
Cover by Johnathan Constanski

Library of Congress Cataloging-in-Publication Data

Names: Roberts, Michael, 1965—author.
Title: Behind sacred walls : the true story of my abuse by Catholic priests / Michael Roberts.
Description: Omaha, Nebraska : Addicus Books Inc., [2021] |
Identifiers: LCCN 2021041677 | ISBN 9781950091539 (trade paperback) | ISBN 9781950091669 (PDF) | ISBN 9781950091683 (KDL) | IBSN 9781950091676 (EPUB)
Subjects: LCSH: Roberts, Michael, 1965— | Catholic Church—Clergy—Sexual behavior—United States. | Child sexual abuse by clergy—United States—Biography. | Adult child sexual abuse victims—United States.—Biography. | Catholics—United States—Biography.
Classification: LCC BX1912.9 .R57 2021
DDC 261.8/3272088282—dc23
LC record available at https://lccn.loc.gov/2021041677

Addicus Books, Inc.
P.O. Box 45327
Omaha, Nebraska 68145
AddicusBooks.com
Printed in the United States of America
10 9 8 7 6 5 4 3 2 1

To Earl, without whose encouragement, creativity, editing, and friendship, this book would never have come to fruition.

To Lee, who has been my greatest support and dearest friend.

To my husband Johnathan, thank you for showing me unconditional love and for encouraging me to tell the world my story.

To the memory of Johnny, who was the spark that ignited my interest in writing. I miss you.

To Fred, for your support, friendship, and love.

To Peter, a warrior, a friend, and a survivor.

The world is full of suffering.
It is also full of overcoming it.

—Helen Keller (1880–1968)

PROLOGUE

When I was a teenager, everyone in my family was a devout Catholic. We never missed Sunday Mass and we were active in parish activities. The walls of our home were adorned with crucifixes and with pictures of Jesus. And we always adored our parish priests. They all but walked on water. Like all good Catholics, I knew that God was watching every move I made. In all of my years growing up, I knew God was sending me messages, telling me to be a good Catholic. I feared God's wrath if I did something wrong.

Never did I think that my life would plummet into an abyss of abuse and manipulation at the hands of a popular parish priest. But sadly, it happened.

"Please no more!" I said, begging him to stop the sexual assault. Perhaps he would see my distress and stop. But, he didn't.

He shoved my body against the back of the chair. "Relax. No one will know. I will never let your parents find out. This is just between you and me."

"This isn't a good idea. I have to go home," I insisted.

He continued rubbing me. He leaned in and whispered into my ear, "God would just love you for pleasing a priest. We all have needs."

INTRODUCTION

All my life, I had believed the teachings of the Catholic
Church. I was a believer even when a priest, whom I
will refer to as Father Gregory, began sexually abusing me. But
my story is more than just a story of abuse by a single priest.
It's also my account about the total indifference I encountered
when I eventually reported the abuse to the officials of the
Catholic Church back in the early 1990s. In one case, I was
even sexually molested by the priest to whom I first reported
my abuse.

To be clear, this is not the story of a prepubescent child.
Quite the contrary. I was a painfully naive seventeen-year-
old boy in 1983, which is when the abuse started. The age of
consent in my state was sixteen at the time, but I was anything
but consenting. My story is more than one of sexual abuse.
Through my years of abuse, I was totally controlled by the
priest who abused me.

As he destroyed my self-esteem with his constant criticism,
I became easier for him to manipulate. I was conditioned to
respond to him with unquestioned obedience. He dominated
me emotionally, requiring me to always report my whereabouts
to him at all times. If I disobeyed him in any way whatsoever, I
would face his rage. I felt totally powerless. I was always afraid
of him. I feared hurting my parents if they learned of the abuse.
I feared being punished by God. I feared the priest. I saw no
way out. I felt like I was a member of a cult.

To further complicate matters, Father Gregory was a charismatic religious figure, who endeared himself to his parish-

ioners. Everyone in the community admired him, especially Catholic boys, like me.

Father Gregory was quite adept at grooming me. The affable cleric easily infiltrated my family, becoming a weekly guest at our dinner table. My mother was enthralled with his down-to-earth nature and with his clever sense of humor. He ingratiated himself into a position of trust within our family. Both of my parents revered him. To them, he could do no wrong, and they made that perfectly clear to me and to my siblings.

This is the backdrop for my story. The names of all the characters in this book have been changed for privacy reasons. Any likeness to a real Father Gregory Burgess, living or dead, is purely coincidental. The names of cities and places have also been changed.

1

*The exact location of your dream lies
entangled in your childhood memories.*

—Vanshika Dhyani
Poet

I can still remember the musty smell of Peter's basement, paneled in dark oak. We sat together on his green-tweed sofa. A single ray of sunlight streamed through old rust-colored curtains. The only sound you could hear was the fizzing of our carbonated sodas.

Peter Sullivan was one of my first childhood friends. Even as a kid, he was a Dick Van Dyke look-alike, and, like Van Dyke, he had a unique comical streak. He was great fun to be around, and he was quite intelligent as well.

Throughout our grade school years, Peter and I spent a lot of time in his room. As little boys, we played with multicolored, circus toys. I was always envious of the fact that he had his own private space. Built-in bookcases filled one side of the room; they held a hodgepodge of his brother's books and model airplanes. Beyond his brother's room, was another small room where Peter slept. A blue cotton comforter covered his bed, which had been pushed against the wall.

Peter had many toys, but no plastic soldiers. No toy guns. No metal dump trucks. He had only bright, gay, fanciful collections of little animals, circus trains, and circus figures—

1

the people we placed under the carnival's big top. The toys were scattered across the braided rug. We separated the pieces between us, arguing who would acquire more townspeople. We would spend many afternoons in his bedroom, playing with his toys. I was envious of Peter for having so many toys.

When I was in elementary school, I had a lot of friends and was fairly well-liked by everyone. My dad Russell, who was a police officer, often dropped me off at school with me riding on the back of his police motorcycle. All of the kids envied me for getting a ride to school.

Peter always arrived at school with a bagged lunch, prepared by his mother. I, on the other hand, received a round token each morning that was required during the class roll call. That token was my lunch ticket. I would hand it to the lunch lady, who, like all of the lunch ladies, wore white uniforms and black hairnets. One lunchroom lady would hand us kids a brown, plastic tray, as though it was a gift from Tiffany. We'd grab those trays like trained dolphins at SeaWorld. From there, we peered through the foggy glass of the steam tables and made our lunch selection.

As we became teens, Peter and I still spent a lot of time in his basement after school. Only our attention had turned from toy blocks to television. We watched our favorite programs.

Looking back, I remember the times when Peter would turn on the TV and begin flipping through the channels. He would pause at soap operas, at sporting events, and at sitcoms that featured beautiful men. I knew exactly what he was doing—like me, he was admiring handsome men. Could he tell my heart would race whenever a celebrity hunk appeared on the TV screen? Was I given away by my reaction to the shirtless man in the commercial? Probably.

As we grew into our teenage years, Peter and I were dealing with an emerging awareness that we were attracted to boys. We hadn't admitted it to each other, but I think we both sensed it. I certainly didn't fully understand my feelings, yet my curiosity was in overdrive. At the time, I had no idea of the internal struggle I would face in coming to terms with being gay. But much worse, little did I know how being gay would be used against me by a Catholic priest who would abuse me for years.

2

2

There were four of us children in the Robert's family, and like most families, we created a beehive of activity in our kitchen each morning. My goal was to grab the cereal box that featured the most colorful design. I loved retrieving the free toy in the bottom of the cereal box.

Living at home with two deeply religious parents, we children were trained early on to obey the rules expected of good Christians. Not the least of these rules was the expression of gratitude for having enough to eat. We had learned to never complain about the meal that was being served. If we ever said that we didn't care for a certain dish, we were admonished with, "Don't like it? Then starve." Whatever food we had on our plates, we were expected to eat or to suffer the Billy Graham–like sermon about the impoverished children in other countries.

"Your father works all day to put food on this table. Children are starving in other parts of the world," Mother would remind us.

My silent retort would be, why don't you invite those kids over some time? We walked on eggshells, making sure we displayed only our best table manners. We knew better than to ever put our elbows on the table.

My dad had a commanding presence in our household. A handsome man, he was thirty-seven and stood five feet ten inches tall. In pictures I'd seen of him when he was a teenager, he resembled the actor James Dean. As he got older, I thought he looked like the singer Glen Campbell. He was a good man and a good provider, but he was a strict disciplinarian. I often thought of him as the "executioner" within our household. I felt like my regular chores should include sharpening the blade of his guillotine. But I wasn't trained to play the role of Anne Boleyn, even though I often thought I might share her fate.

When my dad spoke, his facial expression alone was enough to make me jump. I can still hear his nightly speech at the dinner table, "You're not leaving this table until you eat everything on your plate. When you're finished, you'll do your homework before that TV gets turned on. I won't tell you a second time."

Would that I were brave enough to reply sarcastically, "I'm so glad you won't make me hear it a second time."

My mom Martha was forty-one. She was of average height, and I always thought she had a Spanish look with her dark eyes and her olive skin. She wore her dark hair at shoulder length. We kids knew she loved us; she always had her heart in the right place. She kept a clean house, and we always had clean clothes. She always had hot meals for us, and she was a good cook, but I must say, her knowledge of spices was limited to salt and pepper. The spice carousel that sat on the counter, was only an ornament. I wondered if my mom's objective was to delude visitors into thinking she used these spices to whip up culinary delights.

Mom grew up with four brothers, two sisters, an acquiescent father, and a strong, tenacious mother. I only saw my grandmother, Mary, once a year, but I looked up to her. Solid as an oak tree, she was a stocky Russian-type, who could probably plow the fields with her bare hands. She was an extremely hard worker who cultivated a garden, tended to household chores, and raised seven children. Mom's father was also a hard worker, rather meek, and very submissive to his wife. He had a playful side—I likened him to Charlie Chaplin. He was an unpredictable comic.

With traits inherited from both of her parents, my mom was the strong, silent type—the glue that held our family together. She was also my emotional safety net, a sanctuary in those times when I needed comfort from the ways of the world. I was very close to my mom, and if I could have tucked her into the pocket of my bell-bottom jeans, or into my lunch box, I would have. She was the only person in my life who gave me the attention that I so desperately craved. Unfortunately, the burdensome workload she carried seldom allowed her time to be attentive.

Still, some of my fondest memories are of me nestled in her lap. I can still recall the floral scent of her freshly-laundered blouses. We would rock rhythmically in a black, antique rocker. She would whisper words of assurance that seemed to make everything right with the world.

Because my mother was also a Canadian citizen, when I was a child, I had nightmares—traumatic scenes of her being forced to leave the country. Upon awakening from these horrific visions, I would always run to find her, confirming she hadn't abandoned me. I needed my matriarchal security blanket psychologically wrapped around me at all times.

As I grew older, I began to feel that my mom was probably emotionally wounded as a child. This was surprising because her mother was a strong role model. But, strength has many faces, and my mother's strength was found in her uncanny ability to right any ship and to smooth the turbulent waters. She was the one who would handle any crisis that arose.

My father's vision of his paternal role was old-school. Sovereignty over his wife and silent children was understood. It was difficult seeing my mother subjugated, restrained from having an opinion. She was victimized by the stereotypical male dominance our religion espoused. At times, I resented my father for this unquestioned oligarchy over which he held court. I remember once, in my early twenties, convincing my mother to stand up for herself. Sadly, it seemed to work only for that one moment in time.

"Martha, that was stupid!" my father had shouted from a distance. I don't recall the cause of his anger.

"Dad, that's no way to talk to Mom!" I whispered to Mom, "Call him an asshole."

"Russell, you're an asshole," she shouted, startled that those words came out her mouth.

As he came into to the room, I just smiled, pleased that my mother had stood up to him.

As punishment for our crime, my father spent the next few days not talking to Mother and me. It was as if Mom was Joan of Arc, who betrayed by King Charles VII for her monstrous ingratitude. I, however, got the brunt of his retribution—he completely ignored me whenever I was nearby. I always had thoughts of running away from home.

This ludicrous quote from the Bible is one of many archaic examples of an oppressive religion that reinforces sexism: "I will [say] therefore that the younger woman marries, bears children, guides the house, and gives none occasion to the adversary to speak reproachfully. For some are already turned aside after Satan."

My father was an only child of parents who spoiled him. From what I've been told, his parents never showed much affection to each other; however, my dad's mother, Victoria, was affectionate toward him. However, she had passed away by the time I was born. From photos and conversations, I surmised that she was an emotionally strong-minded woman, but physically frail. I often heard stories involving infidelities between my grandfather, William, and another woman, but I never wanted to believe such stories. I considered it gossip.

My grandfather remarried after Victoria died, and his new wife, Marge, was the only paternal grandmother I had ever known. To deny her would be to deny the importance of Santa Claus, the Tooth Fairy, and the Easter Bunny. It wasn't until I was in my young adult years that my father confirmed the stories about my grandfather—he wasn't faithful to his wife. The gossip I had heard in my youth was true. My grandfather had a mistress, Marge. What a devastating revelation! I grew to dislike the adulterer and his concubine, Marge, whom I had to acknowledge as my grandmother.

When my grandfather died, the family distanced itself from Marge. But I was always reminded of his unfaithfulness when I visited his grave. Interestingly, he had both his wives' names on his headstone.

In my late teens, while working as a busboy at the local steak house, I ran into Marge. She was a poorly-dressed, feeble, old woman, yet I still recognized her as my step-grandmother. I was surprised to feel a connection to her. Was it, perhaps, in my mind, that I, too, was poorly dressed, but in the uniform of a person working in a low-skilled position with seemingly no prospects? Was it her welcoming eyes?

In our brief encounter, she asked how the family was, and I gave her the customary, "Oh, we're all doing fine, thank you." It was in that moment that I recalled how she comforted me and held me in her lap once when I was a toddler. I knew at that moment that she needed to be acknowledged, to be emotionally rescued from her own loneliness. I made a special effort to engage her in conversation. It was soon after our brief conversation that I forgave my grandfather for his infidelity, and I let go of my resentment toward Marge for having been his mistress.

Another powerful memory of my grandfather—his leg had been severed in a train accident when he was younger, and he had a wooden, prosthetic leg. He would often fascinate me by rolling up his pant leg and allow me to examine his prosthesis. He would tell me to knock on his leg with my knuckles. Each time I knocked on it, he would always say, "Come in," and we would have a great laugh about it.

To us children, he was a warm-hearted, loving man who knew how to show his affection to his grandchildren. When he passed away, I went to the wake. For me, it was a double trauma: seeing my dad weep and seeing my dead grandfather. He was dressed in a suit and tie, lying motionless in what I thought was a rather fancy casket. I still remember the muted sobs in the room, the flowers on pedestals, and the strange smell of what must have been preservative chemicals. Was I supposed to cry? I didn't understand death, but despite the emotional trauma, it didn't seem to be all that horrifying.

I think because my own father may not have had all the tender loving care he needed as a child, he may have come up short on knowing how to be emotionally close to his children. But he was a hard-working man and a good provider. He would often take on a second job, so our Christmas mornings would be full of joy. We kids, still clad in our footed pajamas, would run into the living room where we would find piles of packages, all in bright Christmas wrapping. I would virtually dive into the treasure piles, looking for any package labeled: To Michael.

Regardless of the seemingly happy holidays, I lacked the emotional support I craved so desperately. Simply put, I was afraid of my father—the boss. To question or to challenge him would be seen as mutiny on the ship. He would need only to give us that indignant facial expression for us to flee like cockroaches. Provoking him was like waking a sleeping dragon. Growing up with a man who was tough and unapproachable made life difficult for his children. Maybe he thought he was preparing us for a hard world. Who knows?

My father always made himself the center of attention, using vaudeville-like antics, by removing his false upper teeth or by telling politically incorrect jokes, all in order to receive the attention he himself craved.

"Can I have the stage now Dad?" Never. He was the star of his own comedy series *Everybody Loves Russell,* and anyone daring to seek attention at his expense only caused him to silently pout like a child who lost his balloon.

On the other hand, I felt sad for my father. I knew his soul was wounded when he lost his job as a police officer. As the result of a lot of politics, he was pushed out of the police force. Being a cop had been his lifelong dream. He was never quite the same after he lost that job. He seemed rather beaten down and resorted to taking odd jobs such as driving a delivery truck or cleaning offices late at night.

I often accompanied him on some of these delivery assignments to help in any way I could, even if it was just to keep him company. He was the leader, and I was his sidekick—like Batman and Robin. I delighted in riding along when he drove a massive truck that delivered hamburger buns to McDonalds' restaurants. I loved the fact that we often got freebies. Many kind store managers gave us glorious bounties of cheeseburgers, soda, and apple pies. Most likely my adorable smile and prepubescent cuteness had something to do with it.

Looking back, I showed empathy for my father. In a way, I tried to parent him. I could see the pain in his eyes, and I attempted to lighten any portion of that burden I could. I felt guilty that he had to sacrifice so much for his children. Because he and I weren't very close, I thought I was more of a burden than the other kids. A good Catholic boy, I took on some of the emotional burden for the death of his dream. Henry Thoreau once said: "The mass of men lead lives of quiet desperation."

I may sound like I am contradicting myself. On one hand, I wasn't close to my dad, but he also was a Superman to me. Miraculously, he eluded multiple, near-fatal situations throughout my childhood years. First, when I was little, I recall

Dad contracting a deadly fungus that began growing in his lungs. I vaguely remember a priest giving him his last rites because his health was deteriorating rapidly. It was by luck that a young intern discovered that it was streptococcus. Massive doses of antibiotics saved Dad's life.

Another time, my brother was cutting down a tree with a chain saw. My father miscalculated where the tree would fall. The tree landed on top of him, breaking his back. Apparently fueled by adrenaline, my brother was able to lift the tree off Dad, much to the amazement of the firefighters, who responded to the scene of the accident.

My dad had several other brushes with death. He survived a bad car accident—a snowplow hit him one winter, splitting his car in half. Fortunately, he walked away from the accident. Then, once when he was on duty as a police officer, he was chasing a fleeing suspect who fired a shot at him. Fortunately, the bullet hit his holster and spared him of a gunshot wound. I don't recall what the suspect's offense was, but he got away. Our family was grateful that my dad, the Superman, had escaped more brushes with death than the proverbial cat with nine lives.

Dad also worked part-time at a local truck stop. His duties included directing traffic, answering motorists' questions, and checking trucker's paperwork. One evening my father's coworker mentioned that he was building a pet cemetery in a nearby town. He was planning to sell lots to pet owners who had lost their beloved pets. Apparently, it was a trend in California at the time. My dad's coworker was hoping the trend would catch on locally.

He asked my dad, "You know anyone who could do some landscaping for some extra cash, Russ?"

"My son, Michael, likes yardwork. I'll ask him."

The next morning, I accepted the assignment. Dad thought it would be a good chance for me to learn the value of a dollar. I was thrilled. At thirteen, I had nabbed my first job that would give me spending money. Yeah! I could buy the checkered pants and a wide-collar polka dotted shirt like the one Davy Jones wore on the TV show, *The Monkees*.

The next Saturday morning, I was eager to begin my job. I wondered, how high in the corporate world of pet cemeteries can one go? Dad dropped me off at the pet graveyard, and I met the owner. He was a tall, thin, unshaved man. From his raspy voice, I'm guessing that he considered tobacco as one of the major food groups. He explained that he wanted me to make a walking pathway by clearing a strip of weeds. Then, handing me a shovel, he walked toward his truck. A man of few words, he definitely would not land a job in the field of communications. As he stepped into his vehicle, he shouted, "Hey boy, that small building behind you is my office. The side door is unlocked if you need the bathroom."

"Thank you," I shouted back as though going to the bathroom was an extra bonus.

"Just don't touch anything!" were his final words. He climbed into his dilapidated pickup and kicked up a cloud of dust as he sped off.

Alone in the silent pet graveyard, I began the task at hand. As the day started getting hotter, the sweat started to trickle down my brow. I pulled off my T-shirt. I couldn't help but notice I was beginning to develop some muscles. I wouldn't call myself an athlete, but I was an active kid. I guess you could say I was bulking up. For my age, I had a tapered waist and broad shoulders. I gulped down half a bottle of water and continued pulling weeds. Is this what it feels like to be stranded in the Sahara Desert, I thought to myself?

I had been working for several hours, when I noticed, out of the corner of my eye, a dark blue sedan pulling into the driveway of the property. It stopped about forty feet from where I was working.

"Hello, can you help me?" the man yelled from his car.

As I walked toward his vehicle, I noticed, much to my surprise, that the man was wearing makeup—women's makeup! Was he a retired clown or a masculine flat-chested woman without her wig?

As I got closer, I could see that he was wearing layers of caked, bronze makeup. He must have needed a trowel to apply it. And he didn't stop with only the bronze makeup. He had rosy, red blush on his cheeks, and he wore black eyeliner.

Michael Roberts

Nervous at seeing such a sight, I tried to sound calm and avoided eye contact. "What can I help you with?" I asked.
"I seem to be lost. I'm trying to find the entrance to the highway."
"I am not from around here," I responded. "I'm just here working for the day."
"Looks like hard work."
"Yes, it's tough and dirty."
"You look like a hunk without that shirt on," he said.
"Thank you," I said sheepishly. I found the conversation uncomfortable. I could "feel" his eyes undressing me. At the same time, some force deep inside me was curious. I just stood there.
"Can I see more of that hunky body of yours?" he asked.
"I don't think that's a good idea," I replied.
"Do you have a bathroom I can use?" he asked.
In that moment, I realized he wanted to satisfy his sexual appetite, using me as his boytoy. I thought to myself: Is this man gay? Is this what I will become if I'm gay? It was a sobering thought. All my life I had followed a religious, moral path, but what if I'm different? Abnormal? If I were gay, would I find a trail of remorse, disgrace, and damnation?
I pointed toward the owner's office building. "You can use the bathroom inside the building over there."
"Do you mind coming with me, because I'm uncomfortable going inside alone?"
Apprehensive, I walked with him over to the small building, and we entered the side door.
The room was filled with cardboard boxes, piles of old newspapers, and dirty coffee cups. Cigarette butts were strewn all over the floor as if an army of chain-smokers had just held their annual convention here. I pointed to my right, directing him to the restroom.
"I don't need to go to the bathroom now but thank you for showing me where it's located. I just wanted to be alone with you," he said. He must have sensed my innocence, because he moved toward me, positioning his body so that he was blocking my exit.
Oh my God! I was standing next to a deviant, bohemian vampire who wanted to exploit me, drain my innocence. I

11

stood frozen like a department store mannequin. How do I stop him from proceeding with this assault? Does he have a knife? Will he strangle me? Nervously, I moved back until I bumped into a table, further trapping me. He reached for my zipper and began unzipping my pants. Time froze. I could hear the clicking sound of each tooth on my zipper as he slowly opened my jeans. I tried to squirm away as he began groping me.

"Don't you dare," he said, ordering me not to make a sound. With his other arm gripping my thigh, he had me pinned. Giving into my fear, I allowed him to continue the ordeal. Pulling down my jeans and underwear, he exposed my penis. He dropped to his knees and began his oral copulation. Minutes felt like hours. Feeling repulsed, I zoned out momentarily, escaping to a faraway place. Am I a lost boy in Neverland, never growing up to understand adulthood? Just then, I heard the sound of a car approaching. Was it the owner? My father? What if one of them found me like this? Now, I panicked.

"My father's picking me up here any moment. That could be him now."

Without a single word, the man stood up, walked to the door, and vanished.

I was shaken by the experience, but I was also confused by the odd connection I felt with this stranger. He must have been gay. My confusion aside, I mostly felt shame over the experience. Deep shame.

Was this another moment of trauma in my life? Yes! I had never been molested and never understood the emotional complexity and the level of damage it created.

When my father arrived to pick me up after his shift had ended, I was so relieved. Did I escape a situation that could have been more dangerous to me? Could I have been killed? I will never know! I was silent during the car ride home. I felt dirty. As soon as I was in the house, I jumped into the shower and used a brush and soap to cleanse my body. Days passed before the mental fog began to lift. I would have to try to forget this bizarre memory now deep in my psyche. I never spoke a word to anyone about the makeup man until years later, when I told a friend.

Days and weeks passed by as I questioned what the experience meant at the pet cemetery. Why did I let this happen to me? Was this wrong in God's eyes? This sexual experience pained me for a long time—the shame was so deep. But, like any sexually curious teen, I needed answers. I would frequently grab *The Joy of Sex*, a book that my parents had carelessly placed on the highest shelf in the basement bookcase.

Did my parents want us kids to find this instructional book about sex? Maybe! Being an inquisitive teen, I would flip through the pages examining the black-and-white sketches of men and woman in what I thought were bizarre positions. This was no Twister board game from Milton Bradley. When I could sneak to the basement, I would flip through pages, trying to make sense of human sexuality.

At around the age of thirteen, I had begun to touch myself. I didn't understand the autonomic responses or the biological urges of the male libido, but I found pleasure in this "investigation."

In my early teens, I began to recognize that my body was changing. "Why am I growing hair all over? Why is my voice changing? When did I start getting muscles? Why do I wake up with wet underwear? Could someone please explain all this?" Only later would I learn about nocturnal emissions, but there would be no answers to any of my questions about coming into manhood. Such taboo topics would never be addressed in my house.

I grew more curious about the male figure. Thoughts and images streamed through my mind. I was drawn to the sexual messages I saw on TV—men in the shower, lathering up with Irish Spring soap. Fruit of the Loom T-shirts stretched over muscular torsos. Handsome hunks shaving. Half-naked men, appearing out of the shower's mist, promoting a cologne. At school, I watched boys go by in the hallway, noting the shapes of their physiques. After gym classes, I stole glances of naked boys in the showers. Yes, it was becoming more apparent to me that I was attracted to boys and to men.

I also spent a few nights at Peter's house. Although we were both naive and inexperienced, I believe we both knew "something" might transpire during one of these sleepovers. We were like two male butterflies attracted to the same nectar.

At Peter's, we always slept in his basement. This was our secret boy's club. With such privacy and surging hormones, could one of these nights reveal a sexually brave warrior? Often, Peter would make sexual comments and innuendos that we both understood. He'd say things such as, "I'll clean the basement after we sleep downstairs—you know how a vacuum sucks, don't you?" Or, "Want a bite of my Twinkie?" His flirtatious remarks were not lost on me. Once, he deep-throated a banana in front me. Not exactly subtle, but he could sense my reaction. I loved his sexual courage. Would I someday earn a badge for such courage?

Even though a part of me was uncomfortable with his sexual innuendos, I also found them titillating. One evening at Peter's home, we carried down snacks to the basement—Peter with his preservative-filled Twinkies and I with my healthy apple and popcorn. Peter often joked about how preservatives were preserving his insides.

That night, only one small light illuminated the basement. As the minutes ticked by, I wondered who would make the first sexual "chess move." As the evening progressed, we shuffled our positions closer to each other, like two metals attracted by a magnetic field. Was Peter expecting something to happen? Would my hidden warrior awaken? Nervously, I extended my arm in slow motion toward his left. Resting my fingers upon his warm smooth skin, I waited for any reaction. He lay motionless, giving me no signal to stop. My heart racing, I continued advancing my hand toward his stomach, nervously making my way down to his naval. I was like Ferdinand Magellan, preparing to explore a new, uncharted region.

"Am I brave enough to complete this quest?" I took a deep breath and reached further down, wrapping my hand around his young manhood. I did it! I reached the summit!

Then, as soon as I touched him, I immediately let go. Had I gone too far?

"You like touching me?" he whispered.

"I'm sorry. I didn't mean to," I responded.

"Don't be sorry. I liked it."

"I feel weird and nervous about what we're doing."

"Don't worry. No one needs to know."

"What if your mom walks down the stairs? I'm really nervous about getting caught."

"Relax, we would hear movements, creaking sounds; we can cover up with the blanket and pretend we're asleep."

We spent the next several minutes nervously touching each other. We stopped abruptly, however, as though we were nearing the edge of a cliff. We didn't want to fall any further into the abyss of shame and guilt.

The next morning, we awoke, acting as though last night's performance had never occurred. Perhaps we were slightly embarrassed, but I think we both took some measure of comfort from the experience. From that point forward, I felt closer to Peter. Still, I considered my attraction to boys as a sickness. I believed Peter also felt like me—we were defective. A heavy burden to carry.

Peter's home was a five-minute bike ride away, so I did a lot of pedaling back and forth. I needed to be around him. Whenever I stepped inside Peter's house, I took in the scent of home-cooked meals. The interior of the home looked like a Norman Rockwell painting. I loved how Peter's parents were always so welcoming to me. I soaked in the attention they gave me. I desperately wanted to be noticed, to feel like I mattered.

Peter's mother was a sweet woman and was also my den mother for the Webelos Cub Scouting chapter that I had joined with Peter. I had to climb the ranks from bobcat, tiger cub, wolf, and bear until I reached the highest rank of Webelos. Later in life, I found it ironic, if not humorous, that the gay slang dictionary listed gay men in categories such as: bear, pup, wolf, bull, cub, gym rat, or otter.

I also loved the attention Peter's father gave me. Because I was not emotionally close to my dad, I craved any attention I could get from grown men. I remember Peter's father taking me to my first of many observatory experiences. At a nearby observatory, a dome-shaped roof would slide open, exposing the moon and a sky full of stars. I'd look at the night sky through the lens of the large telescope. As I stood mesmerized, Peter's dad would point out planets, stars, and constellations. Peter and I were always joking around. When his dad would head downstairs to the main entry, we would turn the telescope skyward and make jokes about looking at Uranus. And, yes, the pun was intended.

Peter's father was also one of our Boy Scout leaders, who went on area camping trips. I remember one such trip; we stayed in old, wooden lean-to's that were open to the elements on one side. I was no Daniel Boone, but I was willing to man up and to brave the outdoors. The evening was cold, so we all climbed into our sleeping bags. Peter, who had a low tolerance for discomfort, faked a sickness so that his father would drive him home. I knew exactly what he was doing, and I was envious.

Why couldn't I be brave like Peter and tell a white lie in order to leave this awful, forsaken camping trip? A good Catholic boy would never lie. I feared God's wrath. I knew the Almighty watched every move I made. Hello God, can I use the heat from that burning bush right now! I spent the whole night shivering, waiting for daybreak.

I had always looked up to Peter; I believed he was much smarter and more disciplined than I could ever be. I saw myself as an emotional kid, filled with fear and self-loathing. Most of the self-loathing was related to my realization that I was gay. Therefore, I felt I was unworthy of happiness or of expressing my opinion. I believed I was always being punished by God when I least expected it.

Growing up, I was the second child in a family of four. My sister Donna was a year older than me. She was the bookworm in the family. By the time she reached high school, she had rather large breasts; the boys would say, "Hello Jugs," when they saw her in the hall. Although she never talked about it, I'm sure such remarks were hurtful.

My brother Andrew was one year younger than me, and my brother Matt was six years younger. We played together as children, but as we became teens, we didn't have much in common; my brothers were into sports games and liked to tinker with things around the house with Dad; they liked to watch him work on cars. I, on the other hand, tended the gardens, organized the garage, and decorated my room.

Still, I believed we were a fairly normal American family. We argued. We laughed. We played together. We kids tossed lawn darts, climbed a large maple tree in the backyard, and entertained ourselves with the croquet set. Two of my fondest memories are building tents out of blankets in the living room and playing hide and seek. Each of us would take turns going upstairs, while the rest of us would scamper to find the best hiding spots. I often hid behind a black leather bar my father built in one corner of the room. The rest of Dad's stylish man cave featured a refrigerator, deer-head gun rack, ceramic mugs painted with nude women, and a few neon beer signs. To me, it all seemed a bit contradictory to his religious morality.

We spent summers swimming with friends in my family's above-ground pool. We also played street games, such as kick the can, with the neighborhood kids. We spent winters sliding down a snow-packed hill in the backyard. We would build mounds of snow higher and higher, believing ourselves to be daredevil skiers.

I remember, as a child, always feeling that I was the cursed child within the family—a black sheep, who was different from the others. I always thought God was sending me messages, telling me to change my ways, to be a better Catholic. For example, one time I was walking through our backyard when our pool collapsed. In an instant, a wall of water was cascading toward me. I braced for the impact, but the water missed me by inches. This must have been a sign from God. I was Damien, from the movie, *The Omen,* or so I thought. With just one glance, I could make a swimming pool collapse.

I remember another traumatic experience. Our beloved family dog Charlie, a pure white Samoyed Husky, escaped from our yard. He darted between my legs, through the fence, and into the street, where he was hit by a next-door neighbor, who was driving his pickup truck at an excessive speed. Charlie was killed. What a devastating blow. Was this more punishment from God? Was Charlie's death a sign that God wanted me to mend my ways, to do a better job obeying the Catholic dogma?

I think one of the reasons why I was never really close to my father was because I believed he sensed that I was gay. Of course, it was never discussed, but I think he knew. Was he embarrassed by it? Even ashamed of me? For either of my parents to admit that their son was homosexual would mean they had failed in raising me as a Catholic. Homosexuality, in the eyes of the church, was a mortal sin—pontificated from the

Pope in Rome all the way down to the priests in small-town, parish churches. The churche's stance was that such a lifestyle was a moral disorder and completely contrary to natural law. They also believed that children should be shielded from homosexuals at all costs. To me, it seemed that religious people believed Hell was a justifiable end for such deviant behavior.

Maybe if I had been one of the masculine, car-fixing, sport-loving young men in our family, my father and I would have shared a closer bond. We tried many times, but my father was emotionally unavailable to me. On some level, I think we resented each other. I remember the time he took me to see Father Amos, at our parish church, because we were fighting constantly. Dad thought I needed to be a more obedient child, although I believed that my father just wanted me to have a "tough exterior" like him.

Sitting across from Father Amos, my father sought to enlist the priest's help. "Michael is too rebellious and disrespectful," he told the priest. I guess my dad was looking for some "back-up" to show his parental authority. As I recall, our visit to the priest had been preceded by my talking back to my father over something.

"You must honor your mother and your father," replied Father Amos, quoting the Bible.

That quote from the Bible was contradictory and psychologically damaging from my perspective. This advice surely could not be true for all children. I was not physically abused or molested by my parents, but what about children who were? Should they still honor their parents? The Bible is a book filled with topics such as slavery, torment, torture, massacres, plagues, murder, sexism, racism, bigotry, xenophobia, rape, ostracism, killing nonbelievers, death to homosexuals, and even slaying of children. Fun reading for all!

As a teen, growing up in a world that wanted to get rid of gay people was frightening to me. For me, all these thoughts and mind chatter were emotionally exhausting. I was chronically anxious, fearful, and even paranoid.

Despite our trying, my father and I never seemed to connect on a deep level. I spent many years hoping he would notice me in my endless attempts at doing extra chores, gaining his approval; however, my efforts always ended up with no recognition and no accolades to bolster my desperate need for paternal acceptance. At the age of thirteen, I had a paper route delivering newspapers on my bicycle. I loved the idea of having my own money and learning to be self-reliant. My customers liked me. I always liked it when they were available to talk to me. I shared a room with my two brothers until my parents allowed me to move into the basement. The room was only a tiny space off the main room in the basement, but I was happy to have my privacy. The space was exclusively mine. I took pride in my room, always keeping it clean and organized.

3

As a Catholic family, we had framed pictures of Jesus on the walls and statues of religious figures throughout the home. I even remember my mom having a tiny plastic statue of Jesus that glowed in the dark. It was not uncommon to see her in her rocking chair at night, holding her beads, reciting her rosary. I can recall, during part of my adolescent years, I wore a scapular necklace, a devotional cloth, around the house. A few times I wore it to school, under my shirt. The church believed that wearing this necklace would save me from suffering eternal hellfire and damnation. The scapular was composed of two tiny pieces of cloth connected in the middle by narrower strips of cloth. To me, it looked like two tea bags connected by a long string.

From the day we kids were born, we were taught to fear God—it was all I knew. I did love what I thought was the security that a religious home provided. On Saturday mornings, we attended catechism, or as I called it, religious military boot camp. Can I get a dishonorable discharge? Here we learned creeds, prayers, sacraments, commandments, and the difference between venial and mortal sins. How I hated giving up my summers to a boring church classroom. Sunday mornings, we always dressed in our finest threads for church. I would sit in the pew, daydreaming about what we'd be eating for dinner when we arrived home. Sometimes we'd have daisy ham, a boneless, smoked pork. Other times we'd have roast beef, Minute Rice, and Birds-Eye vegetables.

I was a fidgety child during Mass. I considered the words coming from the pulpit an annoyance, like a mosquito buzzing in my ear. But I always enjoyed the singing. When church

Michael Roberts

service ended, I felt as free and happy as Tweety Bird, escaping from the clutches of Sylvester, the evil puddy-tat. I remember how proud my parents were when I became an altar boy. I was now in the big league with God. Being an altar boy brought honor and prestige to our family. And the job had its perks. Every year the resident priest and a few chaperones would take all the altar boys to a nearby amusement park. We used church money to ride the rollercoaster, knock over bowling pins, and eat lobster dinners.

As an altar boy, I always arrived at church fifteen minutes before Mass began. I often thought the massive sanctuary looked like a gigantic, inverted boat, with exposed hull and beams. But, this ship had paneled walls, marble floors, and red-carpeted chancel. The stage was set for the pomp and pageantry. Please, paparazzi, no pics!

The priest would welcome the altar boys one by one, assigning each of us a duty to perform. Our chores ranged from carrying a large candle or cross or pouring the water and wine from a pitcher. The priest would also assign two altar boys to hold the communion plate during communion. This was a round plate, which the priest held under a parishioner's chin to avoid the communion Eucharist from falling to the floor. The Eucharist, which symbolized the body of Jesus Christ, was a round wafer made of flour and water.

Just before the service, the priest would disappear into a room called the vestibule, where he would dress in his ensemble consisting of his cincture, gown, stole around his neck, chasuble (similar to a Mexican shawl), and an orphrey (a scarf-like garment). Was this religious drag or a costume for the pompous?

On one occasion, I was given the task of ringing the hand bells when the priest would hold up the Eucharist and the wine, the symbol of Christ's blood. Once, when it was my time to "Ring Them Bells" (great title for a song), I wasn't paying attention and forgot to ring the bell! The priest glared at me. Believe me, I rang the bell. In fact, I shook the hell out of that bell. It was my "Fuck you" moment. It was, however, a moment that frightened me. Had I once again failed God? It was a moment of shame.

I also remember my first time in the confessional. We kids sat outside in a row of pews toward the back of the church, waiting our turns to confess. When it was my turn, I entered the tiny room the size of a phone booth. (Remember phone booths?) It would have seemed appropriate for the priest to have called out numbers, like at a deli counter. I will take a pound of disgrace, package of humiliation, and a small container of indignity. There were two confessional booths; a light outside the booths would go off when a room was available.

When the light flashed on, I slid back a heavy red curtain and stepped inside. It was dark with only a stream of light coming in under the curtain. I genuflected and knelt on the kneeler—a padded board.

I faced a screened window. Nervous, I was thinking of any sins I should report to this omniscient, all-powerful Wizard of Oz. The sound of the closing door from the other side indicated the priest was finished with the transgressor in the next booth, and it was my turn to confess. I could see only a shadow enter the other side of the confessional. Only the Shadow knows! I swallowed hard and hoped for the best.

As the priest settled into his seat, I made the sign of the cross and said, "Forgive me Father for I have sinned." Then, I listed what I considered my sins. I was obligated to tell the truth because lying to Christ's emissary was a one-way ticket to Hell, a ride to the underworld.

"Father, I yelled at my sister twice," I confessed. "I didn't do the chores when I was asked. I lied once this week." I figured those things would qualify as sins.

Then, the priest read the prayer of absolution. "God the Father of mercies, through the death resurrection of your son, you have reconciled the world to yourself and sent the Holy Spirit among us for the forgiveness of sins. Through the ministry of the church, may grant you pardon and peace. And I absolve you of your sins, in the name of the Father, and the Son, and of the Holy Spirit."

I responded, "Amen."

Now, filled with shame, I waited for the priest, who was both judge and jury, to deliberate and to hand down his verdict. Typically, he listed several prayers for me to say and suggested that I "do better in the future."

Michael Roberts

I thought to myself: Was this a joke? I should have worked harder at misbehaving if the only punishment was my promise to behave. But, I feared the priest and would never talk back to him. I would be punished with eternal hellfire. The church and the pious stature of the priests was always a big part of our family and to question or to dispute those teachings would cause me to be thrown overboard from this ship called religion. I loved my mother so much that the very thought of hurting her feelings, over the faith she so passionately embraced, was out of the question. I chose to believe every word written in the Bible or mandated by the church. I banned any thoughts that confused me about this religious dogma. I continued following the church like a rat trailing the Pied Piper.

In the second grade, I prepared myself for First Communion. This religious ceremony is the continuation of Baptism in the waters of Christ. My parents would witness me accepting the church and the teachings of Jesus. First Communion would reaffirm my faith and destiny within the church as an adult.

April 1981. It was the date of my confirmation ceremony. I was advised to have a confirmation name ready. A confirmation name was to be that of a biblical figure or a saint. I chose Christopher because I had an odd interest with the movie *Blue Lagoon* and its leading, handsome man Christopher Atkins. I figured his tattered loincloth would have made anyone genuflect.

To further my religious bond, in the Boy Scouts, at the age of twelve, I worked for six months to receive the Ad Altare Dei Award; it was a badge for Christian youths who pledged to develop a fully Christian way of life in the faith community. A few years later, on November 29, 1984, I earned the rank of Eagle Scout, the highest rank one can achieve within the Boy Scouts of America. My parents were proud of me that day; they even held a celebration for me at the church hall. My fellow scouts and family members joined me to celebrate my achievement. Standing in front of my scout master, I was presented with my eagle-shaped medal. He pinned the medallion onto my shirt

23

pocket, as though I had single-handedly saved my comrades during battle. I also received a letter "signed" by Ronald Reagan. It was not until years later that I recognized that Ronald Reagan was part of that bigoted tribe that quietly ignored some gay issues. Even though he opposed the California initiative to prohibit gays/lesbians from teaching in public schools, he continued not to speak of the horrific HIV/AIDS crisis that killed thousands of Americans. Only at the end of his second term did he mention this epidemic, but the loss was already too great.

In hindsight, receiving the scout award was another reminder that I belonged to two institutions that promoted bigotry and discrimination. The Catholic Church and the Boy Scouts of America, both of which prohibited gay boys from joining their organizations. Despite the fact that I was being honored, this ceremony added to my confusion about life.

When it was time to enter high school, I went to public school, and Peter went to a private school. But we were somehow able to hold on to a fragment of friendship, seeing each other on occasion.

In high school, I played freshman football for one season. I did it solely to please my father, who was an avid sports fan. I hated every minute of football but marched into battle. My fairly rugged, athletic body certainly allowed me to pass as a legitimate member of the football team, but I had no talent for football. At every practice and at every game, I was miserable. I felt trapped. I suffered the humiliation of name-calling by my teammates. The jocks saw me as quiet and probably gay. They were relentless at provoking me and at harassing me. Fag, queer, and homo were just some of the insults hurled at me. Maybe they saw me eyeing the padding they wore on their buttocks.

Humor aside, I took all of the insults quietly—I didn't want to provoke the bullies. But still, every insult was painful. In today's world, these football boys would be called "bullies," but back then, bullying was, for the most part, overlooked by the school system.

Michael Roberts

Some of the verbal abuse I suffered was likely prompted by the fact that I wore fashionable clothes. I loved clothes, and I was not one to take a fashion risk. Also, my demeanor was, I'm sure, less than macho. While in high school, I had carefully arranged pictures of Duran Duran, an eighties pop group, hanging on my bedroom walls. The band's trademark was their androgynous makeup, teased hair, and snazzy outfits. I remember dreaming that I, too, could be as unique as this group and wear the attire of my choosing. To this day, I have a photo, hidden in a box, that contains photos of me dressed in sky blue parachute pants with a matching vest, white jacket, and a chic hat, wrapped in a scarf. Can I join the band, please? I knew this outfit was "screaming" gay, but the allure of fashion and style was too enticing to resist. I wanted to wear clothing from the decade's well-known designers: Comme des Garcon, Gautier, and Issey Miyake to name a few. In those days, many malls had a chain store called Chess King. It was a store, especially popular with the gay community, where one could buy such flamboyant attire. I considered myself a nonconformist rebel creating my own path...rather than following someone else's path.

I wanted to be a model or an actor and I held that dream deep within the recesses of my mind. As a young boy, it seemed I was always desperate for attention. Realizing how I suffered with those thoughts still brings tears to my eyes. My only escapes were my phonograph records, my love of nature, time with our family dog, Charlie, and my dreams of travel and fashion. *GQ Magazine* and the *International Male* catalog were my "Bibles." Wherever I could find a copy, I would sneak a peek.

Feeling tortured by my fellow schoolmates, I felt the need to kiss any girl who showed interest in me. I believed this would prove to the high school bullies that I was a heterosexual Casanova. My chance arrived one evening at a party given by my friend Patrick, a young man who was also heterosexually challenged. Milling about his front yard, I prepared myself for the ritual of adolescent necking. The reputed high school slut, Regina, was like a 7-Eleven, always open for business, so I was told. She followed me into the

25

dark shadows of the porch. When the time came to kiss her, I braced myself and did the best I could. It was awkward, to say the least. Unfortunately, the kiss did nothing to change who I was. I was still the quiet homo.

The experience with Regina was one of two experiences I had kissing a girl. My second time was toward the end of my senior year in high school. I was still working as a busboy and dishwasher at the local steak house. A tall, thin red-headed girl, Betty, worked there, too. I enjoyed spending time with her on our breaks; we'd laugh and be silly. I only wanted a friendship, but she seemed to hint at wanting more. The ironic thing about this situation was that her brother was gay and her best friend's brother was gay. I was more attracted to them. But, being closeted, I felt I had no choice but to pretend I was interested in her.

One evening, Betty invited me over to her house. I thought we'd just spend time talking and laughing, but she decided to kiss me. I did my best to kiss her back, but I was lacking a key ingredient—attraction. The kiss mustered no feelings in me at all. When she then took my hand and placed it on her breast, I got up and ran out of her house. The moment cemented the fact in my mind that I was gay.

Feeling humiliated, I drove home thinking that now Betty knew I was gay, and I would have to explain myself to her. I was also fearful that she would tell everyone at work. In the end, I never said anything about it to her, and I never heard about her telling anyone. I was safe. However, our friendship slowly faded.

On another occasion, a popular Black girl, Jody, asked me to be her prom date. Interracial dating at the time in my small community was frowned upon. However, maybe this date could be yet another opportunity to demonstrate publicly that I was a straight boy.

That evening, I showed up at her house dressed in a black tux like the agent 007—Bond, James Bond. I knew I was running late. I rushed to her front door and rang the bell, but when Jody opened the door, she was still in her sweats and was finishing her hair and makeup. "God strike me dead now. Please vaporize me with a bolt of lightning." I feared that our late entrance at the prom would bring additional scrutiny to us, the interracial couple.

At last, Jody came down the stairs in a white satin prom dress. She looked beautiful. With the help of her mother, I pinned my orchid corsage on her dress, and we were off to the prom.

From the entrance to the auditorium, I noticed a sea of round tables, covered in white linen table clothes. The room was aglow with strings of soft lights and a large disco ball suspended from the ceiling. Students were mingling, drinking soda from plastic cups.

Perhaps it was my imagination, but it seemed as if the room grew silent as we stepped into the spacious hall. All eyes were upon us. At least I was taller than Tom Thumb and cuter than the Elephant Man. Our table was located at the far end of the auditorium. Passing by our seated classmates, I heard a few practical jokers break out their rendition of "Ebony and Ivory," the song made popular by Stevie Wonder and Paul McCartney. Despite my discomfort, I held my head high and walked confidently with my stunning date at my side. Drawing attention to myself was just another embarrassment to endure.

With all of the psychological devastation I was experiencing during those years, my only saving grace was my belief in the church. I clung to the belief that my tortured life was justified and proportional to my sins. I honestly believed that my desires for other men were a perversion, and if I could overcome this perversion, I would be absolved, delivered free of my attraction to men.

It frightens me, even today, to think how all my self-loathing came from what I had learned in church. But I was a child, who had been so easily indoctrinated into an ecclesiastical cult. How could such an assembly take a person's spirit and keep it from flying free? It's not right that a young person be sucked into a doctrine that limits his ability to question the sacred text.

I would often think back to the times of play-acting with my best friend Peter. We were free to explore and not to separate girl toys from boy toys. They were just that—toys. We allowed ourselves to question and to scrutinize, but not to judge.

Today, I can't help but think about the church and relate it to those circus toys I once played with years ago. In a sense, they are parallel worlds. It was a world of make-believe where clowns, contortionists, lion tamers, and magicians created an illusion—a smoke screen of deception, used to control one's thoughts. The church, just like the circus, has been perpetuating this deception for generations. I had come to see myself as a carnival freak, performing for the Temple of Theological Narrow-Mindedness.

I feel my bitterness and animosity toward religion is entirely justified. Given what happened to me, I am not being overly harsh in my condemnation of the Catholic Church. However, I assure you that it's not a condemnation of spirituality. It's a condemnation of a corrupt institution.

4

Time seems to me a drift, a shifting of sand.
I am wearing away.

—E. L. Doctorow
American Novelist

April 1983. I was a seventeen-year-old boy. I say "boy" because I was quite naive given my strict religious upbringing. However, by now, I had come to the realization that I was gay. It's not something I would have chosen, but it was the hand I was dealt. There were clues along the way, but I missed them. I knew I felt different by the time I became a teenager, but I didn't really understand how I was different. But now, I knew for sure that I was gay. And so was my good friend Peter.

One afternoon, I decided to pay Peter a visit. I jumped on my Schwinn ten-speed and sped off, looking for him. He wasn't home. Where was he? And then, I remembered. He was at the church rectory. Peter had mentioned that he was going to meet the new priest, Father Gregory Burgess, at around ten that morning.

I knew Peter had been doing odd jobs around the church for the new priest. Peter said that the priest seemed friendly and quite approachable. Peter had told him about his own desire to enter the priesthood. Father Gregory welcomed Peter's intention to join the priesthood.

29

Father Gregory said to Peter, "I'll be your mentor. It'll be great. You'll love it. I'll show you how to jump through the hoops and play the game." Peter's home was only three houses away from the church rectory. How convenient that would be for Father Gregory.

Peter hoped Gregory would become the spiritual advisor he needed to counsel him about entering the seminary. Peter had always enjoyed being part of the church; he enjoyed singing in the choir, the teachings of the Bible, and his role as an altar boy. When Peter was just a little boy, he and I would sometimes be excused from class for a few hours to assist the priest at a funeral Mass. His service to the church had started at an early age.

Peter had also made friends with our previous priest, Father Amos, whose frizzy hair reminded me of a poodle. Father Amos was tall and slender. I assumed, upon meeting him, that he was a homosexual, given his soft voice and effeminate demeanor. Peter had also mentioned to Father Amos his desire to pursue a priestly life, but I didn't know how serious Peter was.

What I didn't know was that Peter, now age sixteen, was spending time with the new priest at the rectory. They often went out to dinner and watched TV together. Peter did tell me that Gregory liked "visits." He felt it was important that future seminary students spend time around the rectory. Peter felt obliged to visit.

Climbing back on my bicycle, I headed toward the church in hopes of finding Peter. Without truly admitting it, I knew why I was obsessed with Peter. I was envious! He was part of an aristocratic, religious association to which I had no membership card. In other words, he was friends with the priest who was popular with the parishioners. I so desperately wanted admittance to this exclusive society. I had very few friends, so I was determined to infiltrate Peter's group.

Still on my bike, I could see Peter in the church yard, working with the new priest. I did want to meet the young, new priest. I had only seen him at Mass over the few months that he'd been assigned to our church. I joined other parishioners in believing that he was the most charismatic priest our church had ever had. As I approached the front of the rectory, I saw that they were tearing out bushes in the garden.

"Hello Peter, what are you doing?" I asked.

Looking rather annoyed, he responded, "Oh! It's you." Had I just breached his personal citadel—one that no other could enter? Apparently, I had! Still, I walked through an open gate. I hadn't seen Peter in recent weeks, and his attitude sent a clear message: our friendship was fading. I had feared as much when he had neglected to return my calls. Now, his callous response was confirmation.

Was Peter afraid that I, his gay friend, would embarrass him? Was he afraid his own secret desires, if known, would impede his chance of becoming a priest? I surmised that he was spending time with the new priest who might guide him into the priesthood. Did Peter really want to walk a more hallowed road? I believed the answer at this point was yes, even though I found it hard to believe.

Hurt by his dismissal, I hopped on my bike and began to pedal away. But just then, I heard the new priest shout in my direction.

"Get over here and grab a shovel."

Flabbergasted by the invitation, I climbed off my bike, grabbed the nearest shovel, and headed to the patch of dying bushes they were removing. I joined in chopping dead bushes.

"Hello. I'm Father Gregory Burgess," he said with a grin.

"Nice to meet you. I'm Michael Roberts," I said, extending my hand.

Indeed, the new priest seemed friendly. He looked to be in his early thirties. He was short and a bit stocky. Dark hair and a moustache. But what really surprised me was how he was dressed—blue jeans, a white T-shirt, and white sneakers. Wait a minute, I said to myself. I thought priests wore black clothes and white collars, but this guy was in blue jeans. He wore a gold cross around his neck, but otherwise, he looked like no priest I'd ever seen. What he said next caught me off guard.

"Take off your shirt so you don't get it dirty," Father Gregory said.

Actually, he sounded more like he was giving me an order rather than a suggestion. His demand made me feel uncomfortable; nevertheless, I obeyed. I removed my shirt and tucked it into my back pocket. His request may have sounded rude, but I had been taught to respect priests and never to question them.

The three of us worked for several hours clearing the bushes out of the garden. By the time we had completed the job, I was exhausted. I leaned on my shovel and wiped the perspiration from my brow. Then, I noticed Father Gregory staring at me. It was not a casual glance. With my chest exposed, I felt like I was a museum sculpture he was admiring. Please move on to the contemporary art section. I reached for my shirt and put it back on. His gaze told me: he is one of us. He's gay. Frankly, I was surprised. He was very straight-acting. Most people would never have suspected he was gay.

"Can I help you put away the tools, Peter?" I asked, hoping to move on from the awkward moment between me and Gregory.

"No, I'll take care of the equipment. Thank you for helping us," Peter replied curtly. I knew I had invaded his territory. Peter, with tools in hand, carried the gear to the two-car garage attached to the rectory. I was left standing next to Father Gregory.

"If you ever need help with the yard work, just let me know," I said to Father Gregory as I walked over to my bicycle.

"Thank you for your help, Michael," he yelled.

I was hoping for a handshake, a glass of water, or an invitation inside. Instead, I was just left there, straddling my bike, as both Father Gregory and Peter disappeared into the priest's private residence. Feeling abandoned, I bicycled away. After I got home, I went to my room, closed the door, and stared out the window. I felt as if I had been shunned.

Growing up, Peter and I had always understood that when priests were ordained, they made promises of poverty, chastity, and obedience. Now, Peter was thinking about becoming a priest. Could he really embrace such religious orders? I concluded that Peter would have a difficult time traveling the road toward the priesthood.

Over the next few days, I frequently bicycled past the church in hopes that Father Gregory might be out in the yard and would see me, but my timing always seemed to be off.

As for Father Gregory, I did see him at next Sunday's Mass. He moved around the pulpit before Mass began, adjusting the microphone and his books; his humming or talking to himself was part of his charisma. I always sat in one of the front pews, hoping he would notice me. A couple of times, when at the kneeler, I coughed or cleared my throat, in hopes that he would see me.

I watched him as if he were a celebrity on stage. I admired his confidence. Was his showy display just a ploy to get others to admire him? I thought so. Occasionally, I would see Peter enter the rectory before Mass began. I figured he was honing the skills, learning all he could, to become a priest. Was there something else going on between Peter and Father Gregory? It was a mystery to me. Still, I was envious of Peter—he had a friend who was a priest.

Father Gregory was the second in command under Pastor Gabriel, who also shared the priests' residence. Father Gabriel was referred to as pastor because he was appointed by the bishop to represent the local parish. He was an old, unapproachable man, seemingly oblivious to anything going on around him. His hearing was poor, and he was absent-minded. He was also known for being frugal, if not stingy. He was Ebenezer Scrooge, minus the walking stick. He was known for holding onto every penny of the church bank account. People would joke that he would: "squeeze a five-dollar bill until Abe Lincoln shit."

When he wasn't dressed as a priest, Pastor Gabriel often wore tattered, paint-splatted clothes. His appearance was somewhat shocking for many Catholics. I feared Pastor Gabriel whenever I assisted him as an altar boy, mostly because he seemed cranky. As a product of my strict home environment, I was already an anxious, submissive child with low self-esteem, and the priest's demeanor only added to my anxiety.

As the weeks moved on, I developed a reverence for Father Gregory. I used to wonder if he knew what power he held over me. You bet your ass he did. He knew he could crack me open like an egg, stir in two cups of fear, two tablespoons of domination, and a pinch of lies.

Father Gregory was no ordinary priest. His sermons were unique, sometimes filled with humor. It was a total change from homilies given by Father Gabriel that would last for at least thirty, monotonous minutes. To me, Chinese water torture would have been less agonizing than the Mass said by Father Gabriel.

During some of Father Gregory's Masses, when the weather was hot and humid, he would wear shorts under his vestments. I remember one instance when he moved in such a way that his garment opened, exposing his khaki shorts and his scrawny, hairy legs. This happened to be in view of my aunt, who was seated in one of the front pews. She loved Father Gregory, but she was unable to stifle her laughter. I can still hear her laughter echoing throughout the cavernous sanctuary.

At one other Sunday Mass, on a blistering hot day, Father Gregory walked up to the pulpit to begin his homily. He spoke simply, "If you think it's hot today, it's even hotter in Hell. Please rise." The congregation loved it. He was off and running with another of his compelling sermons.

One might think that his God-fearing flock would have perceived Father Gregory as cocky and pompous. But to the contrary, they found his individuality refreshing, almost bewitching. I was captivated by his personality. I saw him as a religious figure who, I believed, could guide me and provide answers to my deep-seated problems. As a teenager, I sought knowledge and insight, desperately wanting to reach the peak of spirituality. I believed he was the guide who could lead me to inner peace and enlightenment.

No doubt, Father Gregory was the new star of this church, and everyone loved him. Whatever he was selling, they were buying. With the skill of a cunning television evangelist, he could sell sawdust to a lumber mill. He cajoled his parishioners with the flair and the panache of a crooked politician. Vote for me, and you will be assured of your place in Heaven.

Upon leaving Mass, Father Gregory would always stand at the exit, greeting his parishioners as they left. He would tell jokes and laugh, confidently asserting his dominance over his followers. He loved the attention.

Yet, he never acknowledged me when I left the church. Did he know I was secretly gay? The gay issue was most difficult for me. I didn't want to be gay, and I carried a lot of shame, the most destructive human emotion. Anytime someone seemed to ignore me, my default mind-set was that they probably thought I was gay. Was Father Gregory afraid that his parishioners would question his sexuality if he acknowledged me? You know, guilt by association? Possibly. Another conceivable explanation as to why he seemingly ignored me may have been because Peter had spoken ill of me. Michael is trouble, Michael is mentally disturbed. Michael is attracted to men. So, every Sunday, I would quietly slip past Father Gregory when Mass ended. But that was all about to change rather quickly.

On a bright sunny day in late April 1983, after Mass, as I started to slip past Father Gregory, he spoke to me.

"Hello Michael" he said, as he crossed in front of other churchgoers to greet me.

"Hello, Father," I replied.

Shaking my hand, he pulled me closer and looking directly into my eyes, he said, "I may need some help soon around the church. I'll be in touch with you."

"Okay," I responded with both the enthusiasm and the innocence of a child who had just been given a bag filled with candy.

I walked down the granite stairs and then almost danced toward the family car. Sadly, and in retrospect, I realize that was the moment in my life when the wheels of torment and misery were set in motion. Soon to be spinning out of control.

Several days passed with no sign or word from Father Gregory. But being the hopeful person that I was, I jumped every time the phone rang, thinking it's him on the line, telling me I was needed at the church. Yes. He could validate my self-worth.

That Wednesday evening, while Mother was finishing the dishes, the phone rang.

"Michael, you have a phone call," Mom shouted down to me in the basement.

I thought, it's Father Gregory. I ran to the phone, and thanks to the long phone cord, I secluded myself in the laundry room. I wanted complete privacy when I spoke to God's representative.

"Hello," I said nervously.

"Michael? It's Father Gregory."

"Yes Father."

"Are you free to help me around the church this week?"

"Yes, of course Father, anything I can do to help."

"Great…be here Friday around noon, and you can join me for lunch."

"Okay, see you then."

I listened to the dial tone after he hung up. Lunch he said. I was invited to lunch with the priest! I ran upstairs and boasted of my lunch appointment to my mom. I told the entire family with all the enthusiasm of a newspaper boy, hollering the day's headlines on street corners. I was chosen from everyone else in that parish to personally assist the priest. I bragged to whomever would listen.

That Friday, I arrived at the rectory precisely at noon. The church's housekeeper, a middle-aged woman wearing a white apron, answered the door, greeting me with a warm smile.

"Hello Michael. I'm Hannah. Please come in," she said with a French accent.

Wow, she knew my name, I thought to myself. Did I just arrive for dinner at Buckingham Palace, receiving a stately welcome from the royal staff?

"Hello," I responded.

As I followed her into the kitchen, I couldn't help but think of Hannah as a Julia Child—both in manner and dress. I even remembered Julia Child's famous quote: "The only time to eat diet food is while you're waiting for the steak to cook."

As I stepped into the rectory's kitchen, I felt as though I was entering an inner sanctum. I was in the priest's personal kitchen. I slowly gazed around the room. The walls were papered in a green and white-flowered design. White lace curtains framed the windows. A picture of Pope John Paul hung on one wall. In the center of the room, an old kitchen table was covered with a vinyl tablecloth—checkered green. Next to a casserole of steaming scalloped potatoes on the counter, I noticed an empty package of Shake 'N Bake breadcrumbs. Hannah must be a good cook—the aromas were divine.

"Father will be down shortly. If you need the bathroom, you can use the one straight ahead in the small sitting room," Hannah said pointing past the kitchen.

"Should I leave my shoes at the door?" I replied.

"Of course not. Leave them on; sit here at the kitchen table. Can I get you something to drink? We have soda, orange juice, milk, or water."

"Water will be fine, thank you." I responded humbly.

I sipped on a glass of water, mostly feeling that I did not deserve this entitlement. I was in the holy priest's sanctuary. I couldn't help but feel that I was not worthy of such a special, personal invitation from Father Gregory.

"Hello Michael," Father Gregory said as he walked into the room. He was in his street clothes, a light-weight red sweater, jeans, and sneakers. Would anyone ever suspect he is a priest?

"Hello, Father," I responded.

He moved quickly around the kitchen, flipped through a pile of mail, grabbed a tall drinking glass from the cupboard, and poured himself a glass of milk.

"Come. Let's sit in the dining room," he said.

"Thank you, Father, for inviting me for lunch."

I grabbed my glass of water and followed him to the dining room. I knew it! Rhett Butler and Scarlet O'Hara will be joining us for lunch, because the dining room looked like the left-over staging from the Tara mansion in *Gone with the Wind*. In that moment, I would like to have said, "Frankly my dear, I do give a damn."

Once again, I was so impressed that I committed details of the dining room to memory: a large table, covered with lace, a built-in hutch, crown molding, a small chandelier, polished silver flatware, and crystal goblets. As one might guess, one wall was adorned with a wooden crucifix next to a framed print of the Virgin Mary with child, possibly a print of the original *Madonna,* by Roberto Ferruzzi, the famous Italian painter. Seeing the painting reminded me of one I'd seen in my childhood. It showed a ladder ascending from earth to the heavens. Only the holiest of people were on the highest rung and ever so closer to the entrance. I felt at that moment I had officially obtained some advantage over other sinners.

Lunch was served.

"Michael, I hope you like baked chicken, scalloped potatoes, and string beans," Father Gregory said.

As God is my witness, I'll never be hungry again.

"Yes, Father. It looks delicious," I responded.

"None of this Father stuff. Call me Gregory."

"Okay."

This was an extremely peculiar event for me—calling him by his first name. It would take some getting used to. Calling a priest by his real name was totally foreign to me, but I was honored to have been afforded such a privilege.

"Have all the string beans you want. Hannah knows I don't do vegetables and tuna fish. Period!" Father chuckled, as he turned toward Hannah. The remark was a joke intended for her.

I helped myself to Hannah's sumptuous dishes, all served on vintage, fine China. I ladled only small amounts onto my plate. I knew gluttony was one of the seven deadly sins. Before I took my first bite, the doorbell rang.

Father Gregory looked annoyed. "Who the hell is bothering me now?" he said, flinging his arms in the air. He threw down his napkin and headed to the back door. I sat quietly, thinking that this intrusion just awoke a sleeping bear. Then, to my surprise, I heard what sounded like a friendly conversation and then raucous laughter.

Within a few minutes, Gregory returned to the table. Wow! His emotional scale instantaneously tips in either direction, I thought. It all began to make me feel ill at ease, but shouldn't I still be enjoying the excitement of the occasion?

In this moment of awkwardness, I said something in an attempt to assuage some of my own uneasiness. "Father, I mean Gregory, I see Peter over here sometimes. What's he been up to? He and I haven't talked in a while."

Father seemed perturbed by my question about Peter. His frown confirmed it. "You mean that slut, that whore, who drives around the library block looking for hookups?" he asked.

I was shocked at his words about my friend. I was at a total loss for what to say. What did he mean by hookups? What would one find at the library block other than stacks of books? Only later, I would later learn that the public library was a section of town where gay men would drive around cruising for men. Was Peter there to meet sexually-deprived scholars?

Oh boy, I did it. I hit the wrong nerve by mentioning Peter's name. I had recently seen them together. Maybe they'd had an argument.

"I'm sorry for bringing up his name."

He quickly changed the subject by asking me a question, one that I found rather odd.

"Would your parents mind my coming over for an evening meal some night?"

"I think that would be fine," I said, not sure what to make of his inviting himself to dinner. "What time does your family eat?"

"Around five-thirty."

"Good, I'll see all of you next Tuesday at that time for dinner. Make sure they have a bottle of Dewar's Scotch."

Uh...that sounded pompous, didn't it? I thought. "Okay, Gregory," I said, taking another bite of chicken.

As we continued our meal, our topics of conversation ranged from the weather and family to his friends from surrounding towns. He also mentioned that his mother still lived in the family home in nearby Pineview.

Finishing my meal, I folded my napkin and placed it beside my dish.

"Can I help clear the table?" I asked.

"Hannah will take care of the table. Come. Follow me upstairs."

I followed him out of the dining room. As we ascended the staircase, my gaze followed the white painted spindles up to the second floor. I assumed we were heading to his private quarters. I must be one of the lucky few to have visited his inner sanctum.

His private quarters consisted of one big room. Photos of nameless faces covered every wall. One end of the room was a sitting area; the opposite end of the room was his bedroom. I was astonished at what I saw: a waterbed with a headboard, complete with lights and mirror. (No disco ball?) Against one wall, he had a veritable electronics store: a record player, a video tape recorder, cassette player, laser disk player, a large television with large speakers, and a radio.

Alongside a decanter and ice bucket, I couldn't help but notice a bottle of Blue Nun wine (how appropriate for a priest) and a bottle of Dewar's Scotch. Across the room, he had fiber-optic lamp that changed colors, a stack of books, a cluttered desk, and an octagonal fish tank filled with goldfish. And the room was not without snacks. Throughout the room, I noticed a package of pistachios, a package of Oreos, a can of Pringles, and a plastic container of homemade fudge.

I stood entranced, instantly realizing that his priestly life was filled with an abundance of material goods. Unusual, I thought, for a priest. I shared a bedroom with my two brothers until my early teens, and we never had anything other than a few pieces of furniture, clothes, and a few wall hangings.

The priest's surroundings made me feel impoverished. Oscar Wilde said: "The tragedy of the poor is that they can afford nothing but self-denial." My host's possessions seemed out of character for the way I believed a priest lived. If this is a vow of poverty and denial, sign me up.

"You have a nice room. It looks like you have everything you need."

"Not yet. One can never have enough stuff. I only wish I had a bigger room."

Father Gregory then grabbed a bottle of scotch. He dropped a couple of ice cubes into his glass and poured himself a drink. A priest drinking in the afternoon? He has his own ice bucket—how bizarre. When is Happy Hour?

"Sit, Michael," he said, pointing to the chair closest to me.

As I sat down, I couldn't help but see Peter's bedroom window not too far down the street. Interesting, I thought. I could see Peter's house from here.

As we sat facing the television, I continued to gaze around the room, taking in his private treasures. I just hope he didn't plunder and pillage from unsuspecting town's people.

Handing me his glass, he said, "Take a sip of Scotch."

"I am not old enough. I've never had alcohol before."

I was a young, gullible, seventeen-year-old boy. Emotionally I was probably no more than fourteen. My parents raised us by sheltering us from any television programs that portrayed any semblance of immoral behaviors they felt could corrupt us. We'd never had any exposure to profanity, sexually explicit content, or God forbid anything related to homosexuality.

"Relax, it's just a sip," Father said, encouraging me.

Slowly I took the drink in my hand as the ice cubes clinked against the sides of the glass. I took a small sip. Fortunately, it was a small sip because it tasted like high-octane petrol. I handed the drink back to him. "That's awful," I said.

He laughed. Wasn't it illegal for him to give alcohol to someone underage? What would be his punishment? Did he believe his stature could shield him from any harm?

Smiling, he leaned back in his chair, swirled the ice around with his finger, and gulped a mouthful of that fossil fuel. "Ah! It took me seven years to acquire a taste for scotch, so I don't expect you to enjoy it the first time," he said smiling.

Was he planning on having me try this liquid intoxicant again?

"You drink during the day?" I questioned.

"Yep, and I don't give a damn what anyone else thinks about it. If this is my only vice, so be it!"

I wanted to be liked by Father; however, I felt inept with the etiquette of adulthood. I was introverted and extremely naive to the ways of the world. "Gregory, what work can I help you with today?" I asked.

"Follow me. I have a list to complete." It was mostly work around the church grounds.

We worked on the church grounds most of the afternoon. He thanked me for my time, and I was on my way.

A few days later, Gregory summoned me to help him again around the yard of the rectory. He met me at the rectory door.

"Hi, Gregory. What can I help you with today?

"Follow me. I have a list of things I need your help with."

We spent the day weeding the vegetable garden, cleaning the basement, organizing closets in the church, and sprucing up the grounds. I left, not having been compensated for my time and another luncheon prepared by Hannah. I assumed my payment was to be spiritual. The voices reverberated in my brain to be compliant. To help a priest was seen as a benevolent act. Father Gregory was a perpetual reminder that he was nearer to God than I, and that the Almighty instantly knew of my good deeds. But was my goodwill being taken advantage of? As I walked in the door at home, I had a phone call.

"Hello Michael. It's Greggie."

Greggie? Not even Gregory, I thought?

"I was wondering if you would join me for dinner tonight."

"Well, sure," I said, still pondering the way he had introduced himself. Lunch, now dinner in the same day? Was I special enough to receive such attention? I regained my composure and finally remembered to tell my mother about Father Gregory joining us for dinner on Tuesday of next week.

That night, Father picked me up at six o'clock and drove us to his favorite Italian restaurant, Lorenzo's Ristorante. As we walked in, I felt rather important as the guest of a priest. In those days, if you were accompanied by a priest, you enjoyed preferential treatment. You reaped the benefits only priests received, the exalted level of respect they were given by others. From the way we were treated, I recognized that the simple, white plastic collar he wore gave him influence. I grew up believing that a priest's collar was a symbol of trust. That collar was a reminder that he was a representation of Christ on earth.

As we were walking to our table, we passed two men, one of whom was a priest I had seen before and the other, a younger male companion.

Father Gregory stopped to greet the priest. "I see you're having chicken tonight."

"It looks like you plan to have a tasty dish yourself," the priest replied.

"Having dessert later?" Gregory smirked.

I was disappointed that Gregory did not introduce me. Furthermore, as I observed this odd exchange between them, I felt as if the priest was inspecting me. I didn't want to believe that their comments were sexual innuendos. But I later learned that "chicken" was the slang term older gay men used for young men.

As we took seats at our table, Gregory explained to me, "That priest is the soon-to-be Bishop Marcus."

"Is he higher than a priest?" I asked.

"No, he's the auxiliary bishop."

"What's an auxiliary bishop?" I asked, as I glanced back, observing this new religious celebrity and his friend.

"He assists the bishop. The actual bishop oversees the priests, churches, and schools within this geographical area that we call the diocese," he explained.

"Who is the guy he's with?" I asked.

"Let's just say, his escort for the evening."

As we sat at our table, I tried to stay focused on my host, but my attention drifted toward the auxillary bishop's table and his remark about Father Marcus's escort? What did he mean? Did the bishop bring security with him? Was this customary for an older holy man to have a young man as his dinner companion? Was I Father's Gregory's escort for the evening? I couldn't quite figure it out.

Years later, in 2005, I learned that the bishop we had met in the restaurant was accused of sexually abusing a boy three times from the time the boy was eleven up until he was fifteen. The abuse had consisted of genital fondling, anal penetration, and oral copulation. The Diocese supposedly examined diocesan records and stated that it "found no basis of credibility to the claim," even though the bishop had passed away six years earlier, and, therefore, he could not be questioned on the matter.

It was time to order our meal. Our waiter handed me a menu. I opened it and began to glance at its content. When our server returned to take our order, I deferred to Father Gregory's position and rank and waited for him to order first.

"We both will have the Chicken Francaise, angel hair pasta with marinara, the house salad with blue cheese, and two glasses of the house red wine."

We? Who else was he ordering for? I'd never had anyone order for me.

From that point on, I assumed that when dining with a priest, the proper protocol was to allow him to make all of the decisions. That evening would be one of many in which I learned I was to keep my opinions to myself. I had no voice in the matter. Gregory was always the main act on the stage. I was merely an understudy.

Strangely, two days after my going out to dinner with Father Gregory, Peter called and wanted to meet with me. "Do you want to go for a ride?" Peter asked.

"You have a car?"

"Yes, my parent's car," Peter said.

"I would love to," I responded.

It was unusual to hear from Peter. I assumed he had something he wanted to talk about. Had he decided not to go into the priesthood? Was he going to explain his friendship, or lack thereof, with Father Gregory? Regardless, I was just excited to revive our fractured friendship.

Upon his arrival, I climbed into the car, making it a point not to question our seemingly estranged friendship. "Where do you want to go?" I asked.

"I thought we might drive up to Saint Leonard's Abbey."

Peter and I had visited there before. It was only about a mile away. The abbey housed a community of Trappist monks. The church sanctuary was a refuge where Peter and I had found solace in the past. It was also the place where I learned to appreciate the many nuances of the Gregorian chant musical art form. We arrived just before the nightly prayer, called Compline, was about to begin. The chapel was austere. It consisted of five rows of wooden benches. The room was surrounded by stone walls that were only about four feet high. The space behind these walls was the only area in which guests were welcomed. Guest interactions with the brothers were limited to only a few Trappist monks.

The abbey survived on products the monks made and sold. They were well known in the area for the variety of Trappist jams and and later on, craft beers. If they had served these delightful brews during Mass, they would have lines out the door.

Now seated in the secluded chapel, I looked around the room, taking in the crucifix, stained glass windows, and stone barriers that separated me from the cloistered monks. Occasionally, I stood, peering over the chest-high wall down into the darkened hallways, looking to see if I could see any sacred visions that might reveal themselves to the holiest of friars. I fell in love with the architecture as well as the ambiance.

The monastery felt like an old castle from the Middle Ages with Michael-the-Jester here to make merry. At the beginning of the service, I could see monks pouring into the church like a swarm of worker ants descending upon an abandoned

44

picnic lunch. The chapel was quiet with the exception of the muffled patter of footsteps. I loved the haunting echoes reverberating inside the stone enclosure. I found this place to be very hallowed, filled with the fervor that God, in which the Almighty, could actually be present. I smelled the sweet scent of balsam and myrrh burning in the incense holder. The clouds of smoke rose toward the heavens.

Kneeling, I closed my eyes, allowing my thoughts to be focused on the holy, omnipresent savior of mankind, Jesus Christ. In my conviction, he was the embodiment of all that had been created. Pondering his presence in this holiest of places was a blessed moment, which served to strengthen my lifelong resolve and commitment to the faith in which I had been so stringently raised.

After the night prayer concluded, Peter and I returned to his car, where we sat talking for several hours. It was here that Peter revealed to me more of the pieces of the puzzle in his attempt to justify his recent "retreat" from our friendship. He began by telling me that he had enrolled in Saint Luke's Seminary. He went on to explain that he had been working around the church in order to save money. He also told me that he was thankful to Father Amos and to Father Gregory, the two influential figures who convinced him to follow this theological calling.

"That's great," I said. "When are you going to start at the seminary?"

"I start school in September."

"Are you still friends with Father Gregory?" I asked.

"We still chat periodically. Occasionally, we spend time together."

I decided to be frank with Peter. "When I was over to the rectory for lunch, he called you a slut."

Peter was quick to defend himself, "He can't be too mad at me. I have a key to the rectory. He's likely playing us against each other. He gets jealous because I have my freedom this summer to work, to be independent. When he gets mad at me, he calls you. After some time passes, he calls me back. He makes comments to me about you as well. He says you're just a naive boy who helps around the church. He said, 'Michael is nobody important.'"

Oh, that remark was stinging, I thought to myself. Gregory had denigrated me, and I had begun to think I was becoming someone of value to him.

"You've been to my house," Peter said. "You know if you look out my bedroom window you can see Gregory's bedroom window."

"Yes, I responded."

"At night, he places a candle on his windowsill as a signal that he's home. I place one on my windowsill as well when I'm home. I'm just trying to keep the peace between us."

In my mind, Peter should have placed a big, neon sign that said, "Fuck You" in his window.

"Even though he can be controlling, temperamental, and stubborn, I need his support right now. I am sure you can understand. Recommendation letters are invaluable," Peter said.

"I guess," I replied.

Peter dropped me off at home, never speaking a word about the toll his so-called friendship with Gregory was taking on him. Years later, I would learn that although Father Gregory never succeeded in sexually seducing Peter, it was not for lack of Gregory's trying. Whenever Gregory would try to kiss him or to grope him, Peter would fend him off, using humor, trying to not offend him. When Gregory started groping him and placing his hands down his pants, grabbing his penis, Peter would say things such as, "Oh stop that silliness." Or "Oh, stop, Gregory, what are you doing?" In short, Peter feared Gregory. He especially feared that Gregory could derail his dream to become a priest.

Peter also later told me that his parents didn't care for Father Gregory. Peter said his parents may have been suspicious of him. One time, Peter called his dad to ask if he could stay overnight at the rectory. His dad said, "No, you cannot, and if you're not home in five minutes, I'm coming after you."

Peter and I continued getting together, as friends. We were never lovers. However, he would show me how he cruised around the "gay block" in the downtown area as we listened to his cassette recordings of Madonna's "Burning Up and Everybody", and Boy George's "Do You Really Want to Hurt Me?"

Later in life, I developed animosity toward Peter for not disclosing any of the traps that eventually ensnared him. I could have been forewarned. I would eventually fall victim to Gregory's abuse, tenfold. Peter's warning me could have changed the course of my life and perhaps his life as well. In the end, we would both be left with emotional wounds that would never fully heal.

Looking back, I realize that Peter never talked about his problems or displayed his emotions. In fact, I believe that he was unaware of any emotional damage he was suffering. Did Peter have any inclination that his own life could or would be shattered in the aftermath of the tornado named Father Gregory? Should I stay angry at a person who was out of touch with his emotions? Could I ever be truly emotionally detached from a childhood friend? The answer was no.

5

Over the next few days, Gregory called me more frequently.

"Michael, it's Father Gregory on the phone for you," my mother would say.

Was this Gregory's way of seeing where I was, what I was doing, who I was with? I knew he was curious to find out if Peter and I were getting together. Father Gregory's behavior was slightly neurotic, but I cannot deny that part of me enjoyed being the recipient of this attention. When I spoke with him, I did my best to keep my stories accurate, regardless of how I distorted the facts. I would never admit to seeing Peter. I created lies while also being accessible to Father Gregory at any given moment.

But telling lies came with a price for me. An already anxious kid, I was developing stomach aches, anxiety, and paranoia. I was maintaining a balancing act. I didn't want to lose my already-fragile friendship with Peter, who was my kindred gay spirit. So, I would secretly spend time with Peter, without letting Gregory know about it. Why? Because Gregory didn't want me to spend time with Peter. Adding to my anxiety, I didn't want to disrespect or to deceive a Catholic priest, with whom I thought I was developing a friendship, and I certainly didn't want to hurt my parents, who found a close friend in Father Gregory.

Somehow, I found the strength to become a skilled, master juggler of the facts. Soon, I was deceiving everyone around me. Whenever Gregory was busy with friends, Masses, or funerals, I would spend time with Peter. When Gregory was back at the rectory, I told Peter I was busy doing yardwork or housework. I began to think that Gregory's daily phone calls were really just his way of learning who my friends were and how I was spending my time. In my naiveté, I failed to recognize that his true motive was to control me. From my perspective, I simply didn't want to rock the boat or get any one upset.

The following Tuesday, expecting Father Gregory to arrive for dinner, the entire family scurried around the house in preparation. My parents always felt slightly intimidated at the prospect of hosting the priest; my mother always prepared a nice meal and set the table with the best dishes and silverware.

That evening, without even ringing the doorbell, Father Gregory walked right into the house. Dressed in his casual blue jeans and short-sleeved shirt, he carried a bottle of Dewar's Scotch. Did he assume that, just because of his station in life that he had an open invitation to walk right in? Apparently so. His entrance established a precedent for future visits.

"Hello Martha!" he said as he walked into the kitchen.

"Hello Father!" my mother replied.

"Jeez! As I told Michael, none of this Father stuff. Call me by my first name, Gregory. Where are the glasses?"

She selected a large glass from the cabinet and handed it to him.

"I assume you have ice."

"Yes, I'll get you some," she responded, obediently.

"Relax. I'll take care of it," he said. Father Gregory walked over to the refrigerator, pulled the ice cube tray from the freezer, and began preparing his drink. Unscrewing the cap from the Dewar's bottle, he poured a generous amount of scotch then added ice. Clearly, Father had plenty of experience in preparing this drink.

"Sorry Gregory, I forgot to mention to my parents that you like scotch," I said sheepishly.

"Not to worry this time. You all will get to know me rather quickly. Meanwhile, I always come prepared."

We spent that evening around the dinner table, fascinated with a cleric who was unconventional, self-assured, and incredibly charismatic. His sarcasm and wit had us all laughing.

He immediately succeeded in shattering our image of a pious priest. He loved to push our buttons, and we found it refreshing.

Growing up, however, I did have a slight case of hierophobia—fear of holy people and sacred things. It all began as a child. I feared that God was always watching me. Even picking my nose or going to the bathroom gave me anxiety. I believed stories I had been told of religious objects that would weep tears. I learned stories from the Bible about plagues, floods, and destruction.

TV programs presented evangelists who railed on about the infernos of Hell. That expression, "fire and brimstone," scared me to death. Not to mention terms and phrases such as: resurrection, crucifixion, apocalypse, stigmata, exorcism, Armageddon, raising the dead, holes in hands, and beheadings. All those terms terrified me. Yet, this nonconformist priest was one of us, swearing, joking, and laughing. He had a way of making me less afraid of religion. I had never met a priest like him.

After the evening meal, Mom gave Father Gregory a tour of our home. As he looked around, he opened doors and rummaged through cabinets. He repeatedly asked if he could have this object or that object to take back to the rectory for his personal collection. My mother avoided his rude requests by giggling and saying, "Oh no," as if she were joking. Except she wasn't. Frankly, I think she was rather shocked by his request, but she would never say so.

"I love that statue of the Virgin Mary, Martha. I'll get it someday for my collection."

Collection, I thought? Try stamps. They take up less room.

"Over my dead body you'll take it," she replied laughingly.

As the months passed, Father Gregory continued his daily phone calls to me and his weekly family visits for dinner. He was becoming an ever-larger presence in our lives. I sensed Peter was still in contact with Father Gregory, but I wasn't sure what kind of a friendship they had. I didn't want to believe Peter's cautionary warning that Father Gregory was playing the two of us against each other. A priest would never use another person or ever knowingly speak an untruth. I assumed Peter was becoming jealous of my growing connection with Gregory.

June 1983. I began spending more time with Gregory. We watched TV in his bedroom, snacked on junk food, and went out to dinner weekly. My parents totally approved of my friendship with the young, charismatic priest. Did they suspect that I was gay, now that the priest was a welcomed distraction who exempted them from having to deal with this troublesome subject?

My parents seemed to grow more comfortable with Gregory's weekly visits to dinner. I believed they must have felt they had no choice in the matter, because he infiltrated and nearly dominated their lives. But I loved seeing my parents laugh and develop this priestly connection. But what price might I have to pay?

"Michael, it's Gregory on the phone," Mom called to me in my bedroom.

I answered the phone, "Hello, how are you?"

"Just checking in. Where have you been all morning?"

"Just watching TV," I replied.

"What were you watching?"

"Mork and Mindy." What the hell difference did it make, I thought.

Was he keeping a daily activities journal? Will I survive his religious dystopia and the process of dehumanization? Should I call him George Orwell? After all, it was only a few months until 1984.

"Okay! Just checking! I'll be picking you up at 6:30 tonight."

Why did I automatically obey his instructions? Why didn't I have a voice in this matter? I was quick to argue with my father about any number of things. Why couldn't I stand up to a priest? Was I a robot, pre-programmed to follow a shrewd software engineer's algorithm?

"Where are we going?"

"Madison! My close friends would like to meet you. I know them from when I was assigned at my previous parish. So be ready."

"Okay, I'll be ready."

That evening he picked me up in his brown Chevy Nova. It was the first time I noticed he had bumper stickers: One read "I Love the Single Life." Another one said: "Macho." I found his

51

bumper stickers a bit bizarre, but knowing his maverick style, it seemed fitting. He wasn't afraid to be real. I admired that. Because I, on the other hand, was so uncomfortable in my own skin, so painfully introverted. Was he the panacea I needed to boost my self-esteem? No one in the parish ever questioned his unconventional style and his unorthodox behavior. He must be an okay guy.

After a ten-minute ride, we arrived at his friends' house in Madison. The home was not well maintained, compared with other homes in the area. The brown paint was peeling; the grass was overgrown. We walked up a few steps to the front door. Father rang the doorbell and after a few seconds rang it again.

"For Christ's sake, where the hell are they?" he said impatiently.

Then, he opened the door and walked right in. I found his actions rude. Did he enjoy ignoring boundaries among his friends? He seemed to be an unashamed, egotistical authoritarian. I was a bit uncomfortable with this behavior. On the other hand. I knew I had my own flaws, so I deemed it wise to overlook his.

He greeted his friends with, "I see that none of you can get off your asses and open the door."

"Hello Greggie. How are you?" a woman hollered from an adjacent dining room. She was quite obese, dressed in a bright, cat-print sweatshirt. Was her sweatshirt supposed to distract from the spare-tire surrounding her midsection? She could have been the poster child for midriff bulge. As a young man with a sense of fashion, I had images of rolling her down a steep embankment into a fashionable woman's clothing store, where she could put that sad, cat-print out of its misery.

Her name was Sandra. She was in her early forties, a seemingly kind woman, who laughed easily and made me feel welcome. Her husband, Jack, was the quiet, observant type. He was seated in the living room watching sports on TV. He gave us a quick "hello" and returned back to his TV show. Then, Reggie, a young man whom Gregory had met at his previous parish, made his grand appearance. In his early twenties, Reggie was a tall, lanky, well-dressed man with a perfectly sculpted beard. Rather feminine, he was noticeably wearing light foundation makeup and eyeliner. I had no question about his sexuality.

I stared, watching this pseudo-sophisticated, cocksure queen strut around the table. Our eyes met momentarily. Quickly, I glanced away, realizing the new "gay radar" that I had developed. Which part of the brain is responsible for identification of queens? Should I recalibrate my thought process, because Reggie was moving the needle to the far right, pointing to Her Royal Majesty Queen Reggie from Flamesville?

Reggie craved attention, like a peacock during mating season, displaying his feathers, or in this case, beads, ruffles, and bows, in a dance for all to see. He pranced around the room with all the grace of a ballerina in heat. The exaggerated expression of emotions were his signature gimmicks on his life's stage. Would someone please draw the curtain!

Minutes after meeting his three friends, Sandra's sons arrived. Parker was an arrogant, straight, masculine teenager. Jack Jr. was heavyset and unkempt, but a cordial-type.

I was the only member of the party who was slightly reserved, and I found myself receiving lots of attention. I was the new kid on the block, not fully aware that my good looks and innocence were what made me attractive to them.

I tacitly observed the group. I was too afraid to say anything that may be perceived as sophomoric. I kept my thoughts to myself, such as: Why is Reggie wearing foundation makeup and heavy eyeliner? Was he auditioning for the part of Joel Gray, Master of Ceremonies, in the 1930s Berlin musical, *Cabaret?* Why was Sandra so comfortable with Gregory in a display of playful banter? Why is Reggie flirting with Father? Why is Father flirting with Reggie?

Reggie's fawning over Gregory with hugs, touches, and sexual innuendos, was rather unsettling. Was this typical Reggie behavior, or was he displaying exaggerated behaviors afraid to lose Gregory's attention to a newcomer? Did he think he would be yesterday's news? I never quite understood Reggie's motives that night. I found it rather odd that no one spoke or hinted of Reggie's being gay. Gregory's and Reggie's bond seemed strong. I didn't want to be the wrecking ball.

Sandra's husband was an emotionally distant man. I never got to know him because he isolated himself in another room.

On the other hand, Sandra was a fruit fly, also known as a "fag hag", a not-so-complimentary label ascribed to a woman who flourished in the company of gay men. She gravitated toward Reggie, who seemed to give her as much affection and attention that any narcissist could. They both loved the theater and often reminisced throughout the evening about the *Jesus Christ Superstar* musical performance they were in, when Father Gregory was a clerical resident at the church in their town.

We left a few hours later. I had the feeling that I had passed inspection and was accepted into Gregory's tribe.

Over the next few weeks, Gregory's phone calls became even more intrusive. Like an old vintage cuckoo clock on the wall, the little priest popped out at a specific time and said, "Hello, is Michael there?" "Hello Martha, where's Michael?" My naïve parents never questioned the phone calls; they still thought it was great that I had a priest for a friend.

"What are you up to Michael?" he would say when I answered the phone. There was a part of me that loved the attention that Gregory lavishly bestowed upon me, filling the emotional void I felt inside.

My parents continued their infatuation with Gregory. His arrival to their home was always entertaining to all of us. They embraced his nonchalant, bold behavior. He would walk out to the pool in his black Speedo, a swimsuit for which he was not built, and a scotch in hand. The look on his face said, "Look at me. I'm pretty hot." Even though he wasn't.

If anyone had snidely commented on his appearance, they would get one of his well-known retorts such as: "Pound sand up your ass," or he'd simply scowl while pointing to his chin, saying: "This is a look of nonconcern." We would all laugh. He was very good to my parents, always treating them with kindness and with humor. They lived vicariously through him; he helped them to be less timid with the religion they revered. I loved seeing my parents contented.

That was the strange dichotomy for me: Gregory had a good side and a bad side. He created this utopia that my parents loved. I didn't want to shatter that. Yet, I sacrificed my own happiness so that they could enjoy a respite from their otherwise mundane existence. I believed that my two extremely hard-working parents had earned the right to reap such joy. As for me, I felt justly punished. I felt guilt, shame, and worthlessness for being a closeted homosexual, filled with sinful, immoral thoughts.

Gregory was a disciple of the holy church—a church that would never accept me. It was a church that damned an abomination like me to Hell. The church held religious governance over my parents, who in turn, foisted their dogmatic faith upon their children. Our entire family were staunch supporters of this religious charade, marching in step with obedient precision. We believed in the church mandates, most of which were preposterous to me. No meat on Friday—it's Lent. I used to argue with my parents, telling them that Oscar Mayer bologna wasn't really meat. It was just masquerading as meat. And, I had two questions: how does no meat on Friday punish a vegetarian? Does the Vatican own any financial investment in the seafood industry?

Another ritual I considered silly was, when entering the church, blessing yourself with holy water stored in a vessel at the entrance to the church. My mother explained that the priest blessed the water, reminding us of baptism. It calls to mind the joke: How do you make holy water? You boil the hell of it.

Sometimes the priest would use the holy water during special celebrations. He would take an aspergillum, a silver ball—with holes in it—on the end of a stick and sprinkle holy water on the congregation. Shouldn't I stand and sing a rendition of "It's Raining Men, Alleluia!"? Palm branches were given out to everyone on Palm Sunday. You were never allowed to throw them away; you had to burn them. Couldn't we all just weave fabulous hats?

The last one of many, nonsensical practices was Ash Wednesday. The priest would smear ashes, the size of his thumbprint, in the middle of our foreheads. It was a show of mortality and repentance. I say, the priest should have smeared clown makeup instead, and we all could have exchanged balloon animals.

June 1983. I graduated from high school. Most students celebrated, looking ahead to their future. I had no direction and was scared of the lack of possibilities. I felt the heavy chains of the high school bullies being lifted from my life, but I was unable to shed the manacles of Father Gregory's subjugation. How did I move on to a life without him? How do you say no to a priest?

My sister was freer spirited and more adventurous than I. At the age of seventeen, she moved to Washington, D.C., right out of high school, with two other friends. I was hurt deeply by her move because I craved a connection with her that never materialized. She left to make an independent life for herself while I stayed back, filling the empty space left in the family by her departure. I paid more attention to the needs of the house, cleaning, organizing, and monitoring my brothers.

Ultimately, I think I stayed for two reasons; one was my hope to be appreciated by a dad who was unable to relate with his son. The other reason was that I didn't want to hurt my mother who would be losing another child to the world. My mother was my only true friend who cared deeply for me, so staying at home was not a difficult choice.

With summer here, Gregory became an even larger part of the family. His daily phone call agenda was executed predictably. I made myself always available when Father called. I always explained to him where I had been when not with him. I never complained to my parents about his calls or demands to know of my whereabouts at all times. Our happily ever after, peaceful little kingdom was well maintained and perpetuated by the act of me forfeiting myself. Alone in my room one night, I wrote this poem:

> *I feel an undertow beneath my feet.*
> *Shifting sands engulfing my limbs,*
> *burying my soul. My voice muffled*
> *among the waves. I am drowning.*

6

Train to be a model!

It was an ad for the International Modeling Agency. According to the ad, all I had to do was send for their thirty-two-page booklet, which could start me on my way to become a model! Since 1945, the International Schools had trained thousands of models. The agency claimed to help one develop the look, the poise, and the confidence that could make the difference in any career. But, if you wanted to be a model, you wanted the International Modeling School! I had become aware that I was fairly good-looking. People used to say I looked like a young Kirk Douglas. My neighbor's sister who was a casting director in New York City used to tell me that I had the perfect look to be in soap operas. I didn't think I would become an actor, but maybe I could become a model. I would receive the attention I so craved. Then, I would be happy!

Benefit of hindsight told me the ad was a load of bullshit, but I fell for it. I was ignorant of the whole modeling scene. I knew nothing about being a model, how to deal with an agent, or what was involved in casting calls. I would soon learn that a three-hundred-and-fifty-pound gorilla would have been accepted to the school. They probably would have even modified the payment plan to accept green bananas.

Still, I often daydreamed of seeing myself in magazine ads, appearing in TV commercials, and my photo displayed on billboards. I envied all those who made money by simply looking glamorous, feeling confident. Maybe it was my love of fashion and clothing that most attracted me to modeling. But at the core of my dream was my desire to be seen, to be heard, to be loved. I sensed that Gregory would not like my idea, but I held on to the hopes that I could prove him and everyone else wrong. I could be a model.

After my pet cemetery violation, I developed emotional struggles. I couldn't explain them, but I was like Pinocchio, hardened and disconnected, living a shattered existence. I craved to be an innocent boy once again. Untouched and unbroken.

I often found solace with nature and with its living things. I felt comforted when our dog, Charlie, curled up next to me. I would talk to him as though he fully understood what I was saying. I rescued ill-fated bugs from our swimming pool; I think skimming the bugs from the water symbolized me wanting to be rescued, too. I often climbed the large maple tree in our backyard. The old tree was yet another imaginary friend—a momentary escape from reality. Perched on my favorite branch, I watch bees pollinating flowers, carrying their bounty back to their hives. I delighted in the performances of squirrels chasing each other along the fence. In my isolation, these were my vulnerable, kindred spirits, all of us living in an oppressive, hostile, environment.

Could I ever find a career that involved nature? Possibly, but I never stopped dreaming about a modeling career. Was the lure of modeling because it was an industry that attracted gay men? Did I even understand that, as a model, I might be objectified and preyed upon like I was by that man at the pet cemetery? How had I been influenced by that assault?

It was comforting for me to think that becoming a model, was not dependent on my high school grades. In high school, I was often unable to focus in the classroom. Frequently, I would daydream and detach myself from whatever subject matter was being taught. I struggled to maintain B grades. At times, I received C's in English and math, my two most difficult subjects. Geography and science, on the other hand, were subjects in which I excelled. Science was more hands-on, which seemed to hold my interest. Given my marginal academic accomplishments, my assumption was that, as a model, I wouldn't have to rely on a superior intellect to earn fame and fortune.

These two things—the love of nature and the lure of modeling—created a conflict. They represented two very different career paths. Was there a way to combine the two? Had anyone heard of a gay forest ranger who wore only Ralph Lauren or Armani? Or, would I be the first?

The next Wednesday, Gregory picked me up at 6:30 P.M. He drove us back to the rectory, where we sat in our designated chairs, watching TV, like we did every other weekday night.

"Gregory, can I ask you something?" I asked nervously.

"Yes of course."

"I want to go to the International Modeling School. What do you think?"

"Okay," he said, staring at me. Then, complete silence.

"I found an ad in last week's paper. They teach you how to model."

His silence continued.

"I have saved a little bit of money, but not enough to buy a car. I could never ask my parents to drive me into the city. Would you take me?"

"Well," he replied. "It seems that my plan for your becoming a priest will have to be put on hold until you get this dumb, foolish, cockamamie idea out of your head." His words were hurtful.

But, I persisted, "I could make lots of money. Who knows, you may be friends with a famous model someday. Later then I could become a priest. A career in modeling is very short, only a few years." I hoped my reply would persuade him.

"Well, you're definitely handsome enough to make lots of money. Plus, the one benefit is, you'll be able to spoil me with gifts."

Everything was always about him. Thinking I may have convinced him, I continued to use his idea to my advantage.

"Of course, I'll be able to buy you anything you want. Then after a few years, I'll join the priesthood. Maybe even be a priest in the same area. See, friends for life."

It worked. He reluctantly agreed to take me to visit the modeling school.

I signed up for modeling classes the following day. I would begin modeling school in two weeks. The classes were one night per week over the course of a few months. I was excited, feeling I had a possible direction. Was this also my lottery ticket out of this lifeless town?

Gregory picked me up the first day of class. He drove an hour into the city and dropped me off at the front door to the school. I later learned that he went to the local gay bar.

After I was inside the school, I was sent to a room with six other men who were also recent enrollees to this fashion institute. Over the next few months, we learned runway techniques, photo movement, model etiquette, grooming skills, self-confidence development, audition practicing, and improvisation. I also learned that one must be acutely clothes-minded while attending class.

I was frightened about walking a runway, improvising, and doing acting scenes. And, I didn't think I was very good at it, but I felt good that I was even trying. It was something I thought I could never do with a shattered sense of self. I wasn't confident about becoming a model, but I believed that one day I might be able to model, based on what others had told me. Plus, I loved fashion. I "absorbed" pictures from *GQ Magazine* and dreamed of a better life.

I graduated from the modeling class and received an 8 ½ by 11-inch white paper certificate of completion, printed with black and red lettering. I was proud of myself. I actually believed that the certificate had worth. I enjoyed the courses. They helped me crack the "wall of no self-esteem." I built up some confidence.

Yet, when I had completed my modeling course, I stashed my certificate in my bedroom bureau, almost as if I were embarrassed about it. I had received no congratulations from my disinterested family members. I wondered if any of my family was even going to ask me about my experience with modeling classes. No. They didn't. It was as though it never happened.

Even more hurtful was the fact that Gregory did not offer me a single bit of recognition for completing the modeling course. Not even a simple pat on the back. I knew he did this out of spite, in the hope that I would change career paths and proceed to the seminary studies. Once again, I felt lost and isolated.

Over the summer months, Gregory frequently sent me Hallmark cards, thanking me for our friendship. I believed I was content having a caring friend, someone who wanted to spend time with me. The only issue was my growing dependence on him. I was a vulnerable, naive, teenage boy. I was living at home without a clear path to follow. I struggled to extricate myself from the grips of his control, but at the same time, I somehow felt dependent on him for support.

A typical day involved receiving phone calls from Gregory, who expected me to be available. I was an on-call companion twenty-four hours a day. On his days off, he would either call me or just show up in my bedroom. I would often lie in bed considering options for disentangling myself from Gregory. How could I end this "friendship?" My parents loved his company. I had resigned myself to the fact that I would never distress my parents in any way. It was enough that my mother had to deal with a well-intentioned yet controlling and verbally domineering husband. She desperately deserved a friend and confidant upon whom she could rely. I couldn't allow myself to hurt my mother.

I didn't completely dislike Gregory; however, I desperately needed more freedom and time to myself. He was very good to me. He spoiled me with wonderful meals at nice restaurants. He allowed me to binge on junk food while watching TV at the rectory. He took me with him to spend time with his friends in Madison. He often gave me gifts. One such gift was a statue of St. Michael, the archangel who was the leader of all angels, holding a sword in his hand, ready to slay the devil.

My family lived only minutes away from the church; therefore, I was quite accessible to Gregory. On a hot summer's day, it was typical for him to show up, unannounced, with his bathing suit in hand. He would walk in the front door, immediately go to the guest room, put on his black Speedo, and then head for the kitchen to prepare his favorite cocktail. He stepped outside to the pool with his glass of scotch in hand.

As I have previously mentioned, he bonded with my parents and they with him. I was becoming concerned that they favored him over me. Often, as they lounged around the pool, I would hear their laughter. Gregory was cajoling and holding court with my parents. He was using his religious status to endear himself to them. But in my mind, I likened him to a noxious weed, emerging constantly, in the garden of our family's existence. If only I had had one large can of DDT... Defoliant Dominie Toxicant!

When he would come to the house, I would eventually make my appearance with a smile, contrived of course. After his day of lounging in the sun by the pool, he would join us for dinner. He would eventually go home, always asking about my plans for the evening.

Two days later, he called.

"Hello," I said, picking up the phone. It was Tuesday morning.

"Hello Michael," Gregory said. "I'm on my way over."

"What for?"

"Why, do you have plans?" he said sarcastically.

"No plans."

"Be ready, I'll be over in two minutes."

"Where are we going?" I asked.

"Pineview. To my home."

"I thought it was your mother's house," I said.

"No. The house is mine. My mother still lives in it."

Father picked me up, and we drove the back roads to Pineview. Arriving twenty minutes later, he began showing me around the property. We first walked over to the shrine he had constructed. It was an old bathtub that he turned upside down, sunk halfway into the ground, and then covered with a fieldstone. Nearby, he had placed a statue of the Virgin Mary, who was the focal point of a stone grotto. A red glass votive candle was burning in front of the shrine.

In another part of the yard, he had placed another statue. It was a four-foot statue of St. Teresa standing on a pedestal. She was the lucky one. Mary's home was nothing more than an inverted wash basin. She should have stayed at the inn.

Next, he led me over to a covered, double-seated lawn glider, made of stained wood. I climbed in, sitting on one side;

he sat on the other. We begin to swing back and forth for
several minutes.

"Hello," Gregory's mother said welcoming us with a wave
from the side porch.

She was a short, rotund woman. Her hair was covered in
a head wrap, a style copied from a famous pancake lady. She
was wearing a full-length apron, made of a yellow-flowered
print. She wore black, orthopedic shoes with her stockings
bunched up around her ankles. She looked as if she'd just
stepped out of the 1940s. I was intrigued by the whole setting.

"Come inside for a glass of homemade root beer," she
said.

"This is my mother Beth," Gregory said as we walked
toward the porch.

"Hello, nice to meet you," I said.

"Mother, this is Michael, the young man I mentioned to
you. He helps me around the church."

"Yes, that's right. Nice to meet you."

Gregory then explained that he, too, often made homemade
root beer soda in the basement. He used glass bottles with
metal caps he sealed with an old-fashioned hand-press capper.
He explained that he mixed root beer extract, cane sugar,
water, and yeast. Then, he bottled the mixture. The beverage
was usually ready in less than a week after fermentation.

"Remember when the bottles exploded?" his mother said,
chuckling.

"Oh, yes! What a frigging mess. Several bottles exploded
all over the basement. You have to be careful about using
the right amount of yeast and the right temperature. Come
follow me. I want to show you something upstairs," Gregory
said leading the way.

Moving through the house, I was convinced that H. G.
Wells had brought me here in his time machine. The home
seemed stuck in the 1950s. Bread box, kitchen table, canisters,
appliances, counters, and cabinets all chosen from a palette of
pastel colors—mint green, pale yellow, turquoise, and white. I
will not wear a poodle skirt.

We climbed the stairs to the second floor and entered
a room the likes of which I had never seen. The room was
filled with dozens of statues of saints in varying sizes. They

were all displayed on wooden shelves that reached the ceiling. There wasn't a bare spot on the walls. An altar, which he had constructed under the window, was the focal point of the room.

"Wow! Looks like you have every saint known," I exclaimed.

"I wish. There are hundreds of saints. The reason I have this room is because I don't say no to anyone who gives me a statue." He explained to me that there was a saint for almost every cause, profession, or special interest. Grabbing several statues off the shelf, he began to explain what some of them were known for.

"This one is St. Jude, the patron saint of hopeless causes."

Hey Jude, don't bring me down, take a sad song and make it better.

I picked up a small, painted, ceramic statue. "What about this one? It's kind of creepy." It was a woman, holding a plate with two eyeballs on it.

"That is St. Lucy. She's the patron saint of the blind. The story was that, when she refused to renounce her religious beliefs, the governor ordered her execution. But, before she was executed, the governor ordered his guards to remove her eyes."

"That's awful," I said. It looked to me like she needed St. Raphael, the patron saint of healing who intervened to heal any kind of brokenness or pain.

Picking up another statue, Gregory said, "This one is of Saint Regis, the name given to the church where I was last stationed. He's the patron of dogs. Over here is Saint Patrick, the patron saint of snakes. Legend is that he banished the snakes out of Ireland after they attacked him during his forty-day fasting on a hill."

He should have done the Atkins Diet. It would have been fewer days.

"What made you become a priest?" I asked.

"Most priests get the 'calling' at some point in their lives. "Strangely, my calling came when I was seated on the toilet."

"Really?" I said.

"Yes, you heard that right. Strange as it may sound, that's where I got the calling."

Is Holy Shit an appropriate response or was it simply a religious movement?

We headed back downstairs. He picked up some mail, and we chatted with his mother. Then, we departed for the rectory, where Hannah had lunch prepared for us. A special lunch at that—baked scallops, rice, salad, and homemade apple pie. We sat at the dining-room table, at the precise moment Pastor Gabriel arrived. The head honcho.

Now, I was nervous as hell. I knew Pastor Gabriel was the one in charge of this church, the commander-in-chief of all operations. And, he was Gregory's boss. What would he think of me dining at Gregory's table? Was he curious as to why Gregory had a younger man over for lunch? My paranoia reigned supreme. I wanted to hide under the table. I felt I had infringed upon the domain Pastor Gabriel so vigorously guarded.

Gregory greeted the supreme ruler in his usual gregarious manner as he walked in. Gregory then explained that he would be happy to accommodate Pastor Gabriel by agreeing to take the Sunday Masses. The Sunday Masses were held twice in the morning and once in the late afternoon.

Pastor Gabriel left us at the table and headed toward his office, also located in the rectory. Hannah placed slices of homemade apple pie in front of us.

"Father, Mrs. Smith wanted to know if you would be stopping by the hospital this afternoon to give the 'Last Rites' to her father," Hannah asked.

"You should know me by now. I don't do hospitals. Period."

Saying nothing, she turned and walked back into the kitchen. I sat quietly, eating my desert, ashamed for him at his response. I remembered from catechism class the seven sacraments: baptism, confirmation, Eucharist, confession, anointing of the sick, holy orders, and matrimony. All were a priest's responsibility.

The only difference with anointing of the sick and the last rites is that, if the person is not in imminent danger of death, he can receive the anointing of the sick which includes confession, communion, and the last rites. Gregory's disconcerting, callous response still bothers me to this day.

Summer arrived. I was still spending time with Gregory. He tried to spoil and to pamper me. I was feeling somewhat content, or was I lying to myself? At times I felt asphyxiated, by Gregory's religious governance over me. I was either with Gregory at the rectory or with him visiting his friends in Madison. It was difficult to say no to these lavish dinners out, movies, gifts, or to experience my family's joy when he was around. I seemed incapable of breaking away from him.

I struggled to find my voice when I was with him, but he was easily triggered. He became aggressive and judgmental on virtually any subject that I asked him about.

"Gregory, what do you think about women having abortions?" I inquired.

"I'll give them pro-choice! They can choose to close their Goddamn legs," he snapped.

"I've noticed you seem to fixate on the word Christmas. What's the big deal with writing Xmas?" I inquired.

"Keep Christ in Christmas. I frigging hate it when people use the word Xmas. Are they that Goddamn lazy or just plain disrespectful?"

"Do you think women will ever be allowed to become priests?"

"When hell freezes over. Or, when the Pope gets married and has children."

These were just some examples of his opinionated responses in our conversations, which he always dominated. To question him or the church's teachings would always result in his giving me an indignant response. I was a spectator to his sparring contest of words. I would ask him questions, in the hopes of learning something, but most of the time, I found myself silenced by his harsh retorts. The only survival skill I mastered was not to question him. The noose around my vocal cords was beginning to tighten. I was once a free-spirited, innocent boy. Now, I was dominated by a religious despot.

Summer 1983. I enrolled at the local college during the summer, in preparation for the fall classes. I was indecisive on a career choice, so I decided to take basic required courses, which would be transferable once I had chosen my major.

Michael Roberts

I gave serious consideration to attending a major university; I even contacted an admissions office once to speak with a counselor. They offered a career curriculum in forestry, wildlife conservation, and environmental studies. I thought seriously about saving endangered species and the ecosystems in which they resided.

When I approached Gregory to tell him of my plans to register for fall classes, he seemed unhappy. His grimacing facial expression said it all. Today's Urban Dictionary would call it his "resting bitch face." I knew I had disappointed him once again. He seemed distressed that I would choose a different path, not focusing on the priesthood. Little did he know that becoming a priest was the furthest thing from my mind. I cringed at the thought of seminary life.

On the other hand, I was afraid of disappointing him and my parents who seemed sure that I would become a priest. That was another reason why they loved Father Gregory—he supported the idea of me becoming a priest. My parents never questioned Father's motives when talking about my going into the priesthood. Whenever he would mention the topic at the dinner table or while lounging by the pool, they nodded approvingly.

"Go ahead to college. I'll get you to change your mind, and you'll come to your senses soon enough. I can wait. By the way, you will not get any help from me or use my car. In time, you will understand that you're going to be a priest. I'm sure of that." His tone was bombastic.

Say what you will, I thought. I never looked good in black! However, in that moment, I tried to placate him. "I'm open to the idea Gregory. But attending the local college would be a chance for me to get used to college life before entering the seminary. I could also transfer the credits," I said reassuringly.

He smiled.

I smiled back. I was deceiving him again. I didn't care. I just wanted to buy myself more time. More time for what? I began to contemplate how I could emancipate myself from my relationship with him. Having more time would allow me to shape my future and to figure out what I wanted to do in life. One idea that percolated in my mind was the thought of running away. But I was scared, afraid of being homeless,

67

living on the streets. I was city stupid and dimwitted! I knew very little of the world beyond my home.

In late July, I bought a used blue Mustang in the hopes that having my own car would lessen my dependence on Gregory for transportation. However, he wasn't thrilled that I had my own car. He wanted to control every aspect of my life, so he saw any sign of my independence as a threat.

August 1983. It was a Thursday evening. Gregory and I arrived at the rectory to watch a movie we had watched before: *Oh, God!* starring George Burns and John Denver. I sat in my designated chair, waiting for him to start the movie. Gregory sat down, quietly staring at me. His gaze made me uncomfortable. I distracted myself by looking around the room. The silence continued for several minutes. I desperately wanted to disappear.

"Michael, are you aware that I am a homosexual?" he blurted out.

Stunned by his blunt question, I swallowed deeply.

"No, I didn't know," I said, hoping I sounded convincing.

"I had a lover for eight years, Father Anthony. We kept our relationship quiet for all those years, except for close friends, who knew we were a couple. Now, we're only friends, but it was not my choosing. He thinks we are no longer sexually compatible. Ironically, he's dating someone named Michael."

"Oh," I said, as though I had just witnessed a bolt of lightning split a tree in half outside his window.

"I say this to you because I feel close to you. I feel I can share this with you."

"Oh." I said. My chest felt heavy as I pushed my lower back into the seat cushion.

"I'm very attracted to you," he calmly said.

I looked down at the floor then blurted, "I need to use the bathroom for a minute."

I walked into the bathroom and closed the door. Dazed, I sat down on the toilet seat. Time stood still. With my head in my hands, I whispered to myself, "Oh God, this is not good. What do I do?"

Like a tiger trapped in a cage, I began pacing around the tiny bathroom. I began fumbling with the sheer, white curtains at the window. Yes, the thought of jumping out the window crossed my mind. Peering through the small panes of window, I longed for an escape to the freedom of the world outside. Meanwhile, the hunter was just a few feet away, preparing for the kill. I started to panic. I thought of my parents. They would be so upset that I had hurt their favorite priest, whom they thought had done so much for me. I tried to control my thoughts, but I knew there would be consequences. I did not want to leave the confines of that room.

"Michael," I heard him calling from the other room.

"Just a minute. I'll be right out," I responded, my anxiety growing by the minute.

I flushed the toilet and opened the bathroom door.

Moving slowly into the room, I stood in the doorway. "I think it's best if I go home now," I said.

Gregory leaned forward, and he looked directly at me with indignation.

"You'll go home when I'm Goddamned good and ready!" he said angrily.

I stood quietly in the bathroom doorway. I was numb.

Gregory leaned back in his chair with a confident smile. He must have known I would have eventually had to sit back in my chair. He was right! Petrified, I walked back to the chair and sat down. This was the first moment when I discovered that I was actually frightened of my mentor, Gregory.

I grew up as a child of this church, receiving my punishment in the form of penance, through confession by priests. I was already a controlled, desensitized kid, brainwashed to do exactly what the priest commanded. At every turn, this mental classical conditioning was being reinforced. My mind had been ruled by sermons at Mass, the teachings of the Bible, the Ten Commandments, and the almost God-like status I owed to men of the cloth. I so desperately wanted to go home, to feel protected within the safety of my room with my parents nearby.

Quietly, I recited the Our Father and Hail Mary prayers, hoping my request would be heard. Gregory rose from his chair.

"Oh boy, this is going to be good," he mumbled to himself. He stood and leaned into my ear.

"Close your eyes. I have a surprise for you. Don't open until I tell you. I mean it; don't you dare open your eyes," he said.

With a sick feeling in my stomach, I sat motionless, eyes closed. After a few minutes passed, I heard, "Okay, open your eyes."

The lights were off, but there was now an array of illuminated candles positioned all around the room. A tray with cheese and crackers and two glasses of red wine now sat on a small table between our chairs. I was completely dumbfounded, not sure what he was doing. He then walked over to his record player and turned it on. Soft, classical music began to play as he sat back down.

"I hope you like this music. I want to create a relaxed, meditative state for you."

"Nice of you to go through all of this," I said, still confused.

"For you, no trouble at all," he responded.

Was this the beginning of his seduction ritual? I assumed so. I was the innocent victim entangled in a black widow's web, with no clear way out. He then handed me one of the two glasses of red wine.

"Here, take a sip."

I cautiously accepted the wine and took a sip. He took a sip as well. He encouraged me to take another sip and then a third. Within minutes, I had drunk more than half the wine. He placed his drink on an end table and walked over to me. He gently removed my glass of wine from my hand and placed it on the center table between the two chairs. He walked around my chair, standing behind me. Placing his hands on my shoulders, he began to lightly massage my shoulders.

"I want you to just relax."

"But…"

"Shhh… just relax. Quiet. Just enjoy."

His massage continued for several minutes. Then, he started moving his hands slowly down from my shoulders, toward my upper chest.

I felt as though I were suffocating. He slowly unbuttoned my shirt and began rubbing my chest. He maneuvered his fingers toward my nipples. I hated the feel of his sweaty hands rubbing my exposed skin. I leaned forward, pulling myself away from his roving hands.

"Please no more!" I said in my desperate appeal for him to stop. Couldn't he see my distress?

He pulled my body back against the chair.

"Relax, no one will know. I would never let your parents find out. This is just between me and you."

He continued rubbing me. He quietly leaned in and whispered, "God would just love you for pleasing a priest. We all have needs."

I was paralyzed with fear. If my parents learned about my budding sexual orientation, it would certainly burden them with unbearable shame, or so I thought. Would I be kicked out of the house onto the streets? Will God be angry with me for not following an appointed priest's orders? Will this disgusting escapade be the gossip around town? I knew he was ordained by the bishop, who believed Gregory shared in the ministry of Jesus passed down through the apostles. Gregory once mentioned that his ordination ritual invoked the Holy Spirit to visit itself upon him, giving him a sacred character, setting him apart for his ministry. I was a nobody...an irrelevant sinner.

A memory flashed of the sexual abuse in the pet cemetery years earlier. My mind began to drift. I seemed to separate myself from the assault taking place. Detaching myself from my current reality was my survival mechanism. My thoughts drifted. It was as if the ordeal was happening to some other wretched soul, and I was barely a reluctant spectator to the debauchery.

Gregory stopped his exploration, came out from behind the chair, and stood in front of me. He tried to kiss me, but the smell of his Brut cologne and sweat made me want to throw up. He then knelt in front of me, slowly unbuckling my brown leather belt, pulling it off, and dropping it to the floor. Next, he removed my sneakers.

Suddenly, he unzipped my Levi's, then forcibly pulled my jeans and underwear down to my knees. My genitals, his targets of opportunity, were now fully exposed. Then, he rested his hands on my thighs, spread my legs apart and began his oral assault. Taking my flaccid member in his mouth, he began his oral copulation. His extreme lust was evidenced by the firm grip with which he held my most private parts while continuing his intense act of fellatio.

I squirmed, trying to make him stop. Even though I was unwilling, I was still a hormone-driven, teenage boy whose erogenous zone was being skillfully manipulated. He held me tightly. The stubble of his mustache felt prickly and abrasive. The sensation of him slobbering on my penis was grotesque. He pinned me down firmly with his elbows and full body weight. Finally, my body gave way to an uncontrolled biological response—I ejaculated into his mouth. I was thoroughly sickened by his assault. But I believed I could have done nothing to prevent it. He was a messenger of the Holy Trinity, a priest, and my mentor.

He stood up, staring at me. "You are part of me now." He then undressed, laid on his bed, and signaled me to come over. I didn't move.

"Get the hell over here and jerk me off!"

I pulled up my pants then begrudgingly, but obediently, walked over to his bedside. I assumed once he had climaxed this ordeal would be over. Reluctantly, I reached for his erect penis. I found I need only use my thumb and index finger because his member was surprisingly small. As I continued stroking him, I averted my eyes, afraid that his ejaculate would spray and further contaminate me. After what seemed like an interminable period, I completed my assignment. He let out a loud, moan, spilling his venom onto his hairy abdomen.

"Well, go get some tissues, and clean me up," he ordered.

Little did I know that this ritual would be the first of many in the ensuring years of abuse.

I got a handful of toilet paper from the bathroom and wiped his stomach. I walked back to the bathroom and flushed the toilet paper, still stunned by the two-act tragedy that had just ended with me as one of the lead characters.

Gregory bragged, "You see, it's not what's under the hood that matters, as long as the engine works."

I assumed his remark was to let me know that the size of his penis was irrelevant. I silently thanked my lucky stars that Gregory did not ask me to fellate him. I sat back down in my chair and put my sneakers back on. I was totally embarrassed by this act, which was nothing less than an assault.

He began to hum while putting his clothes back on. He then walked around the room blowing out all the candles, humming louder. I thought for a moment that he may have been possessed by the devil. Was it possible that an evil entity had infiltrated his body, causing this sick behavior?

I was also angry with myself for not being strong enough to stand up to him. Did the devil really reside within him? If he were truly evil, under the power of Satan, that would explain things.

"You haven't tried the cheese and crackers I prepared," he said as though nothing had happened.

I took one slice of cheese and a cracker and washed it down with my wine, even though eating his snacks was the furthest thing from my mind. Once again, I felt compelled to obey my master's command. I just wanted to go home. I continued drinking my wine, finishing every drop. I thought that leaving no wine in my glass and sampling a bit of food would satisfy his commands, and I would be allowed to go home.

I struggled to hold back my anger, apparently allowing him to feel content with what had just transpired. I knew my calm response was most likely the best way of placating him and being allowed to go home. But, why did I need to placate him? Why did I want to protect his feelings? In doing so, I was overlooking this lecherous rape. I thought, maybe in time, he would recognize that what he had done was wrong and that he would feel some guilt and regret.

"The wine gave me an upset stomach," I said in hopes of leaving.

"You need the bathroom?"

"No."

"I'll drive you home. You'll be okay. You're just not used to drinking wine."

"I guess you're right."

"Thank you for coming over. Don't worry about a thing. Your parents will never know. I'll call you tomorrow," he said as we got in his car.

On the ride back to my home, we exchanged no words, only a quick good-night as I exited the car. I walked into the house through the back entrance, where my mother was standing in the kitchen.

"Hello, how was your night?" she asked.

"Fine. We watched a movie," I said smiling, as though I needed to be as convincing as an Oscar-award-winning actor.

I climbed into the shower. I stood under hot water, lathering up with as much soap as I could. I scrubbed my skin with a cotton washcloth. How does one remove this contamination? I scoured my body until my skin was turning red. Stepping out of the shower, I still felt that I could not wash away my disgust. I turned the water on in the sink so no one would hear me. I began to cry. I was certain that God was angry with me. This might be my punishment for my sins. It was a furious Deity who was acting through Gregory to chastise me and to teach me a lesson.

I never fully associated the abuse with the abuser. I strongly believed having abhorrent thoughts about men was damnable. Did I deserve this abuse? Did I believe I was pleasing God by allowing a priest to seduce me? Did I believe I was atoning for my sinful nature?

The following morning, I awoke late, only to find a white envelope lying on my bed cover. I knew immediately it was from Gregory. Did he enter my room when I was asleep? Was it an apology letter? Was this a copy of a letter he may have written to my parents, telling them I was a sick, sinful homosexual? I summoned the nerve to tear it open. I slowly pulled out a greeting card, the cover of which featured a rose in full bloom. The generic message inside read: "I will always love you now and forever." He had signed the card, Gregory.

Oh my God. If my mom had opened this before I did, I would surely have been evicted from our home and ostracized by friends and relatives. I, Frankenstein's monster, would not be allowed to show my face. I would be shunned by a moral society. I would be seen only vile and repulsive.

I knew my father would be working all day, but my mother would be home from her part-time job around twelve-thirty. I raced to the kitchen, grabbed a matchbook. and ran outside, still in my pajamas. I grabbed a hand shovel, dug a hole, and dropped the card into the hole and set it ablaze. I watched as the card slowly became ash. Then, I covered the hole with the section of sod I had removed. Out of sight, out of mind. I was confident that no one would ever notice the small, patched section of grass. How could this be? I'm already living a life without direction, and now, I'm destroying a love letter written to me from a Catholic priest.

I was deeply distressed that Gregory would do this to me. Did he even comprehend that his brazen behavior was a potential damning liability for the both of us? If only I had had the foresight to take the evidence to the bishop at that time, my life would have been far different from the hell I was about to endure.

The letters and cards kept appearing every few weeks. I, in turn, literally kept the fires stoked, burning his letters in different locations in the backyard. I went into survival mode, removing all traces of my enslaved, homosexual lifestyle.

The day after the rape at the rectory, Gregory arrived for dinner. I didn't want to leave my bedroom. I didn't want to sit at the dinner table. I felt deeply ashamed for what had taken place. Sadly, I, the victim, shouldered the blame.

Yet, upon his arrival, he walked right into my bedroom.

"Hello there," he said with a smile.

"Hello," I said shocked, but not totally surprised that he entered my room uninvited.

"I have something for you."

He handed me a square, gift-wrapped box, which I reluctantly took. I unwrapped it and pulled out a rather expensive statue of St. Francis of Assisi. "It's alabaster. I know you're aware that he's the patron saint of animals. I thought you should have this because I know you love animals."

"Thank you, Gregory," I said, trying to sound polite.

"Bring it into the living room to show your parents."

I obeyed his directive and carried the statue to the living room where I showed everyone the gift I had just received. Was his act of kindness a way to strengthen his bond with my parents? Probably. Did he feel remorse for his behavior, and was he attempting to make up for it? Probably not.

"That's such a beautiful gift," my mother said.

"Yes, Gregory, thank you," I said again.

Fall 1983. Peter entered St. Luke's Seminary, but for me, nothing had changed. The abuse continued. I never knew on what night he would make his sexual advances. Like a robot, I survived the only way I knew how. I had learned to disassociate. I would let my mind drift away, as if I were anesthetized, not even feel present as I submitted to his desires. I began to realize that to acquiesce to his demands would fulfill his needs for a few days, maybe even a week. It would give me a few days with no molestation. A few days of peace.

Gregory's control began to escalate. His verbal comments became more domineering, "Michael, you should appreciate all that I do for you. You know anyone you meet will only hurt you or use you. Trust no one. You're following a good path by spending time with a priest who can teach you. Your parents seem so happy that we're friends. Your parents would be hurt if our relationship ended. And by the way, your friend Peter is a user. You should stay away from him."

His control techniques worked. The sad thing is, I believed every fucking word he said! Why wouldn't I? I was a naive teenaged boy who was afraid to acknowledge his own sexual orientation. I started to actually believe that Gregory must be right—anyone outside our relationship, other than my family, would hurt me.

I didn't understand Gregory's behavior prior to his first assault. His actions were what is called "grooming" the victim. I was his targeted quarry. His scheme was to first gain access to my parents, to infiltrate their lives, and to establish a connection. Next, he started controlling my way of thinking by suppressing my voice and by buying me gifts, making me feel safe and accepted. Then, it's time for a change up: alternate demeaning comments with loving compliments. I would later learn that these alternating behaviors were classic techniques for indoctrinating cult members. Such techniques tend to make people walk on eggshells, not knowing what to expect. This process makes the victim easier to control.

This rollercoaster made me become dependent on Gregory for my own sense of self-worth. Lastly, Gregory made me financially dependent on him in his selfish effort to influence any decisions I attempted to make.

·

Years later, I did some research on mind control. I came across the acronym, BRAT, which made perfect sense. It stood for Bond. Reliance. Attenuate resistances. Trap. If only the Internet had been available to me during my teenage years, I may have been able to research the warning signs of how I was being manipulated. The term BRAT is explained as follows:

Bond: First, the offender creates a bond and becomes a special friend. They find one of these three sources of desires to manipulate: escape, worth, and companionship.

Did I covet all three? I was trying to find a career, answers about my life, some path to follow. I suffered from low self-worth. Gregory was there to tell me how special I was. He became my only source of self-esteem. I grew closer to Gregory who was the only one to help support this newfound worth. Feeling isolated and lonely, Gregory filled the void of my isolation.

Reliance: Second, the offender increases one's isolation from avenues of support. They keep the victim away from friends, control their finances, make their decisions, and shrink the sphere of influence from outside, interpersonal relations.

Gregory made all of the decisions for me. He used fear and scare tactics to prevent me from fostering other relationships. Becoming involved in all areas of my life, he would eventually find a job for me, choose my car, and even closely monitor my other, more mundane purchases, including my clothing choices.

Attenuated Resistance: Attenuated means having been reduced in force, effect, or value.

Attenuated resistance is made up of several parts:

Progression: The offender uses rationalization and normalization to justify the new sexual activities.

"Michael, it's completely normal to have needs. God is happy when you please a priest. Masturbation is a normal part of life. God created your body. You shouldn't be ashamed of it."

Coercion: The offender has power over the victim—physically, emotionally, and financially. Victims often submit to abuse out of fear of invoking the offender's wrath, being unable to survive without the offender's funds or losing emotional connection with the offender, which equated to: "submission is easier than resistance."

Trap: Victims are held in the abusive relationship through two primary means: their sense of hopelessness and feelings of guilt and fear.

I believed I couldn't survive on my own. I was convinced that, without Gregory, my life would be even worse. I was fearful others would judge me as complicit, weak, or even worse, deviant. How does one hold a deluge of rain in a paper cup?

In the fall, I started evening classes at the local college, taking liberal arts courses. My car was often broken down, and I didn't want to impose on my busy parents for a ride, so I was usually able to borrow Gregory's car. Of course, his favor came with a price. He took sexual advantage of me when I would return his car that evening. That was the deal—I could borrow his car as long as I "repaid" him later.

Thanksgiving 1983. Gregory arrived at our house for dinner. I stayed in my room, waiting until the last minute before I had to show up in the dining room. At dinner, I was seated next to Gregory, which was the normal protocol when he was over for those weekly dinners.

"Heavenly Father, we thank you for this loving family I am proud to belong to. Thank you for the wonderful meal you provided. Thank you, Martha, for all your hard work. We are blessed when so many others are less fortunate."

"Amen," we all responded.

We began passing the dishes around the table. Finally, everyone's plates were filled with the traditional holiday meal, and we began eating. Then, I suddenly lurched forward in my seat. Gregory was groping my inner thigh under the table. What the hell, I said to myself. I pushed his hand away, pissed by his totally inappropriate behavior. Of course, I concealed my disdain. He, on the other hand, smiled, and continued eating as if nothing had happened.

Excuse me Dad, can you please pass me the turkey? Oh, by the way, Gregory likes sucking my cock, but that's a different kind of bird, and it's not roasted or served on a platter. Mom, please pass me the gravy. Oh, and by the way, Gregory loves for me to massage his meat for him until he shoots his gravy all over his stomach, and he doesn't have a gravy boat. If only I were brave enough. Thank goodness no one could read my mind.

The abuse continued. His domination intensified with each passing day. I was becoming dead inside. I was a zombie. I got up every morning, ate my breakfast, and arranged my schedule around Gregory's whims. It seemed as if my future was set in stone and for me to envision anything better was a fool's paradise. I resigned myself to this inescapable, indentured existence. I became a trapped, docile dog, afraid of his master. I learned to roll, to jump, and to sit on command. I was always under a microscope, having to explain daily where I was, accounting for every hour.

7

It was midafternoon when the phone rang.

"Michael, be ready at 6:00. We're going over to Sandra's tonight," Gregory ordered.

"Okay, I'll be ready."

We arrived at Sandra's home, only to be greeted at the front door by her friend, Reggie, in full drag...not a pretty sight I must say. Like a character from an old southern novel, he began his dramatic performance.

"My, my," Reggie drawled. "Hello, there you handsome men. I see you gentlemen-callers are here to escort this lady to the fancy dress ball."

Lady...or did he mean Tramp? He looked more like Scarlett O'Hara after years of swallowing cheap booze and drugs. Fancy ball? A vision of sequins, bedazzling his scrotum, flashed in my mind. It all seemed so bizarre to me.

Gregory smiled. I said nothing.

"Hello, I'm Ms. Jordan Summers. And whom do I have the pleasure of meeting?" Reggie said, extending her limp wrist to me.

I played along. "I'm Michael, your gallant knight in shining armor."

"I do declare, sister's getting the vapors. I'm about to swoon."

"Reggie, get a grip," Gregory said mockingly.

Reggie, staying in character, walked over to the dining room table where Sandra was seated by her son Parker, who handed Reggie, or should I say Scarlett O'Hara, a neatly-rolled joint. Yes, marijuana! After lighting it, they each took a deep drawl on it.

This was my first exposure to any type of drug. I had never tried marijuana, and I was not going to start now. I was disgusted with them doing an illegal drug.

"Reggie, the pastor will be gone Wednesday night, so you and I can host a gay dinner party at the rectory," Gregory said.

"Lovely my dear. What time shall I arrive?"

"Plan on 7:00," Gregory said.

"Fabulous. This will be a party of all parties. People will be dying to get an invite."

I spent the evening observing this drag scene, which was quite unfamiliar to me, played out by Reggie, the Southern Belle, or was it more like a Southern Bella Lugosi?

Then Gregory began chatting about some theater guild he had formed. "We will begin auditions in January. That way we can begin performances late in March," Gregory explained.

I sat back, wondering what this audition talk was all about. They spent another thirty minutes conversing about songs, props, and the title of the show. Gregory then turned to Sandra.

"Sandra, you can choose the solo you want to do. Reggie will direct the show, and Priscilla, the choir director at the church, will be musical director. I'll be the producer. Okay, it's getting late; I have to get back to the rectory."

Why was he in a rush to get back? I was scared…sensing his haste meant that he was planning to make another sexual assault on me.

As we left, Sandra walked us to the door.

"Michael, enjoy your evening," she said with a grin.

Why the odd grin? I thought. Was she a quiet bystander, supporting Father Gregory's illicit behavior?

Arriving back at the rectory, we entered his room. I was tired and wanted to go home. He had other plans. I noticed his body language and his facial expressions—familiar signs that he wanted his sexual needs met. This time I thought, I needed to stand up to him, in spite of my fear. I took a deep breath and threw caution to the wind. In that moment, I elected to challenge him. I knew, however, that I might face serious consequences. And I was so right. I was about to learn the meaning of severe retribution for standing my ground.

"Michael, come lie with me on the bed. Take off your shoes and belt," he instructed.

"I don't really feel up for it," I said meekly.

"Now!"

"I'm kind of tired, Gregory. I want to go home and go to bed."

"Get your cute little ass over here."

"Can you take me home?"

"Goddamn it! Get over here now!"

"Take me home."

He got out of bed, put his clothes back on, and marched downstairs, leaving me alone in his room.

Dear God, what did I just do? What could he tell my parents? Frightened, I went to the top of the stairs. No sign of Gregory. I went downstairs and I stood quietly in the kitchen. Within seconds, I heard the side door slam loudly; then I recognize the lifting of the garage door. I peeked out the kitchen window and watched Father Gregory back his car midway down the driveway.

I walked outside and slid into the passenger's seat. I could see from his expression that Father Gregory was livid. Scared by his silence, I avoided eye contract. I knew I was in trouble.

"Sorry," I said, aware that I had really angered him.

He completely ignored me and began to speed in the direction of my house.

"Please slow down. You're going over the speed limit," I said.

That only angered him more. He pressed the gas pedal even more. The car became momentarily airborne at the crest of each hill, landing with a thud each time.

"Stop it! Are you trying to kill us?" I shouted in a panic.

No response.

He seemed to zone out entirely. I braced myself, pressing my feet against the floorboard and grabbing the door handle. As we approached the turn onto my street, he slammed on the brakes, spinning the car halfway around. I could smell the rubber tires burning. I sat motionless as the car came to a stop.

He leaned toward me, pointing his finger at my face.

"You will pay for this," he raged.

Michael Roberts

He pressed the gas, turned the car around, and continued up the street toward my house.

Dear God, I prayed silently. Please kill me now. I want to die. He is going to say something to my parents. I just know it. Gregory pulled into my driveway. As I was stepping out of the car, he sped off. I fell to the pavement. The passenger door slammed shut on its own. Stunned by his dangerous stunt, I got up, brushed myself off, and walked to the back door. I had scraped my palms on the cement. But my real concern was that my parents might have witnessed Gregory's display of aggression. I was relieved, when I entered the house, that my parents, now in their bedroom, mentioned nothing about the noise or what had just transpired outside. For the moment, I was safe, but nervous that I would face more of Gregory's wrath. I decided to broach the subject of Gregory to my parents.

"Hello" I said calmly.

"You're back early," Mom said.

"Yes, Gregory forgot he had some paperwork to do." I wasn't sure what to say next.

"You going to bed now or watch some TV?" Mom asked.

"I'm tired. I think I'll go to bed."

"Well, have a good night."

"You know, Gregory isn't an easy friend to have." I said. "As a matter-of-fact, I'm not sure if I even like him all that much," I said, hoping they would sense that something was wrong.

"Well, he seems to do a lot for you," my dad said.

"I know. I'm not saying he doesn't, but he's just a difficult personality to deal with."

"He's been a good friend. You should appreciate that and overlook his faults."

"I guess so," I replied.

I walked out of their bedroom, feeling like a coward— not brave enough to tell them about the sexual abuse I was enduring. How does one explain to two parents who never allowed discussions about anything to do with sex, that their son was being sexually assaulted? By a homosexual! I was just not willing, nor did I feel I had the power, to open Pandora's box.

I went to my room, shut the door, and flopped on my bed. Like a broken record, I begin recalling the last words he said to me, "You will pay for this." What was he going to do? I only hoped he meant that our friendship was over and that I was free of him.

Several days passed with no sign of Gregory. I was relieved to think that maybe he wanted nothing to do with me anymore. Saturday evening my parents decided to go to the church service, so we would fulfill our weekend obligation. I was glad that Pastor Gabriel was going to be saying Mass, so I could avoid seeing Gregory. Upon arrival, we sat toward the back waiting for Mass to begin. The organist began to play. Out from the shadows, Father Gregory entered the sanctuary with three altar boys. Where was Pastor Gabriel? I thought he was saying Mass.

Through the entire Mass, I worried about what he may say to my parents as we left the church at the end of the service. Halfway through Mass, Gregory rose and walked over to the pulpit to begin his homily. I stared into the prayer book, avoiding eye contact.

"I would like to ask you all to pray for me."

The congregation was silent.

"Several nights ago, a friend of mine died. It's a very painful time for me. I'll need your support. Please keep me in your prayers and thoughts."

He then began his sermon. I sat in my seat, shocked, realizing that when he said a friend had died, he was referring to me. He used the church to gain sympathy for himself. Was he expecting homemade apple pies, cards, and flowers? I also wondered if he was doing all the Masses, making sure I would be at one of them to witness his display of depravity.

Exiting the church, I walked alongside my parents, hoping to avoid any contact with him. As we approached the exit, I could hear parishioners offering him condolences for his loss. Some gave him a hug. I walked to the car. I never knew whether my parents said anything to him. I was, once again, stunned by his behavior.

The following Tuesday, I walked out of my bedroom to the sounds of laughter coming from downstairs. I walked into the kitchen, only to see Father Gregory, with a scotch in hand, laughing with my mother.

"Hello Michael," he said grinning.

"Hello," I said, not sure what to say, seeing him in our kitchen.

He acted as though nothing had happened. Now, I was beginning to loath this man who had not only violated me, but who had put my life in danger when I fell out of his car. Furthermore, he had played his parishioners for fools and continued to foist himself on my family. He knew how to play emotional chess. I wasn't cunning enough to outwit him. He was the king on this board, clever enough to move in any direction. I was the pawn, able to move in only one direction. If only I could gather support from the knight, bishop, and rook, I could win this game.

Now, he was seamlessly reentering my life. I was not pleased. We spent the remainder of the year getting together with him. I felt my only recourse was to try to make the best of it. Once again, I was trapped.

For me, Christmas was always a magical time, but this Christmas would be one of despair for me. Gregory's assaults on me continued. I still believed deep in my heart that I could tell no one. All I could do was tolerate Gregory in my life.

Of course, Gregory recruited me to help him decorate the inside and outside of the church and rectory. I put up the rectory Christmas tree and a one-hundred-piece manger set in front of the altar. Incidentally, the manger scene included a large plastic squirrel that he took from my parent's garden. I placed dozens of poinsettia plants around the church, hung wreathes, and draped banners on the walls.

Father Gregory spent hours with the choir, preparing them for the list of Christmas songs they would sing. He even rehearsed the children for their role in the Christmas play. The stage was set for his performance. The only things missing were the Radio City Rockettes.

The only response Gregory had from the penny-pinching pastor was that he was spending too much for electricity, used for all of the outside lights. When the pastor complained, Father Gregory had no problem putting him in his place. I often saw Gregory belittle the pastor, slam doors in his face, and yell at him.

The parishioners loved Gregory's Christmas Spectacular! They adored his P. T. Barnum–like circus. Of course, Barnum did say, "There's a sucker born every minute."

The following week, Father Gregory placed a note inside the church bulletin, thanking those who helped make the Christmas program possible. He thanked the choir, the choir director, the organist, and contributors to Toys for Tots. He also thanked me for decorating the church. Always ill at ease, I wondered if there were whispers that might be spreading among the parishioners about the priest spending so much time with a younger man.

At the bottom of the bulletin, he added this:

No Excuse Sunday:

To make it possible for everyone to attend church next weekend, we are going to make attendance very special. A cot will be placed in the sanctuary for those who say, "Saturday I work around the house all day, and Sunday is my only day to sleep." The bulletin continued:

- Eye drops will be available for those with tired eyes from watching TV too late Saturday night.
- We will have steel helmets for those who say, "The roof will cave in if I go to church."
- Blankets will be furnished for those who think the church is too cold, and fans will be available for those who say it's too hot.
- We will have hearing aids for those who say the priest speaks too softly. Cotton balls, to stick in your ears, will be available for those feel the priest speaks too loudly.
- Score cards will be available for listing hypocrites present.

Michael Roberts

- One hundred TV dinners for those who can't go to Church and prepare dinner.
- A selection of trees and grass will be displayed for those who like to see God in nature.
- A putting green near the altar for those who say, "Sunday is my day for golf."
- The Sanctuary will be decorated with both Christmas poinsettias and Easter lilies for those who have never seen the church without them.

Odd as it may seem, most everyone in the church liked his "No Excuse Sunday." They were used to the mundane and monotonous, so they found this new game most amusing.

In *Aesop's Fables,* the wolf disguises himself as a sheep. At night, the wolf, in sheep's clothing, could hide himself among the flock and eat a lamb whenever he wanted. Then one day a shepherd, needing mutton for the table, killed the wolf instantly, thinking he killed a lamb. The moral to the story: Appearances are deceptive.

8

January 1984. I didn't re-enroll in college. Gregory's growing dominance in my life and my lack of funds were the deciding factors. I assumed my parents believed I would eventually find my career path.

One Monday evening in February, Gregory picked me up at my home. I always wondered when his animalistic, sexual urges were fueling his behavior. At the rectory, we flipped through the TV channels and talked about the upcoming church show he was planning with Reggie and Sandra. After two hours, I expressed my concern about the snow fall that was accumulating, but Gregory reassured me that I would be home well before the snow became a problem.

"Gregory, I think you better drive me home, the snow's starting to come down faster now," I said.

"I will, but will you stand up for a minute?" he asked.

"Okay, but why?" I stood up, wondering what was coming next.

"I want you to take off your clothes one piece at a time. Do it very slowly," he ordered.

"The snow is really coming down now. I better go."

"Just do what I say. You like pleasing me."

"I think you better drive me home."

With that, he instantly turned into the rabid wolf.

"I will take you home once, but first you take off your Goddamned clothes right now, before I take them off for you."

"I don't want to tonight. We did this a few days ago."

He got up from his chair, slammed the bedroom door, and lunged toward me. He grabbed my belt and tried to unbuckle it. I placed my hand over his, wrestling him to stop.

"You will take off these clothes?"

"Stop!"

At that point, he pushed me, and I fell back onto the bed. He continued to grab at my belt buckle. When he succeeded in unfastening my belt, he threw it against the wall. He then pulled my shoes off, one by one, as I continued pushing him away. He unbuttoned my jeans, as if driven by an uncontrolled, savage lust. He was much smaller than me and really not very strong. But, when aroused and angry, he was powerful.

After several minutes of rolling on the bed, he seemed to give up. Out of breath, he walked out of the room, slamming the door behind him. I was left in an almost-fetal position atop his bed quilt. I knew he was enraged over my wanting to go home, leaving him without his sexual gratification. I got dressed, and as I rushed downstairs to the kitchen, I heard the backdoor slam shut. He had gone to the church, leaving me alone.

In the hope of getting a ride home, I foolishly followed him to the church. As I stepped out into the cold February night, I realized that I forgot my coat. I turned back but the rectory door was locked. Clearly, my situation was going from bad to worse. I ran to the church entrance, only to find the main church door locked. I knocked to get his attention.

"Gregory, I left my coat in the rectory. I need to get home," I yelled.

No answer! I repeated myself. Again, nothing! A third try, once again, resulted in no response.

By now, I was starting to shiver. I decided to walk around the church, attempting to open any of the side doors. No luck. All doors were locked. I was stuck outside, with no coat, in the dead of winter. I can't believe this, I thought. I walked back to the main entrance and begin kicking at the door with my foot. I shouted, "Gregory, I'm stuck outside. Open the door. It's cold. I left my coat inside the rectory. Please open the door!"

Suddenly, the organ began making discordant noises. Gregory, with no piano skills, decided to take out his aggression by pummeling the keys, drowning out my cries.

I knew, at that point, I was in a dangerous situation. My home was a good twenty-minute walk away, but I realized that walking was my only option. Jogging and at times sprinting, I arrived home fifteen minutes later. I felt frozen to the bone. I knew I needed a good lie to tell my parents, so I told them that I wanted to jog home to get some exercise. They questioned why I had no coat. I explained that I thought it was better to run without being weighed down with extra clothing as a way to burn off more body fat. I was becoming a compulsive liar.

Several days later, Gregory, with my coat in hand, came over to the house. Once again, acting as if nothing had happened. It was his pattern—give him a few days and he would be right back like an unsightly wart.

"Michael, you forgot your coat the other night. And by the way, I signed you up to be in the show."

"The theater show you were discussing with Reggie and Sandra?"

"Yes, that one."

"Tell me again. What kind of show is it?"

"It's a musical, put on by the theater guild I formed in the church. We'll perform: *Join Us at the Cabaret.* It's a compilation of popular songs from various musicals. Rehearsals will begin tomorrow night and continue every Thursday night until the show's performances on the last weekend in March. I expect you at all rehearsals. You can also help the rest of the cast members with painting the sets."

"I have never sung in front of anyone. The thought of doing so makes me nervous."

"Relax. You're in the men's chorus and in the dance ensemble."

"I don't really want to be part of the show."

"You'll do it, and that's that."

He was right. I did exactly as I was told to do. I spent the next few hours wondering why I could never cut the puppet strings he'd attached to me. Maybe, if I could stop all of my own lies and deception, I might lose the strings and become a real young man.

The musical numbers I was scheduled for were "Luck Be a Lady" from *Guys and Dolls,* "One" from *Chorus Line,* and "Hello Dolly" from *Hello Dolly.* He told me there were a few other musical numbers that would involve me.

The show went off without a hitch. I was scared, but I found myself actually enjoying the music. I enjoyed receiving positive responses from the audience. I felt seen, noticed, and supported. The parishioners seemed to enjoy watching the talents of the church members.

After these theater performances, but sometime before Easter, I wrote a letter to Peter, who was at the seminary. I hoped he would write and give me some insight as to what happened between him and Gregory. It was certainly never my aim to make him jealous. If anything, I was hurt that he ever introduced me to Father Gregory. I assumed they were no longer friends, but I wasn't sure. I had seen them talking before Christmas Mass. I thought it was possible that I was being used by Gregory while Peter was away at seminary life. Was he saying the same things to Peter that he said to me? Was I a seasonal play toy while Peter was away?

In the letter, I told Peter about my growing friendship with Father Gregory. I mentioned a dinner party that I attended at Sandra's home. Reggie had made homemade French onion soup. I also told him that Father treated me to dinner at fancy restaurants, whose customers included well-known local celebrities.

A few weeks later, I received a letter from Peter. His letter consisted of one sentence: "Kept item of the Vatican-American Queens." He was referring to gay priests as "Queens" and was calling me a kept man. I wasn't sure what Peter meant. Was he jealous in some way?

Years later, I learned from Peter that he had sent Gregory a letter at the same time, telling him that he was no longer interested in working for the church when he was home for school breaks. It was Peter's way of pulling away.

Spring 1984. I recall one incident when I was left alone in Father Gregory's room while he walked over to the church to help Pastor Gabriel hand out communion during Saturday evening Mass.

"Michael, I'll be back in twenty minutes."

"That's fine. I'll just watch TV."

After he was out the front door, the inquisitive side of me was compelled to look around his room. I wasn't really sure what I was looking for, or for that matter what urged me to proceed. Was I looking for something that revealed itself as gay material? Was I looking for pictures of Anthony, his ex-boyfriend? I knew my time was limited, so I began searching in the closet. My attention was drawn to a faded, brown briefcase hidden, on the floor, tucked behind a built-in bookcase. I pulled out the briefcase and opened it as I took a seat in Gregory's chair.

I was stunned at what I saw. Porn magazines and gay videos. I hadn't seen pornography before, so the scenes I saw were rather shocking. Nervous that he would be back soon, I flipped through a few of the magazines. I saw mostly naked men—porn stars, I assumed.

I wasn't quite sure what to make of all this. I was bothered by a Catholic priest owning such pornography, but yet I was titillated by what I saw. I closed the briefcase and placed it back where I found it. I remember spending the rest of the day worried that I hadn't put the magazine back in the right order, and that Gregory would know that I had looked through his closet.

May 1984. Gregory called me at home. He ordered me to wear some old clothes and demanded that I be ready when he got there to pick me up. I didn't have a chance to question him as to why. Within five minutes, he arrived and commenced honking his horn. I rushed out the door and got into his car.

"Took you long enough," he said derisively.

"It was just a few minutes. You can't wait? What's the rush?"

"We're spending the entire day tearing out sod on one side of my mother's house. Then we need to plant fifty bushes. I'm sick and tired of mowing that Goddamn hill."

"All day, really? Will this be for extra money?"

He chuckled.

"Pay you?" he said, laughing. "You'll do it and that's that. End of discussion." He manipulated me with all of the dexterity of a precocious child playing with a remote-controlled car.

Gregory helped with the work, but I spent the next ten hours in the hot summer sun, doing forced labor. Removing large sections of sod, tilling the soil, and planting the bushes was a grueling effort. The prickly juniper bushes cut up my hands. Sweat poured down my face, and my sweat-soaked clothes clung to my skin. If I dared to complain or to suggest a rest period, I was assaulted by a barrage of snide rebukes. Given his self-imposed deadline of sunset, he worked me harder and faster.

June 1984. I receive a phone call from Peter telling me that he was home for the summer and wasn't sure if and when he would return to St. Luke's Seminary. He also mentioned that he would start working full-time next month at the hardware store in town. We agreed that we should get together soon.

Not much in my life had changed. If anything, things were worse. Gregory continued to show up for dinner; he continued to enter my bedroom without knocking. He would close the door and try to kiss me. I always freaked out, begging him to stop, warning him that my parents could find out. He would only stop if I promised to have sex with him later that night. Extortion was the game he played. He must have assumed I was too cowardly to say anything to my parents. He was right.

"Okay, I'll fool around with you tonight," I would say reluctantly.

One afternoon on his visit, he entered my bedroom signaling for me to follow him. I wasn't sure what he was doing, but I prepared myself for the worst. I followed him to the kitchen where my mom was cleaning.

"Martha, my friend Barry, who lives next door to the rectory, has a house on Cape Cod. Tomorrow, I'm taking Michael with me for a few days of relaxation. I need a mental break."

"You mean Barry, who's one of the lectors at the Mass?" my mom asked.

"Yup! He gave me the key to his summer home. He'll leave me his cottage in his will. It's all how you work it."

"Do I get a say in this?" I asked.

"Why? You don't want to go? Anyone else would appreciate the chance to get away, relax, walk on the beach," Gregory responded.

"I'll go!" my mom said jokingly.

"Ah, too late. Hannah has already packed up food for the two of us for the three days," he said.

I agreed to go—as if I had a choice. I packed my things that night and he picked me up the following morning. I assumed that maybe some fresh air would be beneficial. Again, I was in the position of trying to make the best of a bad situation.

We arrived at the summer home around noon.

"Wow, Barry has a nice vacation home!" I exclaimed.

"He told me anytime I want to use it, just ask him."

"We should eat then go for a walk on the beach," I suggested.

"Let's fool around first. We have the whole place to ourselves."

"No, I'm hungry, Gregory."

"We can make it a quickie."

"Maybe later tonight."

"Tonight, too," he replied.

"Gregory, stop!"

"You want food, then let's fool around," he said sternly.

"Really, you're holding me hostage, not feeding me until I give you sex?"

"Yup, just a quickie is all I ask."

Ignoring him, I decided to make my lunch. I began reaching for the food I had placed in the refrigerator—the luncheon meat and mayonnaise. As I began making a sandwich, he walked over to the counter, grabbed both the meat and the mayonnaise and placed them back into the refrigerator. Then, he stood, blocking my access to the refrigerator.

I looked at him in disbelief. He was really telling the truth about not letting me eat until I satiated his sexual appetite.

He won! I knew I would have to play his game. I had no prison bars, yet I was still his captive. I had no outside walls to scale, yet I was still a prisoner.

That evening, when he fell asleep, I climbed out of bed and searched for a pen and a piece of paper. I scribbled out a plan of escape. This is what I wrote:

8-12 Month Plan

A. Find any job: part-time.
Ask Gregory to pay me for church work.
Part of the money will be hidden in my room.

Michael Roberts

Buy items I will need: towels, toilet paper, pots, pans, plates, flatware, glasses, bowls, sheets, pillow, blankets, microwave, toaster, utensils, tea pot, lamps, TV, chair. *B.* Hide items. I will ask my aunt Wilma if I can use her basement. *C.* Buy a used car to transport items. *D.* When enough money is raised, pack up all items, when everyone is at work, leave letter. Possible locations: Florida (warm weather), Colorado. Live in car until you get apartment and job.

At the end of my list, I wrote another poem:

I was a tree, like no other in the forest.
Roots grounded in the sacred soils of life,
budding forth the branches of individuality.
But my leaves slowly become infested with the poison of
manipulation, my trunk decays,
rots with the fungus of control.
I will soon decompose under the mossy ground, inconspicuous
to even the smallest of creatures.

9

It was ironic that I came across a new line of avant-garde cards in a local card shop. One card showed a young boy in the confessional, "Forgive me Father for I have sinned." The priest responded, "Yeah! Hold on a second while I prepare your priesthood application."

Another card depicted a little boy confronting a bishop, "I was molested by a priest."

"I forgive you," the bishop responded.

Last but not least, another card showed a little boy, saying to a priest, "When I grow up, I want to be a priest."

"That's strange, I'm grown up and I want a little boy." The priest responded.

My life as a zombie progressed. I was forgetting the pleasures in life. Father Gregory controlled me like a voodoo doll he'd assembled. I just tolerated the misery. My dream of going back to college had faded.

July 1984. All I had to show for my life was my involvement with the church theater company and the small, pathetic performance as a cast member, where I was often relegated to the background. Feeling demoralized, my life seemed to fall into a rhythmic repetition. I would continue to give in to Gregory's sexual demands. I no longer argued about it with him. The simplest solution for survival was to give him what he wanted or drown in a sea of clergy-imposed misery.

I was penniless. I had to ask Gregory, in all humility, to help me. I couldn't ask my parents. They were already raising four kids on a limited income. I hoped, with Father Gregory's cooperation, that I could make some much-needed cash. It was critical for me to stick to my covert plan of leaving. I recalled that night when I jotted down all of my ideas on a piece of paper in that Cape Cod cottage. Those goals somehow kept me motivated. Maybe I could escape. I was determined to keep my promise to myself. I had hidden my list of goals in my room.

"Gregory, I need to find a job. I have no income," I said.

"Um," he uttered.

"Maybe you can ask some parishioners who have businesses if I could work for them," I said.

"I don't think so," he replied.

"Sorry I asked. I thought you'd help me."

"I would rather have you around here."

Clearly, he didn't want to loosen his control over me.

"What do you mean?"

"You can take over Peter's job."

"That would be great."

"That self-absorbed slut is no longer around. You can start tomorrow."

"Can I ask what happened between you and Peter? I saw you talking to him before Mass during Christmas week."

"I tried to talk to the slut, to tell him to be more involved with his own church because he was a seminarian for this parish. But he is selfish. A slut is a slut you know. A zebra never changes its stripes."

I knew better than to respond to his remarks about Peter. Did Gregory's anger with Peter having anything to do with his romantic feelings for him or to his feelings of rejection by him? Was I just an unwitting surrogate being used for the time being, lied to, while he spent time with Peter secretly? I had to hold on to the assumption that Peter was no longer in the picture and that Gregory actually cared for me, regardless of the pain he inflicted on me. It was my only chance for survival.

Within a week, I took over the job that Peter was doing for Pastor Gabriel, the head of the rectory. The work entailed cleaning around the church once a week, replacing prayer booklets, and other odd jobs that changed weekly. I made meager wages but was glad to take whatever I was given.

Late one Saturday evening, I received a call from Peter, wanting me to meet him at his home. So much time had elapsed, I was surprised to hear from him. He suggested we go to the local gay gar.

I was really nervous because I had never been to any kind of bar—gay or straight. Being underage, I was afraid I might be arrested; however, Peter assured me we'd be okay. Once I was inside the bar, I was intrigued by the thought of being with other gay men. I also found myself curious, aroused actually, with the fantasy of kissing a man. On the other hand, I was plagued with guilt and shame brought on by my curiosity. This religion I followed preached that such acts of any kind were an abomination.

The timing, however, was perfect to go to the club that evening and to satisfy my curiosity. Gregory was busy with a visiting priest-friend from Pennsylvania. I knew it was safe to leave with Peter, without Gregory ever knowing. The odds were in my favor, so I took the risk.

Before I left, I told my parents that I was going to visit Peter, but not to tell Gregory if he called. I followed that with another lie, mentioning that they were at odds with each other, and I was trying to keep both friendships without either knowing. I told them that if Gregory called, tell him I'd gone to bed early because I wasn't feeling well. Because my car was having an engine problem again, I walked fifteen minutes to Peter's home, taking only back roads that led behind the church. I took every precaution, other than wearing all black, so I would not be seen by Gregory.

Peter greeted me at the door. "Come on upstairs for a minute."

I followed Peter up to the second floor into his room.

"Michael, I want you to watch what I'm about to do."

"Okay," I said. somewhat mystified.

"Do you remember what I told you about Gregory communicating from his window?"

"Yes, I remember. You can see each other's windows."

Peter walked over to a shelf, picked up a tall votive candle, and lighted the wick. He placed the candle on the windowsill. Handing me a pair of binoculars, he instructed me to look out the window toward Gregory's bedroom window.

"Not sure I get what this is all about," I said.

"Trust me. Look through the lens toward his window. Be patient."

A few minutes passed. I saw nothing through the binoculars.

"What am I looking for?" I questioned again.

"Keep watching," he repeated.

Another minute passed. Still nothing. Then, I saw it. Father Gregory was staring out his window, while placing a lit candle on his windowsill. It was like a ghostly apparition peering out from behind the white shear drapes. I blew out the candle on Peter's windowsill. I started to panic, wondering if Gregory had just seen me staring back at him. I literally crawled across the floor afraid Gregory had seen me. Once on the other side of the bedroom, I stood up.

"Michael, are you okay?" Peter asked.

"Not really, if he sees me with you, all hell will break lose."

"Relax, he wasn't using binoculars, so he wouldn't see you, I promise. He would have assumed it was me."

"I hope he didn't recognize me."

"He is playing the both of us."

"What?"

"Michael," Peter said, "I don't know if you're aware that I'm working at the hardware store down the street. I've been trying to break away from Gregory for some time now, and he doesn't like it. He has had the audacity to call me at work a few times to harass me. What's worse, he showed up the hardware store once, with a dozen red roses for me. I was mortified. I was a supervisor; I wasn't sure what to say to my coworkers, so I told them the flowers were for my family. I told him to leave me alone and not to call me at work or at home."

Peter went on to explain a letter he'd received from Gregory. "He sent me a three-page letter a few days ago. It was filled with threatening remarks. He said that I was selfish, not acting like a seminarian. He implied that he wouldn't support me or give me any recommendations unless I changed my ways. He watches me come and go from my house, never giving up trying to control me, always signaling me with his candle at his window."

"I'm confused, Peter. What happened between the two of you?"

"We can talk about it another time. Let's get going to the bar," Peter said changing the subject. He seemed uncomfortable revealing any more details about whatever type of relationship he'd had with Gregory.

With all of these red flags appearing, I never put two and two together to get four. I was so controlled by Gregory that I never suspected that he might be the cause of losing my friendship with Peter.

In my mind, I think Peter was able to escape the bondage of Gregory physically, but not emotionally. I would later learn that victims of abuse often return to the abuser—we accept what we think we deserve. My guess was that Peter was jealous that I was being wined and dined by Gregory. I was his new boy. I also think Peter may have missed not having a priest-friend. As crazy as it sounds, being the friend of a priest did give one a sense of power. Peter told me that Gregory referred to me as his prized possession.

The two of us got into the car. He cranked up the music. We both loved Madonna and sang along to Borderline. Always afraid of being seen by Gregory, I slouched down in the front seat.

"Michael, you're being foolish; he doesn't have bionic sight," Peter said laughingly.

"I am afraid he may see me with you."

"He won't. I promise," he said, reassuring me once again.

Ten minutes later we arrived in the large parking lot adjacent to the night club. I was feeling anxious about embarking on this new experience. I followed closely behind Peter, who was my protective shield. We entered a side door of a plain, cement-faced building. It had no windows and only a light above the bar's entrance.

Peter opened the door. I was now Dorothy from Kamsas, stepping out from her aunt's demolished home into Oz, an unknown, bizarre world that I had never explored. This definitely wasn't Kansas anymore! I was apprehensive, expecting to see that Gregory, the Wicked Witch, may have somehow followed us. We were instantly welcomed into the club by a rugged, masculine bouncer.

"Hello boys," the guardian of the gate said.

"Hello John," Peter said while giving him a tight hug and kiss.

Men actually hug and kiss each other here, I thought to myself.

"Who is this young stud?" John asked, looking right at me. He extended his hand toward mine. We shook hands enthusiastically, and I felt strangely gratified by his gesture. He was personally acknowledging my presence.

"I'm Michael. Nice to meet you," I said. I was shy but was already liking the comfortable feeling I was experiencing. Maybe, just maybe, I was meeting my "tribe" for the first time.

As I glanced around the bar, I noticed men staring at me. I instantly lowered my head, playing one of the bashful dwarves. Peter offered to take me on a tour of the club.

First, we entered a room filled with a mix of older men and a few younger men. Peter explained that this was the piano bar. "This room seems to attract older men who like to have conversations with friends, younger men, or new acquaintances," he explained. Performers packed the piano bar, belting out old favorite musical numbers from Barbara, Liza, and Judy.

We proceeded down the hallway that opened onto the dance floor, packed with men, some with shirts off, gyrating to the pulsating beat of the music. We moved closer to the dance floor to watch others dancing.

I spent the rest of the evening hidden in the dark corners of the dance club. Although I felt the urge to dance, I chose to stay in the shadows. For me, I knew that dancing would be considered as having too much fun, which was a sin. I didn't even talk to anyone. I was as quiet as a church mouse, no pun intended.

Still, I was mesmerized by the crowd. It was all so new to me—seeing a crowd of other young men like me. I felt that I fit in. It seemed everyone could be fully who they wanted to be, without judgment from the outside world. These men could dress in whatever style they liked, they could kiss, or dye their hair any color.

I watched Peter the whole night, captivated by his self-assured behavior. I assumed he knew some of the gay men

101

because he chatted with several during the night. When we left that evening, I was soaring. It was the first time that I'd had any positive feelings about being gay. At last, I knew I wasn't alone in the world of homosexuals. I found the whole evening comforting.

On our way home, I asked Peter several questions.

"Have you seen Gregory recently?"

"I told you I don't want anything to do with him."

"Why did you put a candle in the window then?"

"He does it all the time when he sees I'm home, in the hope I'll respond. I just wanted to prove a point."

"Peter, do you honestly believe Gregory is using me because you're not around?"

"Michael, I haven't been at that church in some time. During Easter break I went to the Cathedral instead. When Father Gregory didn't see me around Easter holiday, he called me. He asked me why I wasn't home, where I belonged, under his care. He then told me to meet him at the rectory on the Tuesday after Easter. After chiding me for ignoring him, he took me to dinner and then back to the rectory. He explained to me how this was the way it should be and how he was so eager for us to be together, with both of us as priests. He told me that he's using you while I'm away at school, so he can get some things done around the church. He told me that you were nothing to worry about."

I was confused. I was once again thinking that Peter was making up this whole story, trying to make me jealous, but another part of me questioned whether Gregory was sincere or playing me for a fool.

"Peter, Gregory said that you abandoned the church and your job at the church."

"Michael," Peter replied, "I heard that you were given my job at the church. Pastor Gabriel called me at the hardware store. He wanted me to clean out the lower storage room under the sacristy."

"I said to Pastor Gabriel, 'Isn't Michael employed there now?'"

"Pastor Gabriel chuckled, and said, 'No, Michael's working with Father Gregory.'

"On my day off, I decided to go over to do the work that Pastor Gabriel asked of me," Peter said. "Michael, you weren't around that day, but Gregory was. He insisted on helping me put the tables and chairs away on movable racks in the storage area. I left saying very little to him. A few days later Gregory called me at work. I told him to leave me alone, not to call me at work, not to visit me, and not to call me at home."

Was this the real story? I was now more confused than ever as to who was telling the truth. Peter dropped me off at my home; I climbed into bed, questioning all the conflicting information given to me by Peter and Gregory. I simply needed to know who was telling the truth.

The following week, I planned to go back to the gay bar with Peter. I just told Father Gregory that I wasn't feeling well. At the bar, I discovered that Peter was a frequent visitor, something that he hadn't mentioned to me.

Peter spotted one of the managers, John. "I'm glad to see you again, Peter. What do you think of the place?" he asked me.

"It's only my second time here. I'm glad to be here. Everyone seems so friendly and welcoming."

"Peter is here all the time; hope we see you as much," John replied.

Peter comes often, I thought to myself.

"Peter's a blithering bar fly," John continued in a humorous, well-intended manner.

I laughed.

It all began to make sense how Peter knew so many people in the club. I wasn't surprised to learn that he was popular there.

Once, Peter shared in confidence, that he fooled around with the trash collector whose job took him to Father Gregory's church to collect the trash. Peter admitted that he would sometimes play with the guy in the room that housed the lawnmowers under the sacristy. It was pretty clear that Peter and I were at the age when we both were exploring our sexuality. Maybe he wasn't anything Gregory accused him of being. Maybe this was a normal journey for any young, gay man.

In bed that evening, I thought about my second experience at the gay bar, and the sense of belonging I felt there. I
was quite impressed with the hunky barman who served me
a Cape Codder, a drink made with vodka and cranberry juice.
Damn. He was hot. I was really attracted to him, imagining
a simple kiss as he leaned over the bar. I later learned that
his name was also Michael. He had a reputation of sleeping
around with all the cute, good-looking men. I didn't care. He
was gorgeous.

The following morning, I received a phone call from
Father Gregory.

"We're going over to Sandra's tonight. Be ready."

"Not sure if I'm up to going."

"You will go. That's the end of it."

"I think another time. I'm kind of tired."

As expected, I had just opened Pandora's box by
disobeying.

"Let me clarify only once. I don't get mad I get even.
You'll go. Period!"

"Okay. I'll go," I said, surrendering to his command.

Unfortunately, I was totally oblivious as to why it was
so important that I go. I couldn't have anticipated the turn of
events that would befall me later that evening.

Keeping true to form, Gregory honked his horn repeatedly
as he waited for me to come out of the house. Once in the car,
I noticed that he seemed a bit subdued. He never spoke to me
during the car ride. I thought maybe he was only tired or had a
disagreement with his pastor. We arrived at Sandra's home. She
welcomed us at the front door. We followed her into the dining
room, where Jack Jr., Parker, and Reggie were seated around
the table, smoking a joint. Gregory immediately poured himself
a drink. The atmosphere seemed peculiar to me that evening.
No one said hello or acknowledged my presence.

After Gregory fixed his drink, he motioned for me to
follow him.

"Where are we going?" I asked.

"We're heading over to Kelly's house next door," Gregory
replied curtly. She was a friend of Sandra's. Why, all of a
sudden, was he acting as though he was incensed with me?

Michael Roberts

I met Kelly. Her gregarious personality was infectious. We all made small talk in her living room. Then, to my surprise, Sandra, Reggie, Jack Jr., and Parker went down to Kelly's basement. I was now alone with Kelly and Gregory upstairs, wondering what this was all about.

"Where did everyone go?" I asked.

"Michael, follow me downstairs," Gregory ordered.

I followed close behind him, but for some reason, Kelly didn't join us.

Kelly's unfinished basement was damp and chilly. As I stepped into the room, I sensed that something was definitely odd about this situation. I wondered why four chairs were lined up in a row with Sandra and her two sons seated in three of them. One empty chair faced them. I assumed the empty chair was for Reggie. I was wrong. It was for Gregory.

"Michael, please have a seat here," Reggie said, pointing to an empty chair.

Still confused, I took a seat in the chair facing everyone. Now, they were all staring at me, like wolves stalking their prey.

Reggie moved to a plant stand, which he used as a podium and announced, "Michael Roberts, you're on trial."

What the hell? On trial for what, I thought? My pulse quickened.

Reggie began his opening statement.

"Good evening ladies and gentlemen. The docket for tonight is the case of Father Gregory, Plaintiff versus Michael, Defendant."

What is this? I thought to myself.

Reggie continued, "Does each jury member swear that you will fairly try the case before this court, and that you will return a true verdict according to the evidence and the instructions of the court, so help you, God?

The three devils and Father Prince of Darkness responded, "I do."

Still trying to keep my wits about me, Reggie then began asking me a series of questions.

"Michael, is Peter your friend?"

"We seldom see each other anymore. I'm lucky if I see him at all."

105

"Michael, have you spent time with him recently?"

"No!"

Sandra, the corpulent she-devil of the jury, giggled. What a bitch, I thought to myself. I hated every single one of them. If I could have personally thrown them into a burning chasm, I would have.

"Michael, where were you last Saturday evening?"

"Home!"

I thought to myself: why does he keep saying my name. He knows who I am. This was all contrived beforehand. They actually spent time rehearsing this play, in order to make it more dramatic and humiliating. Was I being filmed and interrogated for a future episode of *Law and Order: Special Victims Unit?* If so, who was the special victim?

"Michael, what were you doing at home?"

"Nothing. I went to bed early."

"Why didn't you spend time with Father Gregory?"

"I wasn't feeling my best. And, he told me his friend Father Colin was visiting him for a few days."

"Michael, did you see Peter that evening?"

"No!"

"Have you ever gone to a gay bar?"

They knew! They all fucking knew! That's what this was about. They wanted to see if I would tell the truth about going to the gay bar. I was furious with Father Gregory for being so sick that he arranged this despicable exhibition, a so-called trial.

"No!"

"Has Peter ever been to a gay bar?"

"I don't know."

"Have you ever been to the gay bar downtown?"

I decided to play dumb, regardless of what they knew.

"What gay bar?"

"The gay bar on Main Street."

"Oh." I offered no further explanation.

One last question.

"Are you one hundred percent positive that you have never been to the bar in question?"

"I'm sure!"

Michael Roberts

"Were you and Peter at the Brass-Rail bar two Saturday evenings ago?" Reggie asked.

"That's not true either," I replied.

Then, Reggie launched his final assault. "Several people saw you and Peter leaving the bar as they sat in their car. I was one of those people."

"Really," I said with a belligerent tone. I was pissed and wanted these assholes to know it.

"You're committing perjury."

Hey folks, this is pure bullshit, I thought. I'm not under oath here. Fuck Reggie and his accusations. "I don't care," I proclaimed. I should have told them all to fuck off and to stick their perjury up their asses.

"Unfortunately, that wasn't me," I said. I was a controlled, scared, naive, passive teenager trying desperately to find my voice and to fight for myself. I somehow summoned the courage to say to Reggie, "You saw us leaving the club, but not in the club?"

"How long were you in the parking lot?" I asked Reggie.

"Just enough time to see you both leaving."

I decided to play their game, and I knew I had him, using his own statement against him, because he only saw us leaving.

"Peter called my home, wanting to take me for a ride in his car. I decided it would give us a chance to chat. I hadn't seen him in a while. Without my consent or prior knowledge, he decided to drive into the gay bar parking lot. When I mentioned I wanted to go home, he told me he just needed to go in for a few minutes to collect some money he had loaned to a friend. He told me to sit in his car and wait."

"After forty-five minutes elapsed, I was livid that I was still sitting in the car. I finally decided to go to the front door to ask someone to find him for me. I stepped inside, closed the door behind me, and waited by the entrance for Peter. I thanked the bouncer for allowing me to wait. After another ten minutes, Peter came to the front door, and we left. He drove me back home. That's when you and your friend might have seen us. You assumed I was in the club. I wasn't. I just went in to find Peter, standing just inside the door. So, your line, 'Just enough time to see you,' doesn't prove anything; does it?"

Reggie was not happy with my clever retort.

107

Behind Sacred Walls

"Michael, now that I think about it, I was in the car for close to an hour. So, you must have been inside for some time."

I was shocked that Reggie, with his brain's limited gray matter, could reply so quickly, that he could think on his feet. He was able to spew forth such bullshit.

"Do you have anything else you would like to add to your story?" he said with all of the subtlety of a fart in church.

What a creep, addressing me in such a patronizing and sarcastic manner.

"No Reggie, I do not," I said, quite proud of my throwing his shit right back in his face.

"Does the jury have any questions or comments?" Reggie asked.

"Shame on you, Michael" Sandra spoke up. "Greggie has done so much for you, and this is how you treat him? You better step up to the plate, give him more attention, and stop your lying and complaining."

Jack Jr. shook his head in agreement, while Gregory sat quietly smirking.

I'll step up to the plate with a baseball bat, then swing it at your head, you parasitic bitch.

"Michael, please go and sit at the top of the basement stairs while we deliberate."

I resented this whole farce, but in the interest of ending the fiasco, I walked up the stairs and sat, waiting for my fate to be determined by this ragtag jury of miscreants.

I heard the mumble of voices. It was like a paranormal haunting of spirits calling my name from the other side. Twenty long minutes passed of their so-called "deliberation."

Reggie walked over to the stairs. "Michael please come down and take your seat."

Reluctantly, I complied.

Reggie returned to his podium and began to speak. "We all know that proof beyond a reasonable doubt does not mean beyond all possible doubt. It means that you must consider all of the evidence and that you are absolutely certain that the charge is true. Has the jury reached a verdict?"

Wow, brainless Reggie actually did his research on courtroom protocol. He must have watched old episodes of the *Perry Mason* TV show.

Sandra rose from her chair, faced Judge Judy...I mean Judge Reggie, and commenced her oration.

"Yes, we have reached a unanimous verdict."

"Please read it aloud," Reggie said.

"We find Michael, the defendant, guilty of gross misrepresentation and contempt. It's obvious he is lying."

I was mortified at this charade they had put on. I'm guilty? Gee, I wonder if I will be sentenced to hard labor or forced to watch one of Reggie's drag shows.

Thank you, madam foreman, I thought. This court is now adjourned.

The jury stood, folded their chairs, and carried them off under their arms. Passing in front of me, not one single person looked at me, as if this was some kind of serious courtroom hearing. They marched, single file, up the stairs.

Not only was I offended, but I was stunned by what had just happened.

I walked upstairs, just as my entire tribunal was leaving to go back to Sandra's house. Father Gregory was the last to leave.

"Michael, what's going on?" Kelly asked me with a look of confusion.

"Nothing," I said. "Absolutely nothing!"

"What happened?" she asked again.

"They just wanted to humiliate me."

"I'm so sorry. That's not what they told me. They mentioned something about you practicing for a show."

I replied, "That's not what happened at all. Far from it." I bid Kelly a hasty good-bye and thanked her for her hospitality. My assumption was Kelly was an unknowing participant in this fiasco. I never thought to ask her to elaborate on what, if anything, else they might have told her.

I walked a few steps behind Gregory. I could barely see him in the dark as we headed across the lawn back toward Sandra's house. I hated all of them. I would have gone home immediately, but I needed a ride from Gregory. Clearly, the whole group enabled Gregory's sickness. They had supported his staging of this ridiculous inquisition. I arrived at the back entrance to Sandra's house only to find the door locked. I was now certain that the punishment phase of my ordeal was yet to come. I walked around the house, over to the front door, only to meet Father Gregory who was making his exit.

"Bye Greggie," Sandra said with a mocking tone. Although, I knew she saw me, she never acknowledged my presence.

Gregory was my only ride home. I climbed into his front seat. I all but clung to the passenger door, praying no words would be spoken. I got my wish, not one single word was exchanged. He drove to my parent's house, pulled up to the front walkway, and stared straight ahead. I jumped out the car. At least this time I was completely out of the car before he sped off.

As I replayed the events of this comedic trial in my mind, Gregory seemed to delight in chastising me in front of others. His revenge always included anger and contempt for me, regardless of the potential consequences for himself.

As I expected, a few days, he called me, acting as if nothing had happened. It was as if his goofy inquisition had never happened.

10

Gregory had intended for the group's shame and humiliation to affect me, but if it did anything, it repulsed me. I'll be dammed if I would accept any form of punishment at the hands of his ecclesiastical suck-ups. And strangely, there were no further repercussions from my personal inquisition. Still, things were never quite the same after the trial. I resented him even more. Sill, Gregory, the anaconda, was constricting my windpipe ever so slowly.

His emotional manipulation escalated as did his appetite for sex. I am reminded of just a handful of the many lines he used to play upon my insecurities and exercise control over me. "God would love for you to please a priest. Only I will make you happy. Everyone else will use you. You know you'll live on the streets if your parents find out. Peter is a user. Any friends you make will never treat you as well as I do. Trust no one. We all have needs."

I would often lay in bed thinking of Gregory's warnings. He had almost succeeded in convincing me that he was, in fact, my only true friend. I figured that his abuse was the manifestation of his sick idea of love. I was controlled by this "Jim Jones–style" leader of our local church.

Clearly, he wasn't the embodiment of true Christian charity. I was beginning to see his character flaws that I had been conditioned to not recognize. I was so brainwashed that I even remember adopting and repeating many of Father Gregory's favorite lines of derision to others: "Pound sand up your ass. I don't get mad. I get even." When in traffic he would say, "the horn blows; does the driver?" If a car in front of him waited too long to move at a green light, he'd shout, "What are you waiting for another shade of green?"

A couple of his other favorite expressions were: "They're going to do wonders and shit cucumbers" and, "His horns are holding up his halo." One of his favorite gestures for giving people the finger was raising his pinky finger—he said it was "For those who didn't deserve the very best." In other words, the person he was flipping-off didn't deserve his full middle finger.

I was oblivious to the fact my spirit was being broken. Like a moth to the flame, I had become a slave to the teachings of the Catholic Church and to the whims of a diabolic priest. To further my subservience, I also started eagerly learning verses from the Bible. I not only committed a few of them to memory, I believed them. It would be years before I came to see the Bible's teaching as a work of fiction.

Early fall 1984. Father Gregory became more verbally abusive. He commonly called me stupid, dumb, idiot, naive, brainless, and unattractive. He was a master at belittling me. He found amusement in giving me a drag name. I was assigned the name Sally. When asked why that name was chosen, his response was that Sally sounded like a stupid, dumb, blond girl.

He even assigned female drag names for some of his priest friends. Anthony, Gregory's ex-partner, was Uwana. His last name was Doome. Among Gregory's crowd, the name Uwana Doome evoked great laughter. His friend Father Colin was called Patti with an "i" not a "y." Father Gregory's drag name was Helen, which I didn't find the least bit amusing. I thought the whole drag thing was rather disturbing, to say the least.

Father Gregory also became more violent and demanding. One example that comes to mind was when he stood at the desk in his bedroom. He proposed that we have some "fool around" time. I expressed my reluctance and said that I wanted to go home. He was furious with me. In retaliation, he picked up several books and began throwing them at me. Fortunately, I had good reflexes, so I was able to dodge most of them. I wonder if any of the titles were: *One Flew Over the*

Cuckoo's Nest, War and Peace, or *Crime and Punishment.* One book left a bruise along my right side. He seemed to revel in threatening me, slamming doors in my face, chasing me, and swearing at me.

Finally, he became more of a warden of my mental prison. He telephoned more often, kept tabs on my whereabouts, and demanded more of my time. I was now being abused spiritually, emotionally, physically, and sexually by a Catholic priest. Sadly, in my mind, I was powerless. I gave in to him out of a sense of obligation, obedience, and dedication to the Catholic faith he so loved.

One evening, after dinner at my parent's home, Gregory decided to tell me that he was going to buy me another gift. He would be taking me to a high-end clothing store that featured trendy apparel, including designer labels. On several occasions, he said that he wanted me to be more like him, dressed in stylish clothes when we went to dinner. I'm sure he just wanted to show off his younger companion to other priests.

We walked into Arnie's Clothing store and went to the long, dress-coat section. A well-dressed salesperson, with a tape measure around his neck, greeted us. Father Gregory and the salesperson discussed what size I needed. They looked at several fabrics, colors, and sizes, then made a selection. I wasn't consulted. They decided on a long, black and white tweed coat. At the register, Gregory added to the order—two shirts and two pairs of dress pants. At that moment, it dawned on me that Reggie had bragged that Gregory had taken him to this store and treated him to clothes as well.

"You're going to look more and more like a priest, if I have my way," Gregory remarked.

As we left the store, I thanked him for the gifts. I wasn't fond of long coats but tried not to let it show.

"One more gift waits for you back at the rectory," he said.

"That's not necessary."

Again, I was noticing his pattern of behavior. He would give me gifts or dinners, but other times, he would insult, belittle, or otherwise criticized me. He was a master at making me smile one minute, then hurting me the next.

We arrived back at the rectory early that evening, and spent several hours watching TV in his room. I was still wondering what other gift he was talking about in the car. He shut off the TV and stared at me.

I began feeling uneasy.

"Michael, before I take you home, I have that second gift I mentioned."

"You really shouldn't," I started to say.

"Yes, I should! You see only a true friend like me would spoil you. You know I'm always looking out for your best interest. Anyone else would be just using you. In time you will learn."

He walked over to his desk and pulled out a small, gift-wrapped package out of a drawer. He handed me the box. I accepted the neatly wrapped gift, but not wanting to appear too eager or greedy, I opened it slowly. I was shocked to see the contents of the box. It was a silver ring.

"Put it on!" Gregory said, excited.

The ring was a silver crucifix with a red stone in the center. Each side of the stone had Catholic symbols engraved on it. By symbols, I mean a crown, lamb, ladder, and dove. I placed the ring on my right ring finger and looked at it, trying to appear appreciative.

"Very nice. Thank you."

"You're welcome."

"We now have matching rings," he said, smiling.

"Very nice!"

"I thought this would symbolize our love for one another. These duplicate rings will solidify our commitment."

What the fuck was he talking about? Was he telling me that we were engaged? I had no interest in him but was at a loss for words.

"I'm not sure what to say," I said.

"You don't need to say anything. Just make sure you wear it at all times. We need to honor this commitment and to stay loyal to one another."

This would be my Scarlet Letter. I believed he wanted to make sure, by my wearing it daily, I would be loyal to him and have no other friends.

I arrived back at my house, upset over the "gift" he'd given me. I saw no way out. He was reinforcing the prison he had built around me. Whenever he was not around, I removed

Michael Roberts

the ring. I hated wearing it, not only because of what it was supposed to represent, but because I found it gaudy. September 1984. Gregory wanted to go to Canada, where the Pope would be appearing. Of course, he demanded that I go with him. My mom had relatives in Canada, so we could visit them, too. The Pope's appearance would be only about thirty minutes from my grandmother's home.

I was reluctant about going for two reasons. First, the trip would mean a ten-hour drive with Gregory. The idea of spending ten hours in a car with him was difficult. Secondly, I was starting to question my religious faith, in large part due to Gregory. Morally, he was far from what I thought a priest should be, and I had started seeing the church differently—I was no longer such a fervent believer. Accordingly, I wasn't at all enthusiastic about seeing the Pope. I had become distrustful of men who were supposed to be leaders in the church. My discontent was growing. Nevertheless, we headed for Canada.

We arrived late Sunday evening. My aunt and uncle greeted us. I loved my Aunt Nancy very much but despised my Uncle Earl. So much so, that I had fantasized about dancing on his grave when he died. I'd even piss on his headstone. I had never shared my story about the pain he had caused me as a child.

Several years earlier, when I was around the age of fourteen, my family went to Canada to visit my grandmother and my aunt and uncle. We always tried to go once a year. It was the only time my mother got to see her mother along with other family and friends. My grandmother had a home across the street from the rocky shoreline of the Atlantic Ocean. My mother's sister Nancy and her family had lived in the same house with my grandmother for many years.

Behind my grandmother's house was a large field, a portion of which was her huge garden. We kids would run through the field, snacking occasionally on string beans from the garden. I loved walking among the large boulders along the seashore and playing with my cousins.

One day, after going swimming with my cousins, I returned to the house to change out of my wet clothes. As I entered the house, my Uncle Earl grabbed my arm and pinned me against the wall.

115

"You're spending too much time with Laura," he said belligerently.

"She's my cousin," I replied, not understanding his objection.

"You should be playing with the boys."

"I like spending time with everyone. I only get to see them once a year."

"Listen to me. I don't want you to spend time with Laura or to be near her."

"That's not fair."

"Don't you ever back-talk me, you little shit."

Then, he clenched his fist and punched me in the stomach. I doubled over, all but falling to the floor. I held my stomach and started to cry. He stifled my cries by covering my mouth with his hand. He knew people were within earshot.

"If you ever say one word to anyone about this, you'll get more than a punch in the stomach," he whispered as he released his grip on my arm.

Earl walked back into the kitchen where everyone had gathered for lunch. I was silent, afraid to make a sound. I didn't want anyone to know what had just happened. I was fearful of the repercussions it may cause with my parents and with the relatives. I could hear him chatting up a storm, laughing with my family, knowing I had to face everyone and to pretend that everything was normal. I decided to go upstairs, change my wet clothes, and tried to regain my composure before joining the rest of the family in the kitchen.

"Come and eat," my mother yelled up the stairs.

I was trying to gather enough fortitude to hide my contempt for my mother's brother-in-law, the child beater. I knew that this was neither the time, nor the place, to tell her what had just happened.

"I'll be right down," I told her.

I went into the bedroom, lifted my shirt, and looked at the red mark left from the gut punch. I sat on the bed and cried into the blanket. From where I sat, I could see out the window onto the massive gardens, fields, and forest. For some reason, my mind flashed back on my assault by the older man at the pet cemetery. Was Uncle Earl's behavior just another reason to distrust older men? I never understood why I didn't tell my mother about Uncle Earl punching me. If only I had told her, maybe I would have learned the value of standing up for myself. I might have developed a voice of my own. But I never spoke about the incident.

Many years later, we learned that my Uncle Earl, alias Lucifer, had a warrant out for his arrest for years for sexual abuse of his stepdaughter, my cousin Laura. Apparently, the abuse started when she was around nine years old. Was his obsession with Laura the reason why he punched me? Or was he afraid that she would let slip the secret of his abuse if she spent time with me? I also resented my aunt, who most likely knew what was happening to her daughter. Was she so afraid of her husband that she never did anything to challenge or to stop this deviant? After he was charged with child abuse, he fled to Florida, where he died years later.

While in Canada, Gregory and I took walks along the beach and spent time visiting with my relatives. Within two days, everybody liked Gregory. My relatives' friends and neighbors would come to the house just to visit him, as if they were on some kind of pilgrimage. He became the talk of this small town. Everyone was enamored with him. You'd think he was a celebrity. He could make anyone laugh with is offbeat humor.

Thursday morning, we were all excited about seeing the Pope. We arrived in the town of Moncton, near a place called Magnetic Hill, a popular tourist destination. It was known for its optical illusion created by the rising and descending terrain. For decades, the road had baffled visitors, because at the bottom of the hill, they could take their feet off the accelerator, and it would appear that their cars were rolling up the hill. When, in fact, what appeared to be an uphill incline was actually part of a larger downhill road.

We parked the car and walked toward the huge crowd already gathering to see his Holiness, John Paul II. Inside the massive gathering, we worked our way past souvenir shops. I couldn't help but notice one merchant's offering which was a bar of soap, carved in the Pope's likeness. It was called Pope

Soap on a Rope! Hey, I thought, I'll wash my ass with the Pope's face.

We found our place among the swarm waiting for the saintly figure. The Pope finally arrived in his Popemobile; it looked like a fish tank in which he could stand, in all his glory, to be adored by his devoted flock. The crowd roared ever louder as he progressed toward the altar. With all the raucous noise coming from the throngs, one would think The Beatles were performing! Would the crowd break into a chorus of All You Need is Love?

The setting for the Pope was an elaborate display that must have costs thousands of dollars. There was a waterfall in front of the altar. They even used a gold chalice during Mass.

The whole spectacle was ostentatious and a contradiction for the supposedly humble man who wore the "Shoes of the Fisherman." I thought the community should have been ashamed of themselves for this extravagant waste of money. The clergy preached against materialism and encouraged help for the poor in their sermons. This seemed a bit inconsistent with what they preached. High, rubber boots would have been the proper attire to listen to this pageantry of hypocritical, bullshit. All of the money that was spent for his visit could have gone to food pantries and shelters.

After an hour of standing, listening to the Pope pontificate, I was exhausted. I was more than ready to return to my grandmother's house. We got into our cars and left the throngs behind us.

As the years passed, I grew to further distrust all of religion. It was only bigotry and prejudice. In my eyes, the Pope was one of many of the ignorant, but powerful people in the public eye, who were responsible for the degradation of gay men and woman. Members of the gay community were assaulted, judged, and shamed for being gay, especially those who suffered from the horrific disease, AIDS. The Pope, and the institution he governed, never spoke a single sympathetic word, or even mentioned the devastating disease, seven years into the AIDS crisis. There was no Papal solace or compassion for the afflicted.

Michael Roberts

In an article in the *New York Times,* said:

"'The church is doing all that is possible," the Pope had said, "'to heal and to prevent the moral background of this." The remark was widely taken to mean that AIDS was rooted in immorality.

Later, however, the Pope's views appeared to change. His first major statement on homosexuality wasn't made until 1986, at which time he was basically saying it's okay to be homosexual, but that homosexuals should not have sex. Issued on October 31, 1986, by Cardinal Joseph Ratzinger, prefect of the Congregation of the Doctrine of Faith (the new name for the Inquisition), it expressed traditional teachings in very harsh and uncompromising language.

According to his Letter to the Bishops of the Catholic Church on the Pastoral Care of Homosexual Persons:

"Although the particular inclination of the homosexual person is not a sin, it is a more or less strong tendency ordered toward an intrinsic moral evil; thus, the inclination itself must be seen as an objective disorder. Therefore, special concern and pastoral attention should be directed to those who have this condition, lest they be led to believe that the living out of this orientation in homosexual activity is a morally acceptable option. It is not."

The article outraged many. John Paul II was telling people that even if homosexuality wasn't freely chosen by each individual, it was nevertheless wrong. Not a "sin," but still wrong.

September 1984. I performed in a three-night production of *A Night at the Theater,* the church theater guild's second performance. The show was still a medley of show tunes. Father Gregory produced the show. Reggie directed, with Sandra as the musical director. Father Gregory was also the bartender during the church production. He was always looking for a way to make money. He served drinks at a well-stocked bar. He collected money in a metal can with a sign that read: "Tips don't insult me."

119

A few months earlier, I had been instructed to have an audition song, possibly a solo, ready so that I might have a bigger role in this show. Even though I was in the chorus of the last show, I was still terrified of singing alone in front of anyone. I was, however, a fabulous singer in the shower, if I do say so myself.

Right before I walked on stage to audition, I was a nervous wreck. Somehow, I had the wherewithal to listen to the voice in my head that reminded me something I had learned in modeling school: you've always wanted to be an actor. Take this chance. Sometimes you just have to face the fear and to move through it.

I had learned to walk with purpose in modeling school, so I took the stage, looking confident. As I faced fellow cast members, the pianist started playing. I took a deep breath, and I delivered my rendition of Just the "Way You Are", by Billy Joel. As I ended the song, I could not believe I had sung in front of people. I was proud of myself, something I had rarely felt. The cast members applauded and cheered. I felt supported.

The next day, Father Gregory told me that I would play the part of Alonso Quixano, better known as Don Quixote de la Mancha. The role called for me to sing a solo, "I Am I, Don Quixote".

For my number, I was given props that included a horse made from a wooden sawhorse and a cardboard cutout of a windmill. The horse had a burlap vest. I had a fake beard and carried a sword and a shield. Onstage, with my back to the audience, I was to get dressed during my monologue, then turn around, as my character, to face the audience and to sing my solo.

I delivered that night, just as I had done during my audition. Again, I was in disbelief that I had done it and was very relieved that it was over. As parishioners congratulated me after the show, I thought it odd that I heard a couple comments such as: "Michael, great job. You and Father Gregory seem to have a close friendship, don't you?" Or, "Are you planning on becoming a priest? You seem to spend all your time at the rectory and church." One person asked, "Why are you able to walk right into the rectory?"

Michael Roberts

I was bothered by such intrusive questions. It was no one's business. After those three performances, I became uncomfortable whenever parishioners were around the church. I was paranoid, worried that churchgoers may know, or at least suspect, what's going on with Father Gregory. Would they assume that I was the manipulative schemer out to use Father Gregory? Or that I was a parasite, benefitting from his popularity and power? Did they see me as the sick homosexual trying to ruin the church, or for that matter, to corrupt Father Gregory? Most of the members of this church so loved him, I concluded that they might see me as the opportunist.

11

October 1984. I arrived at the rectory, prepared to go to dinner with Gregory at our usual hangout. Greeted at the door by Gregory, I followed him into the office of Pastor Gabriel, who was away for several days. Gregory walked over to the pastor's desk and removed some cash from an envelope in a drawer.

"Are you allowed to take money from Pastor Gabriel's desk?" I asked.

"I take what I want. I'm allowed to take money for dining out. It's one of the perks of being a priest. Plus, it's none of your goddamned business."

"Okay," I said. Then we left for dinner.

I knew that priestly life included food and allowances for a car and clothing, no rent, no utilities, and a retirement plan, not to mention coverage of medical and dental expenses. He also made good money on weddings, funerals, and gifts from parishioners during holidays. I found it unusual that there appeared to be no oversight or monitoring of church funds. No checks and balances? I began to question all the gifts he bought for me: extravagant meals at the rectory, dinners at fancy restaurants, movies, entertainment, clothing, trips, and more. He also provided financial support for his mother. Could his salary support all this?

After dinner, we returned to the rectory.

"Michael, come for a walk with me."

"Where are we going?"

"Down to the church hall."

We walked along a road that led to the auditorium. The hall was mostly used for civic activities such as Boy Scout meetings, basketball games, theater productions, and church fund raisers. Once inside the hall, he ordered me to begin closing off all the window drapes so that no one could see inside. As instructed, I began closing the drapes. At times he would walk over, check my work, then rearrange panels he felt were not closed to his satisfaction. He wanted to make sure that nothing would be visible to the outside. I found it unnerving.

"Michael, do the job right. I don't want anyone knowing what's going on inside."

When I finished, he issued another order: "Sweep the stage quickly before they arrive and also check the bathroom toilet paper."

"Gregory, who is they?"

"The Hollywood Harlots."

"Hollywood who?" I questioned.

"Performing drag queens."

"What do you mean?"

"Reggie and probably two or three of his friends will be here. They dress in makeup and female drag. They lip sync to songs while prancing around the stage to choreography they've created."

They call themselves the Hollywood Harlots? How bizarre, I thought!

"Not my cup of tea," Gregory responded, "But they enjoy it."

It was kind of funny that they were using the church hall to practice such routines. I pictured the woman's church social group arriving at the hall unexpectedly just in time to witness a command performance of the drag queens. Would the church ladies be bothered by the fact that these girls applied makeup better than they did? When all of the chores were completed, Gregory told me it was time to leave, and we left the hall without previewing any of night's performances. He then told me that he always locked the door to the hall once they all had arrived for rehearsal, so he would have to return soon to open the door.

Late October 1984. Gregory and I went over to Sandra's house for one of our regular weekly visits. I hated being there with all of these lunatics, but I did enjoy being able to visit with Kelly, Sandra's neighbor.

I entered the kitchen behind Gregory, only to see Reggie and Parker once again smoking marijuana. Was this a halfway house for pot heads or was it a welcome refuge? I was amazed that Sandra was not uncomfortable over the use of drugs in her home. We sat around the kitchen table; the guys offered me some of their pot. I declined.

"Gregory, do you want a hit?" Reggie asked, offering him the joint.

"No, I have my scotch, my drug of choice."

Gregory then began to talk about performing *Jesus Christ, Superstar,* the musical, at the beginning of the year. Sandra took notes, while Reggie excused himself, telling Gregory that he needed to talk with me privately about the show. Gregory, not paying any attention, dismissed us. He mumbled, "Do whatever."

I was curious as to why Reggie wanted to chat with me privately, but I obeyed his request, following him into the basement. Upon entering the furnished cellar, Reggie motioned for me to sit next to him on a bed in the corner.

"How are you doing?" he asked.

"I'm okay, I guess," I said with questioning eyes.

He placed his hand on my leg. I slid away from him, a signal that I didn't want him to touch me.

"Relax, I thought we could play a little."

"No. I don't think that's a good idea."

"Relax. No one will know."

Reggie was an unattractive, flamboyant gay man who was more feminine than my sister. I was completely repulsed by him. With his eyeliner and pancake makeup, he reminded me of those early technicolor movies where the characters wore too much theatrical makeup. He was the effeminate version of Robin Hood starring Errol Flynn, but more in line with Ethel Flynn.

Suddenly, Reggie leaned toward me and planted an open-mouth kiss on my lips. I was offended by his breath, which smelled of booze and marijuana, not to mention the aroma of his cheap cologne.

Michael Roberts

Using a cough as my ploy, I pulled away, wiping his saliva off my lips.

His next move was right out of a melodrama. He removed his false teeth, giving him the appearance of a much older man. I tried not to smirk when he placed his dentures on the side table. I could only think of the fake teeth you wind up and they would chatter. Then, he started to unbuckle my jeans.

"Reggie, no. Don't do this."

"It's fine, relax."

"I mean it. No."

"Relax, Michael."

"No, Gregory is right upstairs," I said nervously, hoping he would not take a chance at getting caught by a furious priest.

"They are not even paying attention. They're so involved with talking about the next musical. Trust me. Gregory would never believe I would betray him. He would also never suspect you of anything."

"Reggie, don't, please."

"You have nothing to worry about."

Reggie was a clever, self-serving, shameless victimizer. He strategically used fear as his weapon. He insisted that Gregory would never even suspect that I would have come on to Reggie. In other words, Reggie twisted the scenario to make it appear that I was the one who initiated the sexual act. I couldn't believe he would use me in such a manner. Then, he unzipped my jeans. I thought to myself that if Gregory suspected I made a sexual advance on Reggie, all hell would erupt. Would he even believe me? Finding the target of his unbridled lust, Reggie grabbed hold of my private parts.

"Stop!" I said angrily.

He ignored my plea a second time and began his degrading, oral assault. I knew it was too late to do anything. He was just another person exploiting me, objectifying me. One can truly understand the premise of Charles Darwin's book, *Origin of Species,* which talks about the inevitability of survival of the fittest. Natural selection is about the weaker species being vulnerable to the more dominant species in the race to survive. Convinced I was the weaker, I did nothing! After he violated me, he placed his teeth in his mouth and walked away saying only, "See, that was harmless."

125

I fastened my jeans and returned to the kitchen, where Reggie was now seated next to Gregory. I thought, not only did he rape me, but he had the audacity to mock me by sitting next to Gregory. It was almost like he was taunting me with: Go ahead. Tell Gregory.

I knew I had to pretend to be my normal self, act as though nothing terrible just happened to me. I left that night, devastated that I had allowed Reggie to abuse me. A few minutes later, I got into the front seat of Gregory's car. We drove off.

"Michael, what did you and Reggie talk about outside?" Gregory asked curiously.

He didn't even realize I went to the basement.

"Nothing important," I said in the hope that this would end the discussion.

"I want to know. Tell me."

Now, I had to come up with a lie. "He seemed a bit nosey. Wanted to see how things are."

"Like what?"

"He wanted to know what activities we do, my sex life, gifts I received."

"Typical Reggie, jealous that you're getting all the attention now, and he's not."

"Oh, I see," was my only response.

Then Gregory said, "I was involved with Reggie once for a short time. I had hoped we would develop a relationship, but things seemed to fizzle out after a few months. I thought he was too feminine anyway. I never understood the whole drag thing."

"I didn't know that," I replied.

"So, what did you tell him about us?"

"I didn't say very much. Told him we were friends. That I spent a few days a week with you. I avoided answering some of his questions. I mentioned some of the gifts you had bought me: a ring, some clothing, a camera, and two statues."

Gregory replied, "You must have noticed, when we were visiting, he would blatantly and shamelessly flirt with me?"

"Yes," I said, "but I assumed he was just trying to get attention from anyone. Not to be judgmental, but I get the impression that he's a real egomaniac. He wants a spotlight on him at all times."

I hoped Gregory wouldn't take offense to that comment. He didn't. He simply smiled in agreement. In fact, he never suspected that anything had happened with Reggie, but I always wondered if one day he would find out that Reggie had used me. Eventually, I learned to view Reggie as a pathetic human being, whose narcissism was revolting and a frequent source of embarrassment to everyone close to him.

One night at one of Gregory's dinner parties, Reggie went as far as pulling down his pants during dinner—just to get attention. He exposed himself to all of us, including Father Colin from Pennsylvania. For many reasons, I developed a real sense of loathing for Reggie.

A few weeks later I received my retribution for the anguish inflicted on me by Reggie. I arrived at the rectory one weeknight, after a phone call from Gregory instructing me that the door would be unlocked and that I was to come right upstairs. I assumed he was having a meeting and wouldn't be able to greet me at the door.

From the foot of the stairs, I heard a loud wailing. I moved slowly toward Gregory's room. My thought was that he might be consoling a distraught parishioner. I was, however, a bit confused as to why he would do this in his private quarters. I finally recognized that the distressed voice I was hearing was Reggie's. I walked into the bedroom only to see Reggie on his knees with his arms wrapped around Gregory's legs. Usually, when Reggie is on his knees, his mission is far more salacious. I looked on at this comedy-drama, trying not to smirk. Now, Reggie was screaming and then begging. What the hell for, I thought.

"Reggie, you have to accept that it's over. It's over!" Gregory was saying.

I was speechless, not knowing what had just happened. Had someone passed away?

Whatever it was, I had very little sympathy for this man who raped me and who played a role in humiliating me on more than one occasion.

"Randy broke up with Reggie," Gregory explained to me, figuring I should know what was happening.

I remembered Gregory mentioning that Reggie was dating Randy, who worked at a florist shop downtown. A gay male florist? How highly unusual was that? Next, I'll learn that some hairdressers are gay.

I stood listening to Reggie's dramatic performance. The only thing he was missing was a black veil and rosary beads to complete his role of the grieving widow. Reggie cried, "Once they leave, they never come back. I don't want to live anymore. I can't live without him." It seemed strange to me that I was feeling no compassion for this sobbing man, but, given the circumstances, I just could not muster up any empathy.

More than an hour later, Reggie, now emotionally exhausted, exited Gregory's room. Gregory followed behind him. I could hear them both chatting in the kitchen.

"Reggie, you call me any time, any hour of the night. If you need to stay over, let me know. We can cuddle. You know that everyone will use you. I've always been your loyal friend."

It was typical Gregory, only thinking about having a man in his bed. Now, I knew more about the manipulating games he played to get his carnal needs met. And now with Reggie, sobbing in his arms, Gregory cared only about his needs, as he feigned his compassion for Reggie, a fellow Christian.

Gregory came back upstairs with a glass of milk and turned on the television. "He should have listened to me. Goddamn this is going to be one long night."

I thought to myself: this is his definition of a caring friendship?

We watched television for a while. He then told me he was tired, and it would be best if I leave. He didn't feel like driving, so my only option was to walk home. I was okay with that, pleased that I didn't have to offer myself to him that night.

October 1984. Father Gregory invited Reggie and me to a costume party to be held on Halloween night. I was obligated to go, but I was concerned that I had nothing to wear. After much deliberation, I decided I would dress up as Boy George, lead singer of Culture Club.

Halloween night, Gregory, Reggie, and I agree to meet at Sandra's house, where all three of us planned to suit-up in preparation for the party. Gregory and I arrived with the costumes we were planning to wear. Sandra greeted us at the door.

"Hello," she said smiling.

"Move, you blimp. I need my scotch," Gregory said, barging through the door.

He was never nice to Sandra. He seemed to delight in belittling her. When I first met Sandra, I liked her. She seemed kind, but now I only tolerated her. She had shown her true character to me with the basement inquisition. As silly as it was, it was still hurtful.

Gregory made a beeline to the kitchen, made his drink, and returned to the dining room.

In her feeble attempt to inject some arcane, gay humor by way of a clue as to Reggie's costume, Sandra announced, "Reggie will be out shortly. She's making sure she looks perfect."

We all sat around the table, waiting for Reggie's grand entrance. Gregory shouted for him to move his ass and to get the hell out of the bedroom. Gregory's patience had grown thin after only thirty minutes.

"Goddamn you, Reggie, get the hell out here."

I just sat thinking to myself: making a bony, feminine man into a woman should only take a few minutes.

After another ten minutes elapsed, he/she appeared. What pronoun does one use?

"Hello dahling," Reggie said, as he sashayed out of Sandra's bedroom. Then, in true Hollywood fashion, she grabbed the door frame with one hand and assumed the position of a 1940s, leading lady. To me, she looked like she was telling Mr. DeMille she was ready for her close-up. Talk about a WTF moment!

"Who the hell are you supposed to be?" Gregory asked mockingly.

"Joan Collins, of course, my dear," she said as she stepped out into the living room. Our resident diva was wearing a red taffeta dress, a wide black belt, red earrings, and black pumps. He looked ridiculous. He looked like a mixture of *Moulin Rouge* meets Minnie Pearl, the fancy-hatted, sassy comedian from the old television show *Hee Haw*. Jesus, Mary, and Joseph! Could it get any worse than this? Yes, it could.

After Reggie's grandstanding subsided, he began helping Gregory get into his cat costume. Gregory was adamant about not competing with him by wearing another of Reggie's hand-me-down cat costumes. Gregory wanted to stand out at the party. He would be the only one there from the musical *Cats*. Reggie went to work on Gregory. He painted white stripes on his beard and covered his face in white powder. Then he drew large, black, eyebrows and one black stripe down his nose. He finished it off with a teased wig with cat ears.

Reggie then began to work on my makeup, transforming me into Boy George, the androgynous lead singer from Culture Club. My costume included many ribbons attached inside my black hat. Several long strands of hair were attached to the front of the hat. These hairs hung down in front of my face. The rest of my costume consisted of baggy clothes, cut off gloves, and what seemed like pounds of costume jewelry. To Reggie's credit, I did look like Boy George. It was finally time to go.

We arrived at the party, which was being hosted by Father Gregory's ex-boyfriend, Father Anthony. I wasn't sure if this was Father Anthony's home or his new boyfriend's place. Father Gregory still had feelings for Father Anthony, but he knew it was over when Father Anthony insisted that, for him, there was no physical attraction and that they were no longer sexually compatible.

Father Anthony greeted us with hugs, telling us he was expecting seven or eight other priests to show up. First, I met Father Anthony's partner. We made drinks and mingled around the table exchanging small talk.

Over the next hour, the other priests arrived, some with their own partners. Four of them were wearing nuns' costumes. One of them looked like the *Flying Nun* from the television series. I decided she could be called Sister Mary Bitch. Another nun wore what looked like seagull wings atop her head. Another nun had added tree branches to the top of her costume, signifying that she was with Sisters from the Woods convent. As the party continued, raucous laughter erupted each time another guest arrived.

The party was now in its second hour, and I was getting bored. I felt as isolated as a Democrat stuck in the corner at a Republican Convention. Eventually, Father Gregory noticed my boredom and suggested that I lose the Boy George costume and change into my street clothes. I wasn't opposed—I'd had enough with wearing the pore-clogging makeup and the itchy hat. I knew, however, that Gregory requested this only in his effort to me show off to all the other priests, especially to his ex-boyfriend, Father Anthony. I went into the bathroom, removed my costume and washed off all the makeup. I combed my hair and returned to the nunnery.

As I entered the room, the crowd became silent. No one spoke. They just stared at me. I soon realized that they found me attractive. Over the next two hours, I was grabbed, pinched, and gawked at. I was the target of sexual innuendos. I felt like a piece of flesh, surrounded by vultures.

Reggie was obviously jealous. He sat quietly in a corner, in a Queen Anne chair, no less. I was relieved when it was time to leave. I no longer wished to be a target of sexual objectification. My worth to these few lecherous priests was only my appearance. No one really wanted to know me for who I was. These religious men, who were closeted within their own parishes, became hungry homosexuals when surrounded by the like-minded peers.

The following week, Gregory, Sandra, and Reggie invited me to go with them to a gay bar in the city. I think Gregory might have planned the evening in an effort to keep Reggie from thinking about his now defunct relationship with Randy.

I found myself having conflicting feelings. On one hand, I thought going to the bar was sinful. On the other hand, I felt a twinge of excitement because I could live vicariously through all of them. I was underage, so getting into a gay bar in the city was titillating. After all my years of hiding who I was, I once again could join a large, happy group of men who were like me.

When we arrived at the club, we were greeted at the door by the security guard.

"Welcome," he said.

Reggie, Sandra, and Gregory moved past the doorman into the club, but the security guard stopped me.

"Can I see your driver's license?"

Thinking quickly, I responded, "I don't have it with me. I came along with my friends."

"I'm sorry, but I can't allow you into the club."

Gregory signaled all of us to step outside. "Damn. It figures you would screw this one up," he said, now pissed.

"I'm underage. I need an ID to prove my age. You never said I needed an ID. Either way I wouldn't get in. It's not my fault."

"Forget it. The night's ruined now."

"Go in. Enjoy yourselves," I responded. "It's a beautiful night. I can take a walk, window shop, and hang around.

Reggie and Sandra said nothing. I was hoping they would support me and go inside for a drink.

"Let's head to the other bar," Reggie said.

"Goddamn it! We drive all the way here and can't even enjoy one night out in the city," complained Gregory.

We all got back in the car, heading to the other bar. We had to listen to Gregory madly huff and puff all the way to the other club. Near tears, I sat in the front seat, feeling humiliated and disgraced. I was the sole person who ruined everyone's evening. Again, Gregory was publicly shaming me.

Luckily, I was able to get into the club across town without my ID; it was the same club I'd gone to with Peter. Gregory was dressed in ordinary street clothes. No one would have ever guessed he was a priest.

He clung to me. He would hold my hand or lean in and kiss me. He wanted to make sure that everyone in the club knew that he had a good-looking guy by his side. Every time he tried to move toward me, I created a diversion. I commented on the music, took a drink of my water, or talked to Sandra and Reggie. I did anything and everything to avoid his mouth and his roaming hands. I didn't want anyone suspecting that we were a couple. I was repulsed by the thought of this man assuming that I was his lover.

As the hours passed, I watched the priest, with scotch in hand, trying to dance. Was he dancing or having a seizure? Frankly, I was surprised that he took the risk of going to the bar, where someone might have recognized him.

132

Michael Roberts

After I was back home in my bedroom, I wrote another
poem.
My weary, vacant, cadaverous body stands
on the edge of the abyss.
This ethereal subterranean world pulls me in.
Deep, narrow, sharp cavern walls lacerate
my skin.
Voice strangled by the noxious air of malice.
Eyes bleed from the swift river of animosity.
Ears impaired with the piercing vibration of disparagement.
My soul now severed into fragments, now fallen into shadows.

133

12

His was an impenetrable darkness. I looked at him
as you peer down at a man who is lying at the
bottom of a precipice where the sun never shines.

—Joseph Conrad,
Heart of Darkness

January 1985. The ground was covered with a fresh
layer of white, powdery snow. The temperature was in
the mid-twenties. The night sky was so clear and crisp that you
could see every star shining in the winter sky. My entire family,
along with Father Gregory, decided to spend an evening at the
ski resort, about thirty minutes from our house. Father Gregory
rode with my family. My brother Andrew drove ahead of us
with his girlfriend.

Upon arrival, we donned our skis and snow gear, all
except Gregory. He preferred to stay in the lodge, next to the
wood-burning fireplace, where he could kick back in a recliner
and sip his scotch. He was probably an alcoholic. He had a
scotch in his hand morning, noon, and night.

I loved the sport of skiing, getting bundled up in my heavy
layers of winter clothing, strapping on my boots and skis, and
preparing for the evening run down the slopes. This particular
evening was perfect for skiing because a fresh layer of snow
covered the slopes. Better yet, the slopes weren't crowded.

I remember going skiing the first time as a little boy. I was with my father. We took skiing lessons together. We spent hours mastering the skill of not falling flat on our faces. But now after years of practice, both my father and my mother were somewhat skilled in maneuvering a downhill slope. My dad even found that he had the courage to take the main ski lift to the top of the mountain. As I looked down the slopes, they resembled a maze of snow-covered Christmas trees. It was a Burl Ives moment, for sure. From there, we slowly descended the mountain side, making it back to the lodge without incident.

Once back at the lodge, we warmed up by the fire with hot chocolate. And of course, Father Gregory had to swill down his third or fourth Dewar's on the rocks. About twenty minutes later, we climbed into the car to go home. It had been a delightful evening of family fun.

As we turned the corner on to our street, we saw flashing red lights. They appeared to be near our house. Something was on fire.

"Oh my God, please don't let it be our home!" I said.

Then, my father let out a shriek. "Our house is on fire."

Oh my God. It was our house. My heart was pounding. We weren't permitted to get within a couple blocks of the house. The streets were blocked with fire trucks. We all sat, paralyzed, in the car.

A few minutes later, we stepped outside of the car. Three or four firefighters were spraying water on the front of the house. No flames were visible, only black smoke billowing out from my bedroom window. The house was pitch black—a lifeless shell that, only yesterday, was the heart and soul of our family.

"We've lost everything. Everything we worked for is gone," my father cried aloud, as tears streamed down his face.

"It's alright, Russ," Mom said. "We can rebuild the house. We should be glad no one was injured," my mom said, her voice quivering. She tried to console him. She was the strongest member of the family in any crisis.

I was numb. My mind was trying to process all that was taking place.

Just then, my brother Andrew, who had arrived home a few minutes before the rest of us, came running toward us.

"Where's the dog?" my father questioned.

"The dog's fine," my brother Andrew said.

"What happened?" my mother asked.

"When I arrived at the house, I found it odd that no lights were on," Andrew replied. "I walked to the back entrance, and as soon as I opened the door, the fire erupted. Our little Corgi-poodle mix, Bandit came running outside. Thank God he was alive. I grabbed him, ran next door, and asked the neighbors to call the fire department. The neighbors took care of Bandit. I ran back to the house, waiting for firefighters."

When the fire scene was secured, the fire chief told us what he thought had happened. He explained that because the house was completely sealed, the fire burned very slowly, smoldering, generating intense heat.

We all stood with Father Gregory as inquisitive neighbors gathered. I decided to walk around to the backyard. I ignored one firefighter who told me it was best to wait out front. I needed time to myself and, Goddamn it. I walked to the backyard, stood at the back porch, and began to sob.

I was overcome with anger. The trauma of the fire had broken any personal defenses I had left, laying bare raw emotions. I was angry at Gregory for the suffering he had just caused me, and I was angry at God for hurting my parents. They had worked their whole lives building a home for our family—buying furnishings and collecting memories, only to lose it all in the course of an evening. The home they'd planned to live in during their retirement years was in ruins.

Then, a young firefighter opened the back gate. He stopped in his tracks, looking at me. Our eyes locked. We immediately recognized each other. We'd seen each other at the gay bar a few nights earlier! Could this moment get any stranger? I think he was there to deter me from going into the house. I could see the compassion in his soft gaze. He seemed to want to approach me, to hold me as I cried. Then, he turned away and returned to the front of the house. I followed behind him. We never spoke to each other that night, but we exchanged several glances. I could still see the sorrow in his eyes.

About an hour later, one of the firefighters gave us the okay to go inside. We followed the fire chief. With his flashlight in hand, he led us through our burned-out home.

I entered first, followed by my parents and my brothers. We were shocked at how the walls and all of the furnishings were covered in black soot. It looked like someone had used black paint to spray everything.

I walked into the kitchen. The plastic on the microwave door had melted. In the bathroom, the shower curtain had melted into a puddle. Anything plastic had melted. We walked into my bedroom. Nothing seemed salvageable. I was heartbroken. Because the fire had started in my room, all of my cherished possessions were forever gone.

The firefighter explained that the fire had started in my bedroom. "The cause of the fire was mostly likely a faulty electric floor lamp. A spark from a wire ignited the fabric of the comforter on the bed."

The fire chief continued, "The smoke was so intense that when your son opened the back door, a huge fire broke out. The oxygen fed the smoldering flames. Your son was very lucky he didn't get hurt. Your dog probably survived because he was low to the floor, and he escaped the smoke."

We were all grateful that our beloved Bandit had survived.

"Thank you for saving as much of the house as you could," Mom said.

"We did our best," he said. According to the fire chief, the house had extensive damage, but all of the walls and the roof were still intact and structurally sound. Mom was still being the strong one. I heard her say to my dad, "It will be okay, Russ. We just need a little Spic and Span," her household cleanser of choice. She was astoundingly positive despite the calamitous circumstances. I so admired her.

In his effort to reassure us, the fire chief explained, "We will write up the report for your insurance company. I'll have some workers over within the hour to board up the broken windows. It's important to assure that the property is protected from further damage or from vandalism before the insurance adjusters have had a chance to assess the damage."

Our family huddled in front of our house, trying to figure out what to do next. Where would we all stay?

"Michael, you can stay in the guest room at the rectory," Gregory offered.

"What about Pastor Gabriel?" I questioned. I was hoping this would be an excuse to pass on his invitation.

"I don't care what that cheapskate thinks. It's about time that pain-in-the-ass does something other than sock away money in the church bank account. You're staying in the guestroom. End of discussion."

"Russ and I can stay with Russ's aunt, here in town. But it would help us if Michael could stay at the rectory," my mom observed.

I wasn't surprised that Gregory was able to convince my parents that I should stay with him at the church rectory. I knew he was only interested in one thing, and it wasn't my awesome singing. My parents never realized that they were throwing meat into the lion's den.

My brother Andrew was invited to stay with his girlfriend's parents. My youngest brother stayed a few houses up the street at a friend's home. All of the neighbors were so obliging, they even took in the family dog until we figured out what to do next. My dad's aunt and uncle were glad to take in my parents.

Before we all parted ways, my father called my sister Donna, who was living in Washington, D.C., to tell her about the fire. I clearly remember him telling her that the house burned down. I was miffed that he exaggerated the truth. The house had not burned down. It just sustained fire damage to the interior.

I disliked that trait about my father—always putting the worst possible spin on things. I never understood his need to always be the harbinger-of-doom. He seemed oblivious to the emotional devastation he could inflict on others. I felt he could have saved her the suffering by simply saying the house had some fire damage, but that it could all be repaired.

I climbed into Gregory's car, ski clothes now smelling of smoke. At that moment, I realized that the only things I now owned were the clothes on my back. We arrived at the rectory, where Gregory showed me to the guest quarters. He told me to make myself comfortable and that he would join me momentarily. The entrance to my room was off the kitchen, up a steep, narrow staircase. The guest room had two bureaus, a closet, and a four-poster bed. The room had three windows. From one of them, I could see Peter's bedroom window.

Gregory then reappeared carrying some snacks and a glass of milk, which he set on the dresser. He then handed me a T-shirt and underwear that he had taken from Pastor Gabriel's room. I couldn't be finicky at a time like this, and I gladly accepted the under clothes. Father Gregory then left me alone to take a shower. He said to come to his room if I needed him; otherwise, he would speak with me in the morning.

I showered and climbed into bed. The clean sheets smelled nice. I spent most of the night tossing and turning, tortured by thoughts of all of the damage to our home and all of the possessions we had lost. Hours later, I drifted off to sleep.

The next morning, I had no choice but to dress in my ski pants and T-shirt. I went downstairs to the kitchen. Hannah was at the refrigerator, pulling out items for breakfast.

"Good morning, Michael. Father Gregory told me what happened last night, I'm so terribly sorry. I'm so glad no one was hurt."

"Thank you, Hannah."

"You must be hungry."

"Yes, a bit."

She then began to run down the list of my breakfast choices. I settled on cereal, toast, and orange juice. It would be rather strange calling this place my new home while our family home was being restored.

I was deeply sad about the house. It was more than sadness. It was grieving the loss of our home. To make matters worse, I was trapped with Gregory, but I had to pretend that I was grateful for the sake of my parents. How could I mention the abuse to them at a time when they were already overburdened? Still, I was frightened with the thought of Gregory having twenty-four-hour access to me.

The rectory was old with no locks on any of the bedroom or bathroom doors. That was one reason why Gregory had installed a lock on the door to his personal quarters. Other than escaping through a window, my only way out of the rectory was down the stairs off my bedroom and out through the kitchen door. But, under current circumstances, I had a place to stay and had food, heat, my own phone, and bathroom. I just had to tolerate my abuser.

Later that morning, I went back to our family's brown, ranch-style home to assess the damage in daylight. I felt an overwhelming sadness at seeing what we had called home was now a soot-filled abandoned shell. Several windows had been boarded up, and a thin layer of black soot coated the remaining panes of glass. I then sat in the front stairs waiting for my parents to arrive.

Within an hour, they arrived to meet with an insurance agent. Mom handed me a few items of clothing that she had purchased for me. After the adjuster viewed the destruction, he explained how the reimbursement coverage on the house policy would work. While they talked about repairs to the house, I walked to the front of the house, where I found an ash pile. It was ashes and debris the firefighter had scooped out of my room to make sure they hadn't left any burning embers behind.

I shifted through the rubble, searching for anything that was salvageable. I found very little that survived the blaze. There were a couple of singed pictures and a few pieces of melted costume jewelry. And then, I came upon a religious statue that Father Gregory had given me. This figurine of St. Michael was charred, except for the devil, carved into the base of the statue. Ironic.

The insurance company was most helpful and worked closely with my parents. On the next morning after the fire, the adjuster asked the whole family to list every single item destroyed in the fire, from a safety pin to a piece of furniture. They needed this information to get a rough estimate on the total cost of replacements. They would then reimburse my parents on a percentage-based scale. The adjuster also mentioned to my parents that they would have a mobile trailer, delivered in a week or two, to provide temporary housing for the family.

Unable to endure any more of the bickering between my dad's aunt and uncle, my parents left after only two days of staying with them. For the next week, they stayed with the Smith family, friends who lived nearby. After my folks left, the Smiths, or should I say the opportunists, sent my parents an invoice, itemizing costs they incurred while my parents stayed in their home. My parents were hurt, if not furious, and completely ignored the letter. I heard my mother say that they could stick their invoice up their ass. Understandably, after that, their friendship with the Smiths was never the same.

What truly saved my parents, were two amazing friends by the names of Jack and Cathy who told the insurance agent that he could have the trailer delivered to their side property. They would connect the water and sewer lines through their home. I remember the day I went to see this travel trailer, with several plumbing pipes tethering it to the main house; I noticed the wheels of the trailer damaging their otherwise, neatly manicured lawn. Jack and Cathy didn't seem the least bit worried about the damage to their yard. We were truly glad they could help. I have never forgotten the kindness they showed to my parents during that rough time.

Now, as comfortable as they could be in the mobile home, my parents and two brothers settled down for a few months' stay. The trailer was cozy for the four of them, so adding me to the mix would have resulted in overcrowded living conditions. More importantly, I was never even asked if I wanted to move in with them. I'm convinced that they all assumed I was better off than they were, residing comfortably at the rectory. In fact, I wondered if they were a bit envious of me living "like a king" with the saint-like protector, Father Gregory, as my guardian.

Over the next few weeks, while my dad was at work, I would return to our damaged home to help my mother with the clean-up of any items that we could save. Mom and I were able to retrieve cooking pots and pans, silverware, and glassware. In the laundry room, I even salvaged a few articles of my clothing in the basement.

The insurance company also sent workers to help clean and to wash kitchen items and pack them in boxes. A lot of items had to be tossed into large dumpsters. We were tasked with disposing anything that was made of fabric such as mattresses, sofas, chairs, curtains, carpeting, and clothing. The smoke had infiltrated everything, so very few of those types of items could be salvaged. The items we could save were to be stored in the rectory's basement. This kind gesture by Father Gregory only strengthened my resolve not to say anything negative about him to my parents. I didn't want to create any more hardship for Mom and Dad.

A week later, in the presence of my parents, Father Gregory presented me with two new statues to replace the ones lost to the fire. I feigned being appreciative. He also gave me a duplicate key to the rectory because I was now living there.

Over the course of that month, my mother and father worked closely with contractors. They altered the floor plan slightly, adding a second bathroom. They chose light fixtures, cabinets, appliances, and flooring.

Word spread around town about the fire. Because I was constantly bullied in high school, I felt I had few friends when I graduated. So, I certainly never expected a random act of kindness from anyone in my class. But, a classmate, named Kenny, who was also a closeted gay man, sent me a package containing a replacement copy of our graduation yearbook and high school diploma. What a considerate thing for him to do. I was profoundly grateful.

I would often visit my parent's temporary shelter to dine with them and to get updates about the progress on the house. Every time, I would ask them when the house would be finished. I never got a definitive or encouraging answer.

I desperately needed this respite from church life and Gregory. The noise from the church bells, numerous phone calls, and the door buzzing with inquiring parishioners soon became annoying. When I wasn't obligated to be with Father Gregory, I retreated to my room at the rectory. It was quiet there.

But after about two weeks at the rectory, any relaxation I thought I might enjoy was slowly dissipating. At first, Gregory started eavesdropping on my phone conversations. At that time, all telephones were land lines, and most homes had one or two extension phones. I had one in my bedroom. I could tell when Gregory was picking up his phone receiver to listen. I could hear his heavy breathing.

Then, one evening while showering, I noticed a shadow on the other side of the shower curtain. Oh my God! Was this a scene right out of Alfred Hitchcock's horror film *Psycho,* in which the main character was stabbed to death while showering? Was Gregory playing Norman Bates, the man with the knife? I slowly opened the shower curtain, but Gregory was gone. I dried off and headed back to my room. I decided to walk through the side hall that led to Pastor Gabriel's private quarters. I was not given permission to enter the pastor's room but didn't care. Upon entering, I could hear Gregory exiting the pastor's other door. Of course, it had been Gregory. The lecherous son of a bitch was trying to see me naked while I showered.

Should I confront him? Would he become violent? As usual, I remained my passive self and said nothing, hoping this was a one-time event. Unfortunately, his behavior didn't stop. So, I made it a point to always push the shower curtain tightly against the wall, preventing him from seeing me in the shower.

I also decided to make sure he wouldn't be sneaking into my bathroom again. Because the door had no lock, I took a wooden chair from my bedroom and propped it up against the door. That evening, thinking I had stopped his peeping behavior, I decided to shower before bed. I placed the chair against the door and showered. As I dried off, I happened to glance out the window. There stood Gregory on the sunroof, staring at me.

I looked right at him. He was busted. A few minutes later, I heard Gregory coming up the stairs to his room. Once again, I decided to say nothing. After catching him watching me that night, I hoped his peeping Tom days might be over.

Unfortunately, peeping Tom may have been gone, but Gregory's games were just beginning. One night, I turned off the light, and I crawled into bed, only to collide with Gregory's hairy legs. I let out a shriek and jumped out of bed. Gregory laughed, so very pleased with his prank.

"What the hell are you doing? You scared the Goddamn crap out of me!"

"I just love it, You're so cute." He left the room, still laughing.

I would never have any peace while under this roof.

For the following two weeks, while his pastor was gone, Gregory played this little hide and seek game at my emotional expense. He would hide in different locations.

143

One night when I turned off the lights and climbed into bed, I heard the creaking sound of my closet door opening. He crept across the room. When he eventually touched me, I screamed like an injured child. Once again, he erupted into gales of laughter.

Another night, he played the same game, but this time he was under my bed. I'd had enough. From then on, I inspected the room thoroughly before going to bed. Once again, I placed a chair against the bedroom door as I had done in the bathroom. One night, when I was in bed, I heard him jiggling the doorknob. After a few seconds of trying, he walked away. Unfortunately, my actions were a challenge for him to devise even more diabolical methods of distressing me. Was it even possible for things to get worse? Hell yeah!

One evening, after jiggling my door handle, he became angry, and he began pushing on the door. Really throwing himself into it. Panicked, I started to slide the big bureau in front of the door, but I was too late. He managed to push through the door.

"What the hell are you doing?" I yelled.

"I want to fool around, you cutie," he responded.

"No."

"Oh yes, you will."

"I'm not in the mood to play this game. Leave me alone!"

"You will be in the mood if I have anything to do with it, so get over here, you cutie."

I didn't move.

Then I ran out the bedroom door. He followed.

"I'll get you!" he yelled.

How preposterous. Here I was, almost twenty years of age, playing tag with a priest. I ran through Pastor Gabriel's private room, past Gregory's room, and down the stairs, only to come face to face with Gregory in the dining room.

How the hell did he get here before me? I wondered.

"I just love playing this game of catch me if you can," he said laughingly.

"I don't."

"It's so much fun, you cutie, you."

As he ran around the dining room table, I ran the opposite way. He reversed course. I reversed course. We were at a standstill. I was on one side of the table. He was on the other. He smiled, gasping for air. He was not in good shape. Maybe I could use this to my advantage. The game proceeded; we continued to run around the table. Then, I found my escape. I had a chance to get by him. He could not catch me by the time I ran out of the dining room. It worked! He had lunged at me, but I made it past his grasping hands. I dashed to the front of the rectory and up the stairs. I heard him huffing and mumbling behind me.

"I surrender!" he shouted.

Sure, I thought. That son of a bitch was lying.

For a moment, I thought that if I hid behind the bed in his room, he might not find me for some time. I crawled behind his bed. Maybe he'd calm down and eventually give up this psychotic game of cat and mouse. I was wrong.

Then in his now-enraged state, I heard the door to his bedroom slam shut. Next, I heard him lock the door. The sly cat had cornered the frightened mouse. I had no other means of exit. I stayed quiet. "Goddamn son-of-a-bitch. I'll show that bastard," he shouted.

He sat down at his desk.

I thought to myself, if I jumped over his bed and unlocked the door, I could flee back to my room. I even thought about running out of the rectory and hiding in the room above the choir loft. Unfortunately, I never got the chance. I had been discovered behind his bed.

"Well, I'll be damned. Look who's hiding," he said.

"Enough of this game now," I demanded.

"It's so much fun."

He walked over to his bed and patted the bed with his hand, inviting me to take a seat.

"Come join me on the bed."

I will make a run for it, I thought to myself. I got up from the floor, but before I knew it, he grabbed my wrist.

"Stop! That hurts!"

"I said, get on the bed."

"Stop Gregory! You're hurting my wrist."

I tried to break his grip on me, but he became irate and grabbed my hair.

"Stop pulling my hair! That hurts!"

He latched on to my arm with his other hand. I tried to push him away, but the more I tried, the more his anger escalated. He abhorred being rejected. My attempts to push him away only heightened his resolve. I knew he was normally rather weak, but I was no match for his rage. As he wrestled me onto the bed, I decided to surrender. Perhaps, under different circumstances, I could have overpowered him, but I knew I could not assault a priest. It would guarantee me a one-way ticket to an eternity in Hell. He won! I stayed motionless, while he sexually assaulted me. As the assault continued, my mind drifted off, like so many times before.

Years later, in therapy, I learned in order to psychologically protect oneself during an assault, the brain "separates" from itself during traumatic events. You may be physically present, but emotionally, you are drifting somewhere else. I knew I was being orally raped, but I disconnected from the reality taking place. Reflecting back, I remember during the rapes I thought about such things as my career path, what I was going to do for lunch the next day, and places I wanted to visit someday.

My therapist said that many people who are unable to disassociate increase their possibility of becoming schizophrenic. She also explained that chronological age does not equate to developmental age when someone is being traumatized or otherwise abused. In other words, one's emotional development ends the moment the abuse begins. Gregory could take this toy named Michael out of the toy box whenever he wanted to play.

13

February 1985. I snuck out of the rectory late at night and walked over to Peter's house. He had told me he wanted to talk. We got into Peter's Camaro and drove off. We talked about our broken friendship, which we both realized was skillfully and deliberately fractured by Father Gregory.

"Peter, Father Gregory is nasty," I said to him.

I told him about a letter that Gregory had sent me. He had scolded me for not being nice to him after all he'd done for me. He said he was the only one who would ever love me. He said I was fucking up my entire family and that I better change, or else. Then, he threw in a few of his degrading remarks.

"Michael, you need to get away from him. Gregory is a bad person. You have to get out."

"Yes, I know," I said. I wanted to believe Peter, but I was so controlled that I didn't know who was telling the truth, Peter or Gregory. However, I started to think that Peter was right, especially since he was free—with no ties to Gregory.

That night, Peter didn't tell me all that had transpired between him and Father Gregory, but I had a pretty good idea of what Peter had gone through before I came along.

Peter asked me if I would be willing to pray with him. I said yes, so he consulted a prayer book he kept in his glove box.

"Let's pray, O God, come to my assistance. O Lord, make haste to help me know. Glory be to the Father, to the Son, and to the Holy Spirit. As it was in the beginning, it is now and ever shall be, world without end. Amen."

He continued reading. "Into your hands Lord I commend my spirit. You have redeemed me, Lord God of truth. I

147

commend my Spirit." He ended with a plea to Mary, Mother of God.

"Peter, thank you for caring," I said.

Peter leaned over and hugged me.

"I love you."

"I love you, too."

I was struck by his kindness. He drove back to his house. With another hug, we said our good-byes. I walked back to the rectory and snuck in quietly.

I wasn't sure what to make of that night. How could I break away from Father Gregory, who was now intertwined in every aspect of my life? Living at the rectory was like being a refugee in a war zone. I wasn't sure when another bomb would fall around me. I lived with constant anxiety, always feeling like I was teetering on the edge of a precipice.

One evening, Gregory instructed me to stay in his room for several hours and to watch his television if I wished. But he made it clear that I was not to bother him under any circumstances. He would be hosting a conference with other priests downstairs in the living room. He was emphatic about my staying put until he came back. He left a glass of milk and snacks on the side table, then handed me the remote to the television.

"I do not want you leaving this room, period," he admonished.

"Okay. What's this meeting you're having?" I asked.

"Several of us priests, from different parishes, get together once a month. We rotate locations. Tonight, it's my turn. We discuss important issues within the diocese. This is a private group of priests, so the subject matter is none of your business."

"Okay, have a nice meeting."

When the doorbell rang, Gregory promptly left me secluded in his bedroom. It was rather odd being left alone there. He trusted me enough to allow me in his room. Of course, I was very curious. I lowered the volume of the television, hearing the doorbell ring six more times. After twenty minutes, I quietly opened bedroom door and tiptoed to the landing, where I could hear laughter coming from the living room. I moved closer to the top of the stairs, where I could hear better. For the

Michael Roberts

next twenty minutes, I heard a group of priests gossiping and criticizing some of the church leaders.

"How's your boyfriend doing?" one priest asked. "He's so handsome," another one said. Another said, "I saw the bishop with some younger guy a few nights back. He's such a closet case." "Are you going to Provincetown this summer?" "Pass the wine." "I heard that Gregory has a new boy toy."

I gasped when I realized they were now discussing me. I headed back to his room. Again, it was clear to me that I was a possession, a second-class citizen to Father Gregory.

I was angry with his sequestering me in the confines of his bedroom. Fuck him! What an asshole! What was I, a house boy, enslaved by this sanctimonious prick? Now indignant, I decided to leave Gregory's room. I'd go to the kitchen and brazenly walk right pass the group of priests. Was I on the verge of weakening some of his control over me? I didn't care what Gregory thought. I'll be damned if I was going to hide like some kind of hostage.

I sucked up my courage and walked down the stairs. Passing the living room, I glanced casually at the visiting priests as I headed to the kitchen. The silence that momentarily fell over the priests' meeting was surprisingly gratifying, bordering on hilarious, given my belligerent state of mind.

"Wow, is that your hunk, Gregory?" I heard one priest ask.

"You've done well, I see. Living the *Life of Riley,*" another one commented.

"How is he in bed?" a third asked, while the others snickered.

"Quiet, please, I think we need to censor our comments," Father Gregory said to the group.

"He's the gay boy you told me about. What's the problem?" one priest questioned.

"I would like for you to say nothing more about Michael," replied Father Gregory.

"What's it like being with a young guy?" still another priest inquired.

Gregory avoided the question, changing the subject to vacation plans for the summer.

I stayed close to the kitchen door briefly, listening to the priests cackling loudly.

149

In the kitchen, I filled a glass with orange juice, and casually walked upstairs to my own room, not Gregory's. As I climbed into bed, I could still hear their muffled laughter. Was this the gay Knights Templar, or was it Robin Gregory Hood and his band of gay, merry men? I knew they wouldn't steal from the rich and give to the poor, but I was convinced that they were not above plundering the innocent and lavishing the spoils upon themselves. I would come to learn that the meeting in the living room was an underground society of gay priests. Earlier, Gregory had told me that these gay priests met at different locations as sort of a support group.

After the priests had left, I heard Gregory stomping up the stairs to my bedroom. He flipped on the light and glared at me.

"Why the hell did you go against my orders?" Gregory asked.

"I was thirsty," I replied.

"I left you milk. I'm Goddamned pissed with you."

"I wanted juice, so be pissed."

He stormed off, slamming the door so hard that a picture fell off the wall in the hallway. His dramatic performance was predictable. I was thrilled to be left alone and didn't care if he was pissed.

The following week, Gregory's priest-friend, Father Colin, from another state arrived for a visit. He was just in time to join Gregory and me for lunch. They discussed the dinner that Father Colin would be preparing that evening. I knew Reggie would be joining us but hoped that he would take his drama down a notch. Reggie was quite fond of Father Colin, telling him to his face that he wanted to have sex with him. I believed they connected several times, but I was never interested in learning anything more about it.

Later that evening, Reggie and a few friends, minus the drag apparel, arrived for the dinner party. Father Colin had made a veal dish and a Caesar salad. The meal was sumptuous. I was cordial but said very little. As usual, rude Reggie perpetually sought attention. At one point, he dropped his pants and brazenly exposed himself, flaunting his meager attributes. I couldn't speak for the other guests, but I was not impressed. It seemed that whenever Father Colin was visiting,

Reggie acted like a classless fool, all in his effort to seduce his clerical object of desire.

After everyone had left that evening, Father Colin joined Gregory watching TV, while I retired to my bedroom. A couple of hours had passed when Gregory appeared at my bedroom door.

"Michael, you can sleep with me in my room. Father Colin will take your room for the next two nights."

"No. I'm not giving up my room," I said firmly.

"You will sleep in my bed. End of discussion."

"I won't! Sorry. I like sleeping alone!"

"Excuse me?" He wasn't used to me disagreeing with him.

"I am not leaving this room. You sleep on the sofa or in Pastor Gabriel's room. Give Father Colin your room."

"Goddamn you! You will pay for this. You'll be living on the streets after I have a word with your parents about your deviant tendencies."

"Go to Hell," I said. I surprised myself! I was standing up to Gregory.

Furious with me, he stormed off.

I had no clue where my courage came from. Part of my courage came from recognizing his patterns. More than once, he had threatened to tell my parents that I was gay, and I would be worried for days. However, he never would mention anything to my parents. I was, however, not one hundred percent certain that he wouldn't reveal my homosexuality to my mom and dad. The possibility was always in the back of my mind. He always seemed to delight in terrifying me when he was angered. Threatening to out me to my parents was his favorite weapon.

But that night, for the first time, I finally stood up to the son of a bitch. Now, I had created a crack in the wall. I just needed enough intestinal fortitude to tear down the wall completely, to find my own voice—the voice that I'd buried for so long.

Father Colin knocked at my bedroom door. "Michael, may I speak with you?"

"Yes," I said, inviting him in. He took a seat on my bed. "Here, come sit next to me," he said.

I sat down beside him, and he rested his hand on my leg, about mid-thigh. I was uncomfortable—his hand was close to my crotch.

"Gregory loves you very much. He would do anything for you. He wouldn't have bought you gifts, a ring, and dinners if he didn't love you."

I was annoyed with Father Colin's approval of our so-called relationship. He had to have known about Gregory's pattern of abuse. He knew Gregory had first forced himself on me when I was just seventeen. He had to have noticed my reluctance to engage with him. He had heard me make comments about not wanting to be intimate with Gregory. More than anything, he'd observed how Gregory controlled me with degrading, humiliating comments. Yet, Father Colin had said nothing.

Father Colin moved his hand a couple more inches further up my inner thigh. I didn't move. I so hoped he would leave me alone. He then placed a hand on my shoulder and started a deep massage of my shoulder blades. He spoke softly. "Go to Gregory's room. Spend some intimate time with him. He's hurt by the way you talked to him. I'm not sure what took place, but I know he's distraught over your behavior."

"I don't want to have sex with him."

"That's what you do when you love someone."

With that, he moved his hand even closer to my crotch. I jumped up in order to escape any further advances. I went across the hall, into Pastor Gabriel's room; I knew he wasn't there. Now, I was being told by another priest to go comfort Father Gregory. If I didn't, would I pay for disobeying another priest's command? Just then, Father Colin entered the room.

"Michael, go into Gregory's room. You both love each other."

I did not like Father Colin's intrusion into my life. My heart began to beat faster. My mind raced. What if I were to disobey him? I was taught to never disobey a priest. If I disobeyed, would I anger God and face the eternal fires of Hell?

Now, here I was, dealing with one priest, who was telling me to go comfort another priest who was waiting for me in the next room. Father Colin knew about Gregory's behavior, and he should have reported his abusive behavior. I began to fear that Father Colin was not unlike Gregory. I also believed that Father Colin had to have known what was going on at the rectory. Father Colin knew I did not care for Gregory. Why didn't he report the abusive behavior? He used to tell Gregory that he hoped he found a handsome guy like me someday.

I'd had enough of Father Colin's hand on my thigh. I ran out of the room, leaving the priest sitting alone on the bed. Ignoring the dictates of both priests, I did not go to Gregory's room. I went back to my room and closed the door. I moved the heavy dresser against it. I added the side table and chair to further bolster my blockade. Damn, I wished someone had installed dead-bolt locks on these frigging doors. I knew that Gregory would not be strong enough to open the door this time.

The following night, after Father Colin had left, my door rattled as Gregory tried to enter the room. I added my body weight to the barricades at the door. I said nothing, even as he ordered me several times to open the door. After several minutes, he left. I climbed into bed, thinking I finally achieved some advantage over my opponent.

I anticipated I would, at some point, receive my punishment for having disobeyed Gregory's orders both for not letting him into my room and for not staying in his room while Father Colin was downstairs. I was almost asleep, when Gregory stormed into my bedroom. He held me down by my wrists and forced his tongue down my throat. I tried to break away from him, but he had become the wild, untamed beast once again.

I thought quickly, telling him I was embarrassed to do anything with Father Colin in the house. Then I told him to climb into bed with me so we could cuddle and make up. My plan worked. As he walked around to the other side of the bed, I jumped out of bed and fled down the stairs to the kitchen. Like a mad bull, he chased me into the kitchen. I stood on one side of the island. He was on the opposite side. Here I was again, caught up in a game of catch me if you can.

"I just love this," he said giggling.

"Asshole, this shit has to stop. I hate you."

"Your parents would be really upset with your language and behavior, Michael."

Here we go again: SOSDD—same old shit, different day.

As he moved in my direction, I moved in the opposite direction. We played several rounds of this back-and-forth game. Finally, I ran up the stairs and hid in the back of my closet. I heard him enter the room and then leave. He must have assumed I was still running around the house. I jumped out of the closet and crawled under the bed just in the nick of time. He came back into the room. Below the bed skirt, I watched his feet as he walked along the bed. Then, he left again. I was surprised he didn't look under the bed. He was obviously horny, but probably drunk, too.

Hearing him downstairs, I tiptoed into Pastor Gabriel's bedroom and hid in his closet. Hiding here would be considered extremely unacceptable behavior, even sinful in the eyes of any devout Catholic. Entry into a pastor's private sanctum was strictly forbidden. Regardless of the rules, I seemed to have escaped Gregory's assault. I heard him climb the stairs and slam his bedroom door.

I stayed in the closet for about thirty minutes. I knew the slightest sound could initiate another chase scene. Tired, I curled into a fetal position, where I decided to spend the night. I did wonder what Pastor Gabriel would say if he caught me in his closet. I could say, "Just trying on some old priest clothing. How do I look in black?"

I was always happy when Pastor Gabriel was back from his days off. His presence in the house always deterred Gregory's assaults.

14

April 1985. Our entire family moved back into our rebuilt home. The contractors had finished remodeling the house from top to bottom. We had freshly painted walls, new carpets, all new appliances, and a modern bathroom. We were all ecstatic. We had a new home!

During the rebuild, I salvaged all of the aluminum siding from the house. I was quite proud of my work, and I made some cash for my recycling efforts.

Furthermore, I was so relieved to have my own room again under my parents' roof. I was free, having been emancipated from that rectory—the hell house. I could finally breathe without the fear of a lecherous son of a bitch lurking in the next room.

The next month, Gregory mentioned that his housekeeper's husband managed the grounds for a big nearby cemetery. He was looking for summer help to maintain the lawns of the cemetery. I knew a job would take me away from the rectory during the day, and I'd also be earning money, which I really needed.

"Thank you, Gregory for recommending me for the job. I've been looking for work."

"You know I'm always looking out for your best interest. Remember that others will just use you. When you start working, I won't say no to any gifts," he said smiling.

"What do you mean, gifts?"

"Now that you're working, you can spoil me."

"Oh."

Hannah informed me that I got the job. I could start the next morning. My job required me to spend the entire day

155

mowing the huge lawns. It took one week, with four others working eight-hour days, to mow the entire grounds. By the time we finished, it was time to start all over again. It was tiring and tedious work, maneuvering around head stones. I didn't mind the job, but within a few weeks, I was growing rather bored. Working long hours in the summer heat was no picnic. At the end of my workday, my sweat-soaked body was covered with dust, bugs, and grass clippings. But, things were about to change.

Early one morning, I noticed a car parked on one of the side streets in the labyrinth of roads within the cemetery. It was fairly close to where I was working. Peripherally, I could see a man waving at me from inside his car. He seemed to be beckoning me to come over. I assumed he might have questions—perhaps about planting or watering. I finished the row, then turned around to make my way back to the end of the next row where he was waiting.

I turned the lawn mower off and approached his car. The man stepped out of his vehicle and leaned against it. His white collar was a dead giveaway. He was obviously a priest.

"Hello, I'm Father Oliver."

"Hello, Father, I'm Michael."

I know Father Gregory from your parish. I just finished talking to him. I was telling him that I needed help at our church. He suggested that I come here and speak to you. I'm here to offer you the job. We need someone to work a forty-hour week."

"I would love to," I replied almost immediately.

"Your title would be head sexton. The job requirements include setting up the Mass, setting up and cleaning the bingo hall, cleaning the church, passing out the missalettes, 'which were small prayer books', and answering phone calls when no one else is around. In addition, you'd be responsible for bathroom cleaning and garbage collection. Of course, there would be a small amount of yardwork, the removal of trash from the parking lot, and numerous other small chores."

I smiled as I thought to myself: head sexton…that sounded more like a pornographic title, but I was thrilled to have a full-time job.

Michael Roberts

"You can start on Monday. You'll meet with our parttime helper George, an elderly man who works for us and is in charge. He'll show you everything you need to know. I'll check in with you at some point to see how you're doing."

"Thank you, Father."

A few days later, Gregory went with me to the car dealership to help me find my own used car, because my Mustang was always breaking down. He cosigned my loan for the car. Yes, it gave him even more control over me, but I needed a car. I bought a Plymouth Horizon that turned out to be another lemon, needing continued repairs over the next few years.

It wasn't long after I started to work as head sexton at the church when Peter and I got together secretly again. We drove around the city in his Camaro. Out of curiosity, Peter decided to drive by the library. As I mentioned earlier, it was a well-known gay cruising area where like-minded men drove around in their cars trying to "hookup" with other willing, gay men. Driving up and down the side streets adjacent to the library, we passed a sedan. Its occupant had a very familiar face.

"Oh my God! It's Father Oliver," I said with surprise.

"How do you know him?" Peter asked.

"He's my boss, where I maintain the church."

Father Oliver turned into the library's parking lot. I hoped he hadn't seen me. Nevertheless, I crouched out of sight in Peter's car.

"Can we leave Peter?" I asked.

"Yes of course. Let's head to the club."

We arrived at the parking lot, went into the club, and headed directly to the dance floor. I always took a chance that Reggie wouldn't see me then report back to Gregory, but I began to not care. Upon entering, I was excited that the handsome bartender, whom I'd seen the last time I was there, was working. I followed Peter to the bar, where the sexy bartender was busy serving drinks. We found a spot at the bar that was several feet away from him. Within a few seconds, he spotted me staring at him, and he walked toward us. A neophyte when it came to making eye contact with another gay man, I quickly looked away. I didn't have the courage, or the know-how, to hold the eye connection.

"Hello, what can I get for you to drink?" the barman asked.

I wondered if my nervousness was showing. "Umm... I'll have a Cape Codder."

"What's your name?" he asked as he extended his right hand.

"Michael," I said. "Nice to meet you. What's your name?"

"I'm Brandon."

"You're one handsome guy," I said, surprising myself that those words just came out of my mouth.

"Thank you. You're very good-looking as well. I'm sure you get hit on by everyone."

"Not everyone. You're the only one I've met," I replied.

"That's true," he said with a grin.

I so admired how uninhibited he was. He was definitely putting on the charm. I, on the other hand, was trying to hold it together.

"You here with anyone tonight?" he asked.

"I'm here with my friend Peter."

"What are you doing afterward?"

"I'm headed back to Peter's house."

"Would you mind if I join you? Maybe spend the night?"

I hesitated momentarily, startled by his question.

"I'll have to ask him. I'll be right back," I said nervously.

"Okay, let me know."

I walked away, searching for Peter who seemed to have disappeared somewhere in the sea of men. Finally, I found him at the bar in the piano lounge, chatting with an older, attractive man. I rather rudely ignored the other man as I grasped Peter's arm and pulled him aside.

"Peter, that cute bartender wants to come back with me to your house. What should I do?"

"Just tell him that I'm taking care of a friend's home. I can't let anyone know it's my parents' house. The two of you can follow me. My friend Frank is coming home with me as well."

"Frank?" I asked.

"The man over at the bar I'm chatting with. I met him a few weeks ago. He wants to hook up tonight."

"You mean sex?"

"Of course. My parents and brothers won't be back for two more days. You can have my parents' room. Frank and I will be in my bedroom."

"He wants to spend the night," I said.

"That's fine. Frank does too. They can leave in the morning."

Peter took me over and introduced me to Frank. We shook hands, and then I excused myself.

I proceeded back across the dance floor, to the back bar. I stood, waiting for Brandon to see me. He noticed me immediately.

"Hello again," I said. "My friend Peter said we could come over to his friends' house. His friends are on vacation for a few more days. He's housesitting while they're gone."

"That's great. I'll leave a bit early tonight. I'll meet you in the parking lot at midnight."

"That should work. We can follow Peter back to his friends' house."

We left the club and drove to Peter's house. We parked on the opposite side of his house. We didn't want to draw any attention from Gregory, who could see the front side of Peter's house from the rectory. Before getting out of the car, Peter grabbed my arm.

"Michael, I'll run inside, while you distract them for a minute."

"Why, what's wrong?"

"I need to get inside and hide our family pictures. I don't want them to suspect I live here. They can never know that this is my family's home. I want us to stick to the story that I'm taking care of my friends' property while they're away. Hurry, get over there and stall them."

"Okay, I'll do my best."

I walked over to Brandon and Frank. I introduced them to each other and initiated a bit of small-talk before we started to walk toward Peter's front door.

"The church over there is the one I attend," I said, continuing the small-talk. "The elementary school I went to is about an eight-minute walk away. The mall is about a ten-minute walk in that direction." My conversation skills were a bit lacking, but it was the best I could do. I was new at this.

As we approached Peter's door, I hoped he had finished hiding the family photos. He then opened the door and welcomed us.

"You guys can take the master bedroom here on the main floor. We're going to my room upstairs," Peter said.

Not surprisingly, I found I was afraid to be alone with this beautiful man. As we walked toward the bedroom, I was becoming increasingly nervous. I had never had an intentional encounter with a man.

"I'll be right back," I told Brandon. "I need to talk to Peter for a few minutes." I rushed out of the bedroom, finding Peter and Frank still in the kitchen.

"Peter, can I speak with you alone for a moment?"

"Yes, what is it?" he asked motioning me into the dining room.

I was so nervous, I was almost shaking. "Peter, I'm so scared. What should I do?"

"About what?"

"This is my first real experience."

"Relax."

Peter was very kind. He told me to just relax and to follow Brandon's lead.

When I returned to the bedroom, Brandon shut the door, and began to kiss me. It was obvious to me by the way he moved that this was not his first time. In spite of my shyness, I loved this new adventure. As we continued our embrace, I was completely captivated by him—his manly scent and his gentle nature. He was definitely skilled in the art of seduction, which ultimately stimulated all of my senses.

"You're a good kisser," he said.

"Thank you."

I didn't even think I was doing it correctly, but I was pleased he was enjoying it.

We spent the next few hours appreciating our time together, reveling in the intimacy of mutual exploration, admiration, and gratification. Some may simply call it lust, but for me, it was much more. Even though this man was someone I barely knew, I was having my first taste of intimacy. It was powerful. We chatted for a while, then I fell asleep, admiring his hair and broad shoulders.

The following morning, we all exchanged pleasantries, then Frank and Brandon were ready to leave. Yes, we'd had a wonderful night together, but by morning, it was simply time to go our separate ways.

As Peter walked the two men to the door, I stayed in the kitchen, smiling like a Cheshire Cat. I had an amazing feeling of satisfaction that I'd never felt before. I was finally able to explore my sexuality, if only for one night. I had just experienced a new taste of freedom, and I loved it. My brief encounter with Brandon had taught me so much, most of which was that I could overcome my insecurities and start to live life fully. Brandon had shown me that he knew how to live his life fully. Maybe I could, too. I deserved a full life.

Tomorrow came too soon. I was once again Gregory's prisoner. How could I free myself if I had no appreciable job skills or experience to list on a resume. I felt hopeless and helpless. I resigned myself to the fact that I must return to my indentured misery. I would be headed back to the rectory with Gregory, who was completely unaware of my night at Peter's.

Monday morning, I went back to work. But something inside me was different this time. This caged bird wanted desperately to fly free. I decided that I would tell Father Oliver, who I assumed was gay, about Gregory's abuse. I felt a connection with Father Oliver. He always put me at ease. I trusted him. More importantly, I trusted he would listen to me and help liberate me from Gregory.

August 1985. It was early morning when Father Oliver arrived at the church to say morning Mass. He entered his office, as I was finishing setting up for the service. My duties included lighting the candles, preparing the wine and water on the altar, counting out communion wafers, playing the soundtrack of calming religious music, and delivering one or to readings during Mass. The music was my favorite part. It was an open channel that seemed to help me feel closer to God. After Father Oliver finished dressing in his vestment, I approached him.

"Father, I wanted to know if I could speak with you after Mass?"

"What would you like to speak about?"

"It's a rather personal matter."

"I have an appointment after Mass, but let's plan around two o'clock this afternoon. We can meet in my office."

"Thank you, Father,"

I entered the church with him and took my seat at the left side of the altar. The Mass ended, and I reminded Father Oliver that I would see him that afternoon.

At around one forty-five, I heard the side door open as I was removing old bulletins from the pews. Father Oliver stopped in the doorway, waved, and walked back to his office. I finished picking up the bulletins and headed to his office. I noticed the door to Father Oliver's office was ajar. I stood just outside, feigning a cough to get his attention.

"Michael, please come in."

"Thank you, Father."

The phone rang; he answered it and told the caller to contact him tomorrow. He then unplugged the phone from the wall.

"You have my undivided attention, Michael. What would you like to talk about?"

I was slow to speak. How was I going to express my dilemma and the pain and suffering it was causing me?

"Michael, take all the time in the world you need."

"Father, I'm not sure how to say this."

"Do the best you can."

My mouth was dry, but I began to speak. "Father Gregory is not treating me very well."

"Please explain," he said.

"He gets very angry, yells at me, insults me, blackmails me, and sexually assaults me."

Father Oliver rose up from his chair, closed the office door, and returned to his chair.

"I think it's best if our talk is totally private. I'm sorry you're going through a difficult time. What has he done to you physically?"

"Like I mentioned, he forces me to have sex with him."

"Forces you?"

"He told me that he was gay and attracted to me. I feel I am being controlled by him. He uses God and my parents against me. He threatens to tell my parents I'm gay if I report the abuse to anyone. He would be surprised to learn I am telling you."

"Michael, what is said between us goes no further. Being gay is not the issue here."

"Thank you," I said.

"The issue is forcing another person with threats or intimidation."

I felt he understood my situation. I was also confident that he would not divulge any of this information to Gregory. Then, I waited for him to say something. I dropped my gaze to the floor, not wanting to make eye contact with him.

"I understand why Gregory would find you attractive; however, he should never force himself on you. Michael, you need a hug."

He stood up beside his desk and extended his arms. I stood up as well, thinking a comforting hug was his way of showing he cared. I moved toward him, but then he grabbed me pulling me to his body into a tight embrace. I assumed we would hug, but instead he tried to kiss me!

I pulled back, confused as to why he would do this right after I revealed that I was being sexually assaulted. Was he just another selfish, libido-driven priest? It didn't take a Sigmund Freud to understand the psychological impact Gregory's repeated assaults were having on me. I was a mess. Was it possible that Father Oliver simply chose to ignore the mental anguish I was experiencing? I was stunned. Father Oliver was my boss. I was worried he would fire me if I rejected his advances.

"Father, I don't think this is a good idea."

"I'm rather a good kisser."

"I have work to do. I don't want to do this."

"Relax. You'll get overtime."

Once again, I was the powerless Michael.

He kissed me again, this time trying to stick his tongue in my mouth. I turned my head, trying to resist. He stopped kissing me but reached down and pulled at my zipper.

"I don't like this," I said in protest.

He said nothing as he kept pulling at my zipper.

"Stop. I don't think this is a good idea."

He lowered my pants then my underwear just enough to liberate my private parts. I stood exposed, vulnerable to yet another hedonistic priest. He knelt and performed oral copulation until I climaxed. Then, he stood up, reconnected the phone, said 'good afternoon', and walked out of the office.

I was left devastated and alone. I knew Father Oliver was not going to be reporting my abuse by Father Gregory to the diocese—not after molesting me himself. In a mental stupor, I pulled up my jeans. How could this have happened? I came here to report a sexual assault. Oh my God! It took all the courage I could muster to speak with Father Oliver. Now what do I do? Where do I turn to get help?

I moved into the open sacristy area, took a seat at the desk, and spent the remaining time of my shift wondering why I had done nothing to stop him. Why was I paralyzed in the moment, unable to deflect or to stop what had happened? Had Gregory told Father Oliver how easy it would be to exploit me? Why did I allow these priests to molest me? The sad, but simple, truth was that when they both took advantage of me, I did nothing. After that afternoon, Father Oliver never spoke a single word to me. He always left quickly after Mass if I was in attendance.

The morning after my encounter with Father Oliver, Gregory arrived at the church, where I was preparing for the morning Mass. He startled me when he walked into the sacristy.

"What are you doing here?" I asked.

"Good morning to you. I'm saying Mass this morning."

"That's news."

"Father Oliver asked if I could fill in for him."

This was rather odd. Was Gregory saying Mass to check up on me? Was Father Oliver saying fewer Masses here, knowing what he had done to me. The truth became more apparent over the remaining months of summer. Father Oliver did reduce his morning Masses. He enlisted several substitute priests to fill in for his weekday morning obligations. Father Gregory seemed to be doing Masses more frequently as well.

After that, Gregory ended his Mass, and started looking in closets, cabinets, and storage areas in the church.

"What are you doing?"

"Seeing what I can take," he replied.

Michael Roberts

"You mean you're stealing?"

"As I said to you many times before, I am redistributing the wealth."

He left with two, three-foot angel figurines he had found in a side cabinet. He took a few other trinkets, too. I was not sure what to do. What would I say if asked where the items were? Was I to lie? Gregory placed me in a precarious position. I risked the possibility of losing my job for allowing these items to be taken, or much worse, I could be accused of taking them. If I reported this theft, would anyone believe me? Worst of all, I would be the target of Gregory's wrath. Either way, I would suffer some form of retribution.

The following Saturday morning, Gregory came over to our house early, even though he knew I slept late. When he arrived, I was still in bed. My parents and brothers were out grocery shopping. Because he always had access to our home, Gregory let himself in, then made his way to my bedroom.

He scared the crap out of me, shouting, "Michael, get your ass up! You're coming with me to Pineview!"

'I'll pass," I answered.

"Get your ass up or I'll get it up for you."

I didn't move. I just lay in bed, defiant to his demands. Again, I was testing the waters, knowing that I might drown. He kept telling me to get up, but I stayed quiet. He became more belligerent.

"Goddamn you. Get your fucking ass out of bed!"

He was furious, but I didn't care. My shunning him had worked. He walked out of my room, and I heard him slam the front door. Then, I heard tires screech as he sped away.

I just poked the bear, I thought to myself. I climbed out of bed, went to close the front door, and was shocked by what I saw. Gregory had thrown the front door open so viciously that the doorknob had punched a hole in the wall. Oh God, what am I going to do? My parents will be home any time.

I didn't want them to know Gregory and I'd had any altercation. I first ran down to the basement and then on to the garage, looking for anything I could use to fix the hole. I was in luck. I found a container of premixed plaster that the contractors had left behind when they refurbished the house.

165

Many areas of walls had applications of what I call "swirly plaster." I always likened the walls to a cake with a layer of white frosting swirled on top. I grabbed the can along with a putty knife.

I opened the can of plaster and began applying it to the hole in the sheetrock. But each time I tried to add the plaster; it fell down inside the gap between the frame of the house and the sheetrock. I needed a mesh of some kind to fill the hole before applying the plaster. I searched the house again, finding no mesh. As an alternative, I stuffed the hole with crumpled newspaper. I jammed each rolled wad into the hole as far as I could. I continued until the newspaper was showing just above the hole in the wall. I then began to apply the plaster once again. It seemed to work momentarily, but then the newly applied plaster started to bulge out like a rising souffle. Finally, I got my hair dryer and applied a stream of warm air to my handiwork. About thirty minutes later, the hole was repaired, or so I hoped. If anyone could spot the hole, it would be my mother.

When my parents arrived at home, I prayed that neither would see the difference in the wall pattern. I was victorious! They saw nothing, nor did they mention anything. When my folks went to bed that night, I went back to the wall and applied another layer of plaster, trying my best to re-create the swirl pattern in the rest of the wall. The following day, when no one was around, I found the bucket of leftover paint that had been used on the wall. My secret was safe. No one but me knew about the hole in the wall. For days, I was a nervous wreck, worrying that my parents would notice the new plaster. Father Gregory had created even more stress in my life, and I hated him for it.

I often thought of a lesson learned in science class. The teacher said that only ten percent of an iceberg is seen above the water. Ninety percent of it was hidden under the water. That fact had stayed with me for years.

The analogy was parallel to life as I knew it. Ten percent of the people of the parish might have had some suspicion of Gregory's private life—the lies, the cover-ups, the possible

Michael Roberts

thefts, not to mention gay clergy at a time when homosexuality was considered a sin. But such acts would go undetected by most of the people of the congregation. It was all part of what I had come to see as a model of hypocrisy—the institution known as the Catholic Church.

15

Satan's successes are the greatest when he
appears with the name of God on his lips.

—Mahatma Gandhi
Peace Activist

August 1985. Gregory and I saw *Agnes of God,* a movie starring Meg Tilly as a novice nun Sister Agnes. The mystery took us moviegoers on a journey about how Sister Agnes conceived a child. Was it a virgin conception, or was she raped by an outside male figure? Agnes displayed a childlike innocence, unaware how the baby was conceived. In one scene, Sister Agnes blamed God for raping and impregnating her. She told God that she hated him.

I, too, hated God for the suffering he put upon me. I often thought Father Gregory, who was one of His messengers, was apparently ordered by God to carry out His "loving punishment" on me. Like Sister Agnes, I was innocent to the world around me. I grew up believing in God's love, but also understood that He could be vengeful. I recalled stories of God killing everyone in Sodom and Gomorrah, God drowning the Earth, God killing men and women, helping the Israelites destroy Jericho, God helping the Israelites slaughter the Amorites by sword, then finishing them off with rocks from the sky.

These are just a few of many stories of God's wrath in the Bible. I concluded that God was carrying out his grand design by pushing me on a holier path. I was being raped, tormented, and controlled, yet somehow strangely enough, I felt I deserved it. Like Sister Agnes, I felt I was a mistake. Gay people were seen as an anathema, never to make it into Heaven.

When we arrived back at the rectory, Gregory wanted to fool around, but I didn't want to, especially after seeing this disturbing film. He suggested that we should expand our sexual repertoire—try new things. He wanted to explore anal sex, sex toys, and erotic games. I was repulsed by his fantasies. Discretion being the better part of valor, I chose not to add fuel to his fire; therefore, I remained silent while he spewed forth his lascivious thoughts. Sensing his heightened state of arousal, I decided that the path of least resistance would be to agree to allow him to violate me once again. In my fear and low sense of self-worth, I capitulated.

Fall 1985. I was still working at my job at the church. I continued to save as much money as possible, in preparation for the day when I could make my escape. I also wanted to work out more at a gym—I needed it for my mental health, and I wanted to stay in shape; I often had used my parents' membership to a local health club.

Then, on my lunch break one day, I discovered a workout gym I wanted to join. It was different from the health club I had been going to and was closer to my home.

Later, one evening, after finishing my shift at the church, I contemplated asking Gregory for permission to join this gym. But I was reluctant to ask him because I expected him to resort immediately to his playbook of threats, ultimatums, and shaming me. Gregory demanded my full compliance, and if I denied him, I would face his wrath. I decided to wait for a better time to ask him…if it ever came along.

Gregory's paranoia about me was intensifying at an alarming rate. An example that comes to mind was an incident that occurred one evening around midnight. I was in my room, at my parents' home, when I heard a car slowly moving up the street. Something urged me to take a peek out the window, because any traffic on our quiet street at this hour was highly unusual. Peering out the window, I saw Gregory drive by, most likely spying to see if I was home. Fortunately, my bedroom light wasn't on, so I knew he would not be aware that I was watching him. Over the next two weeks, I caught him doing this again. But I often wondered how many times I didn't catch him. I made the conscious decision to stop looking out my window. I thought it best not to speak to him about this. Moreover, I simply had started not to care. I just accepted the fact I would be on trial the rest of my life in a court presided over by Gregory—the Honorable *Judge Judy* of the diocese.

The evening after I had discovered the gym I wanted to join, I found Gregory relaxing in his bedroom chair. I summoned the courage to broach the subject of joining the gym.

"Gregory, I've decided to join a local gym. I'll go right after work."

"Really?" The implication of his tone was: Are you serious?

"It's a rundown place, but it's close to my work, and it's cheap. I want to keep in shape. I stopped by to check out the place the other day. It was rather odd to see very few customers. To be honest, I'm not even sure how they stay in business."

"Umm," he said, staring at me.

"I'll go for an hour or more after work."

"I don't think so. This doesn't work for me. Sorry."

Pulling Psychology 101 out of the back of my brain, I decided to placate him. "I have to keep my body in tip-top shape for you. I don't want you to be embarrassed to be seen with me in public."

"I like that," he replied.

Suddenly, he wasn't so worried about me being at the gym, if I was keeping in shape for him. The lack of clientele working out at the gym and its proximity to the church were all positive in his mind. Then he segued to several other subjects, such as his schedule for the upcoming week and his plans for Labor Day. When he finished his litany, we watched a bit of TV, and I left for home.

After my church shift ended the following day, I showed up at the new health club. Upon entering, members were greeted by Steve at the front desk. He was a nice man and based on the earring he wore in his right ear, I assumed he was gay. In those days, it was commonly thought that a man wearing an earring on the right ear meant he was gay. A man who wore an earring on his left earlobe was straight.

Steve had a thin, meticulously trimmed mustache. His overall demeanor would lead one to believe he might be vying for a vacant position with the Village People. His was dressed in a pink, form-fitting polo shirt, tight jeans, white belt, and sneakers. His comportment was obviously more feminine than masculine. He seemed to fit the then-typical stereotype of a gay man. After I paid the gym fee, Steve showed me around the facilities, explaining the proper use of the machines and club etiquette.

On my third day at the gym, seated at the bicep curl machine, I noticed another man working out. He had light-brown skin and a tall, thin frame. I couldn't help but observe his improper use of the leg machine. He was locking his knees when extending them. I had learned from a previous instructor that the correct form was to keep your knees slightly bent. I was inclined to share this bit of information with him but decided to mind my own business.

I did find it odd that, instead of wearing some sort of gym clothes, he was wearing a black T-shirt, tight black jeans, and black Converse sneakers. Those street clothes would make it difficult to achieve a full range of motion, I thought to myself.

The following day, the tall, thin man was back in the gym. I found myself being critical of him—not as genteel and Christian-like as I should have been. Still, to me he looked like a member of some street gang. Was he a hoodlum, a tough guy? I chided myself for my racist mind-set. Clearly, I was not a racist. My prom date was a Black girl, whom I considered a dear friend. Determined to prove to myself that I was not judgmental, I started up a conversation with him.

"Hi. Not many people here today," I said.

"It's never busy at this time."

I extended my hand. "Michael. Nice to meet you."

"Lee. Nice to meet you."

"I work right across from the park. I take care of the church. What do you do?"

"I'm a puppeteer," he said.

"Wow, that's interesting."

I mentioned that I lived ten minutes away with my parents. He told me that he lived in an apartment just past city hall. He said he traveled all over the state, performing at schools, libraries, private birthdays, and at small theaters. This man was proof that you could not judge a book by its cover. I was fascinated by what he was telling me about his craft and the breadth of his experience. We both spent about an hour working out, periodically chatting.

When it was time for me to go, I mentioned that I was there about this time every day. He also decided to leave and followed me out to the sidewalk. We exchange good-byes and headed in different directions.

A few days later, Lee and I ran into each other at the gym. I changed into my gym clothes, came out from the locker room, and approached the triceps-extension machine. Lee was close by.

"What are you working on today?" I asked.

"Just arms, not up to doing much more."

"I understand. I feel like leaving right now. I'm kind of tired."

"I'm tired as well. You want to skip today, head over to the mall?" Lee asked.

"Sounds good to me," I replied. By now, I assumed he was gay; however, we never discussed the topic.

I changed into my street clothes, and we left for the local mall. It was only a two-minute walk. We meandered around the mall, passing by several department stores and specialty stores. We passed by Fanny Farmers, a bakery and candy store, that had always been a favorite of mine. We entered only a few shops. It so happened that Spencer Gifts was a favorite for both of us. It catered to our sense of humor. Here, one was sure to find a distinctive product mix of silly novelties and gag gifts, some of which were quite ornery. We ended our mall excursion at Orange Julius, where Lee ordered us both a creamy, orange, drink called a Creamsicle. It was delicious.

Over the coming months, our friendship developed, but there was something rather special about our connection. We seemed to enjoy each other's humor, often giggling like little boys. Our silly, spontaneous banter usually brought on more laughter. We were two magnets gravitating toward each other. I loved having developed a new friendship. Our friendship remained purely platonic, but I was always worried that Gregory would find out about Lee and not approve. Whenever Lee and I would get together after my shift at work, I would only have about an hour and half before I'd have to head back home to my parents' house. Even after I had moved out of the rectory, I had to account for every minute I was away from Gregory. Otherwise, he would launch a barrage of questions, making sure I could explain where I had been. It was an arduous task keeping up this charade, all in an effort to avoid his rage. On the one hand, I didn't want to lose a friend like Lee, but on the other hand, I was afraid of Gregory. I was constantly devising ways to maintain any friendships that didn't include Gregory.

The following Wednesday, I met Lee. We decided, again, to play hooky from the health club and walk to the mall. As we were leaving, he invited me to his apartment to meet his mother and to see his handcrafted puppets. I delighted in doing something completely new to me. I was doing something with a friend I had made on my own.

We entered his apartment building across the street from an old department store and took an elevator to the seventh floor. As we entered Lee's apartment, I was greeted by Lee's mother. She was quite pleasant.

"Michael, this is my mother."

"Nice to meet you," I said. Jokingly I added, "Do I call you Mother? Or do you have another name?"

She responded with a chuckle, "Nice to meet you, Michael. My name's Joan."

I was quite surprised at how small the whole apartment was. The tiny kitchen opened into the small living room, which seemed to have a dual purpose—a living room and his mom's bedroom. It was the first time I realized that not everyone lived in a three-bedroom home, like I did.

We babbled a few minutes longer, and then Lee offered to show me his bedroom. The room was just big enough for a twin bed. The rest of the space was his workshop, in which he had thread spools, spray paints, and remnants of fabrics. Also on display was his collection of puppets, all of which he had made. He removed several more puppets from a large canvas bag. I was flabbergasted by his artistry.

"How did you get into puppetry?"

"I became fascinated with puppets after I saw a puppet show when I was little. My mother encouraged me to make some puppets of my own. For my first puppet shows, I was allowed to use some space in a nearby barn. I charged a few cents for admission. Over time, my hobby grew into my life's work, my passion."

That evening at home, I kept thinking of how talented Lee was. I admired how he had built a business from the bottom up, designed his own puppets, and took care of his mother. Most importantly, he said something that resonated deeply with me. He mentioned that he didn't care much for material things...he preferred to spend his money on experiences.

The following day, Gregory asked me to go for a ride with him to his home in Pineview. When he picked me up, I could immediately sense his anger. He sped off, swearing.

"My Goddamn fucking sister!"

I knew of his sister only by her name, Mary. I knew she had a seven-year-old son, Gregory's nephew.

"Calm down. What's wrong?"

"Don't tell me to calm down!"

"You're speeding. Slow down, or I will get out at the next light."

"I'll speed through the light, so there."

"Why are you taking this out on me?"

"She has the fucking, Goddamned nerve to accuse me of touching her son inappropriately."

"Oh boy," I said.

"That bitch will rot in Hell before I forgive her."

I tried to agree with him to assuage his anger. "You have the right to be furious. I would be pissed if I was wrongly accused. How dare she?"

"She better fucking apologize to me and admit that I never laid a finger on her son. She has torn this family apart. Mom's very angry."

"Why the hell would she say this?"

"My bitch of a sister told me that her son said that I touched his buttocks."

Michael Roberts

I wondered if his nephew mistakenly misinterpreted a simple pat on the bottom or if it was more than that. Maybe his hand brushed up against the child's buttocks or maybe they were playfully wrestling together, and Gregory's hand inadvertently landed in the wrong place. Gregory had molested me, but even I could not envision him molesting his little nephew. I was convinced that he didn't touch the little boy inappropriately. Here I was, defending my molester.

We left his mother's home only after Gregory placed another statue of a saint on a shelf in the upstairs bedroom along with his collection of religious statuary. I wondered, how many of these statues were purchased. How many had he stolen?

Gregory drove us over to a popular fast-food restaurant, Jeremy's Kitchen, well known for its barbeque. We had a quick lunch. We arrived back at the rectory where, for the first time, I saw pain on his face. I managed to find a modicum of empathy in my heart to tell him I was there for him. Shortly thereafter, I left the rectory and headed home.

Gregory never again mentioned his sister's accusation. Mentally drained from my own struggles, I was inwardly relieved that he never shared any further details of the incident with me.

January 1986. I continued my friendship with Lee, although I would only see him briefly after work. Over the years, I had improved my craft of deceiving Gregory. Lying became an art form for me. When I did see Lee, it was during the time that Gregory assumed I was at the gym. My best opportunities were when I knew Gregory would be gone for three hours or more, officiating at weddings, funerals, and performing other priestly duties.

One evening, I was able to sneak down to the local gay bar. Now that I had reached the legal drinking age, I no longer feared being arrested. Apparently, I was well-liked by the management and staff. They all seemed to stare at me and to drop sexual innuendos whenever I was around. Entering the club, I spotted Lee dancing with a short guy, who was wearing a black hat and a long coat. Good for him, I thought. He's having a good time.

At this point in my life, I was aware that I was still judgmental of others. I questioned the moral fiber of the club's patrons. Drinking, smoking, touching, and flirting—all were forms of debauchery, according to my teachings. I believed even too much dancing was sinful.

But I also began to realize that Gregory had contorted passages from the Bible to fit his needs. He was critical of having excessive fun. He convinced me that if I witnessed others reveling in gaiety, they were sinful. He lectured me to be distrustful of people whom I believed were seeking only pleasure from the external world rather than from the kingdom of Heaven. I justified Lee's behavior as his not being aware of what it was like to have a relationship with Christ. Lee danced for hours. I reasoned that God would overlook his immoral manner and forgive him when he became enlightened.

I stood under the disc jockey's booth, hoping Lee and his friend would take a break from dancing, so I could say hello. They gyrated to the beat of the music under the psychedelic light show. I admired his confidence and stamina, even though I thought Lee's dancing bordered on having too much pleasure. Just then, Lee and his dancer partner left the dance floor. I caught their attention.

"Hello, Lee." It was rather odd seeing him here because we had never discussed being gay. I guess we were officially out to each other now.

"Hey, it's nice to see you."

"Michael, this is my friend Adam."

"Hello Adam."

"Hello," he said. He seemed to be sizing me up.

Adam excused himself and headed to the restroom.

"He seems like a nice guy."

"Yes, he is," Lee said, catching his breath.

When Adam returned, they both decided to leave. I followed them out to the parking lot. We said our good-byes and left in different directions.

The following week, Lee and I met for our typical quick visit. He explained to me that Adam was planning to have a sex change, only the breasts for now. He was contemplating "bottom surgery" sometime in the future. He was rather concerned about the complete removal of Adam's male genitalia, but Adam firmly believed the sex organs he had received at birth were a contradiction of who he was. Lee went on to tell me that Adam had chosen the name, Mae, as his new first name.

Admittedly, I was a bit baffled by the notion of sexual reassignment and the delicate medical procedures required to accomplish the conversion. At that time, in the United States, the only famous male-to-female transsexual was Christine Jorgensen. Her surgery took place in the early 1950s in Copenhagen, Denmark, and she eventually became a notable entertainer and spokesperson for true-to-yourself, personal identity.

I did, however, recognize a direct correlation between Adam and me. We would both be considered different, but for different reasons. And for all the LGBTQ community, the struggle for acceptance continued.

I was impressed with Adam's fortitude. I thought about him many nights, thinking about his determination to be his authentic self. It then crossed my mind that in the animal kingdom, within every species, there are thousands of variations of color, size, weight, adaptations, uniqueness, and sexualities. I remembered, from my science classes, that some snails are hermaphrodites, having both sex organs. One textbook explained that clownfish, moray eels, gobies, and other aquatic species were known to change their genders; and when males turn into females, they can even lay eggs. According to science, this occurs when there are not enough members of the opposite sex available.

As I researched further, I learned the animal kingdom had hundreds of examples of asexual, bisexual, and homosexual behaviors. An estimated one-quarter of the black swans that mated were males. More than twenty species of bats had been documented to engage in homosexual behavior. Bottlenose dolphins were documented to have engaged in homosexual acts. African and Asian male elephants would engage in same-sex bonding and would mount each other. Courtship, mounting, and full anal penetration between bulls had been noted to occur among American bison. The list also included giraffes, marmots, bonobo, primates, reptiles, insects, and penguins.

The result of this research triggered an enlightenment within me. There was nothing wrong with Adam or with any of us, who were gay. We were all part of this one spectrum. It seemed that we were judged as freaks-of-nature only by most religions, and in my case, the Catholic Church. More and more, the church was no longer playing a major role in my life. I refused to accept the church's bigotry and discrimination. My spirituality was still strong, but I chose to denounce the dogma of any institution that called itself an organized religion.

16

April 1986. Gregory bought tickets for us to see Liza Minelli in concert. What self-respecting gay man wouldn't delight at seeing Liza? It was thrilling to see the daughter of Judy Garland perform old standards. Arriving back at the rectory after the show, we sat and chatted.

"I am hosting a dinner party on Saturday night. You will be there," Gregory commanded.

"I'll skip this one, please."

"You have zero say in this. As I've told you before, this church is not a democracy but a bimonarchy," meaning only he and the Pope ruled the parish. "What I say goes. You will be there. Period!"

"I'm always uncomfortable."

"It will be fine. I hired the bartender who works at the gay bar."

Mmm, I thought. Maybe the bartender would be Brandon, whom I connected with awhile back.

"You know the bartender?" I asked.

"Yes. His name's Chuck."

I was disappointed that he wasn't hiring Brandon, my favorite bartender.

"He's one of Reggie's friends. He works the bar."

For several reasons, I detested attending these events that were planned and catered by Gregory and Reggie. It was the same old scenario played out at all of their parties. I was surrounded with Reggie's gay friends who always felt they had to prance around like women, flail their limp wrists, and speak in annoying falsettos. If I had a dollar for every time someone used the word "Mary," I could buy a Caribbean Island. Mary was the typical salutation these gay men used to address the feminine sides of their friends. Moreover, they usually referred to their gay male companions as "she." Their favorite fallback lines from a popular gay movie, *Boys in The Band,* was: "Who is she? Who was she? Who does she hope to be?"

I often wondered where Gregory was getting the funds to host these exclusive, open bar dinner parties at the rectory. Would the parishioners be disturbed if they knew the church was being used in this manner? Yes! They would have been both furious and devastated that their dear, sweet, funny Gregory would betray their trust in such a decadent and perverted manner. Little did they know that Sodom and Gomorrah had been visited upon their hallowed parish grounds.

The parishioners in our small and tight-knit community knew everyone else's business. The church ladies, whose gossip I deplored, would spread any rumor or scandal within minutes. Gregory's den of iniquity would have been descended upon by a rioting mob, brandishing torches and pitchforks. They would have been hellbent on vanquishing the beast from within. However, Gregory was immune from any gossip or whispers about him. He knew his parishioners adored him, and he ruled the church accordingly.

I arrived at Gregory's party early that evening. I mingled quietly, pretending to enjoy myself. I smiled when others smiled. I laughed when others laughed. Please God! Send a lightning bolt now. Zap me or them. Either way, it was a win-win situation.

Monday, after surviving the party at the rectory dining room, I decided to share an idea I'd had with Gregory. I had helped teach aerobics at a gym I had attended. I thought it would be nice to offer an aerobics class to the church members. I would broach the subject, saying I thought I might serve the church in a broader capacity to offer an exercise class, an aerobics class. I would tell him that I had already begun teaching a few aerobics classes at my gym. And, recently I had begun making appearances on a local cable TV program about health and exercise.

My well-rehearsed presentation went something like this: "Gregory, I should teach a few aerobics classes here in the church hall. I have plenty of experience now. I think the parish would appreciate it, and I could make a few dollars. Of course, I would donate a portion of whatever I made back to the church for the use of the facility."

"Sounds like a good idea," Gregory said without hesitation. I was surprised that he would agree so quickly.

"Really?"

"I'll add information in next week's bulletin."

"Awesome. Thank you."

He was always quick to approve anything that benefited him, often giving little thought to it. I'm sure his approval of this suggestion had everything to do with his ability to keep an even closer watch and control over me.

That Saturday before Mass, I went to see him at the church to discuss details of the exercise class. I found the week's bulletin on the table in the vestibule. It read:

"Aerobics Class in the Hall on Tuesday and Thursday 6:00–7:00 P.M. If you are interested, call Michael for more details."

I was excited to see my name mentioned in print. I felt like an entrepreneur in the making. I wanted to make extra money to add to my savings. The idea was well-received by parishioners. I went on to teach the classes for several months.

May 1986. I sat in Gregory's room waiting for him to finish hearing confessions in the church. I knew he would be gone for little over an hour. We each had a chair where we usually watched TV and ate pizza. His was a big recliner; mine was a small, swivel rocker. A small table sat between the two chairs. As I sat down in my chair, I noticed a letter on the small table. I couldn't help but pick it up. Much to my surprise, it was a letter Gregory had written to Peter.

In the letter, Gregory was chastising Peter. The whole ordeal was based on the fact that Gregory thought Peter had discarded what Gregory considered a most important gift. Because Peter intended to become a priest, Gregory had given him a ciborium, a metal vessel that looked like a goblet with a lid; it was used to hold communion wafers during communion services.

Years later, I would learn that, for reasons unknown, a friend of one of Peter's brothers had stolen the ciborium, and the lid ended up being tossed into some bushes outside the home of an area man, who happened to be a Lutheran minister. The minister recognized the ciborium lid as part of a vessel belonging to the Catholic Church. He dutifully returned it to Father Gregory at the rectory. Holy ciborium lids! Gregory was convinced that Peter had casually discarded the precious gift, and he let his feelings be known to Peter in a letter.

Gregory opened his letter by telling Peter that by discarding his gift, he must hate him and the church. Gregory's letter told Peter that he would never be a priest in this diocese or in any other in the nation and keeping Peter out of the priesthood would be his mission until the day he died. He ended the letter by saying that if Peter didn't change his ways, he might have to tell Peter's grandmother and Peter's friend Father Amos that he was gay.

I was shocked, but not surprised, by Gregory's ugly letter. Didn't he know that Peter could easily expose him for sexually abusing young men and possibly stealing things, including cash, from the church? I left a note on Gregory's bed, saying I wasn't feeling well and had to go home.

June 1986. I was feeling guilty about keeping my friendship with Lee a secret, so I decided at some point soon to tell Gregory about him. It was an innocent friendship, and I felt I had kept the secret long enough.

Several weeks before, I had briefly mentioned to Lee that I was friends with my local priest, and that he paid me forty dollars a week for cleaning the church. I suggested that we should all meet sometime. I filled in Lee with a few more details about my close friendship with Father Gregory as well as my family's fondness of him. I guessed that Lee was not particularly religious; I hoped my disclosures about my faith would not make him uncomfortable.

"Lee, you know that I have a priest-friend. I was introduced to him a few years back by my friend Peter."

"Do I know Peter?" Lee questioned.

"He often goes to the Brass Rail; you might recognize him—he used to be a regular there. Peter and I have been friends since elementary school. He was the first one to take me to a gay club."

"Do you still hear from him?"

"No, we lost contact. Plus, he's been working full-time at the hardware store."

"Do you see your priest-friend often?" Lee asked.

"Unfortunately, I do see him quite often. My parents are friends with him. He integrated himself into my family."

"You don't sound like you care for him very much."

"He can be difficult to deal with, but I try to see the good side of him." I was lying, of course. "It would be nice to have friends other than him. I think you might like him; he's rather unconventional." Then I said, "You up for a movie some time? Maybe we all can go together."

"That's fine. If he's a friend of yours, I'm sure I'll like him."

It didn't seem to me that Lee was a Catholic, but I hoped he was at least Christian. I never asked if he went to church.

Over the years with Gregory, I had learned to be a more loyal follower of Jesus Christ. I believed the Bible was the absolute truth. However, I simply ignored any beliefs that spoke negatively against homosexuals. I reasoned that if a truly devout priest like Father Gregory could rationalize and accept these passages, why shouldn't I? Ironically, I wasn't knowledgeable enough to defend that position.

Gregory, the preacher, would often pontificate, instructing me on his interpretation of the Bible. He indoctrinated me with his beliefs, even though he contorted religion to suit his needs. Brainwashed, I began to preach the gospel according to Gregory and to my family members. I was fanatically narrow-minded, and no one could change that. I believed Gregory when he said that dancing too long or enjoying oneself too much would anger God. Simply put, having too much fun was a sin. Any excesses of lust, gluttony, pride, and envy were shameful.

At night in bed, I would read passages from the Bible. I even wore a scapular around my neck—a religious necklace that would protect me. I would say the rosary and whisper to God, Jesus, Mary, and a few saints, hoping they heard me. I continued holding steadfast to my convictions. I never thought to question Gregory about his religious views or for that matter confront him about sexual abuse, excessive drinking, and flagrant misuse of money.

I felt compelled to tell Gregory about my friend, Lee. I wanted Gregory's approval of my friendship. Yet, I was apprehensive about mentioning that I had a new friend. I was certain he would go into a jealous rage. I met Gregory at the rectory for our regular get together before a dining out. Prior to departing for the restaurant, throwing caution to the wind, I said, "Gregory before we leave, I want to discuss something with you."

"What?"

"As you're already aware, I love working out at the gym after work. I don't like lifting heavy weights without someone to help me. Such a helper is called a 'spotter.' Safety protocol dictates that another person spots for you when you lift heavy weights. Having a spotter reduces the risk of the lifter being injured."

"What the hell does this have to do with anything?"

"I met a guy who's been helping me."

"You would betray me like this?" was his immediate retort.

"Listen, he's a nice person. We chat a bit while we workout."

"I don't give a Goddamn who the hell he is. As I mentioned many times before, he, like everyone else, will just use you. I am your only friend here! Got it?"

I was angry that he disapproved of me talking to someone at the gym, let alone having a friend. I fired back. "I don't care what you think. He is a good friend."

"Now he's a friend. Before he only helped you lift weights."

"We enjoy each other's company."

"Heed my warning! He will hurt and use you. I won't have this! Period!"

"You're my best friend. I just thought it would be nice if I had another acquaintance I could see once and awhile."

"Go to Hell. We're not going to dinner."

He got up, walked out of the bedroom, and slammed the door, his signature move. I looked for him around the entire rectory with no luck. The only other place he might be was locked in the church, like he had done several times before. I was determined to change his mind about my new friend.

Gregory was just like a spoiled child in a toy store, who had been told "no."

I walked across the church's parking lot and pulled on the building's front door handle. To my complete surprise, it wasn't locked. Inside the church, I heard sounds reverberating from the sacristy. I headed to Gregory's office. I was acutely aware that it was considered a sin to walk on the red carpet near the altar, but I didn't give a shit. I wasn't quite sure what state of mind Gregory would be in, but I was ready, in that moment, for him to swing at me or to throw something. As I entered the sacristy, he went into his tirade.

"You son of a bitch! This is how you treat me after all I've done for you?"

"Gregory, stop!" I demanded, in a tone of voice I hardly recognized in myself.

At this point, he was furiously flailing his arms around as he glared at me and yelled.

"Goddamn you!"

"He's a talented puppeteer."

"Whoop De Doo."

"His name is Lee, and he's just a friend. A nice friend, that's all. He is an older Black guy who lives with his mother. His father left when he was little. I have no interest in him at all—we're just friends. You and I will always come first. I talk with him on occasion. I have no attraction to him...only you. Maybe you could use his puppetry to teach or to entertain the children of the parish."

Now, he seemed to calm down. I had his attention.

"Look, let's get together with him sometime and go to a movie. You may end up liking him. If you don't, then I'll stop seeing him."

Gregory's mood changed mostly because I had said that I would end my friendship with Lee if he didn't like him. But I was desperately hoping that once he met Lee, he would like him.

I realized that this might be a good time to leave. I followed my instinct and left with a simple, "I'll leave now. Please don't stay mad at me. Good-night, Gregory."

"Good-night."

A few days later, Gregory, Lee, and I got together for a movie night out. We decided to see *Ruthless People* starring Bette Midler. An hour before the film was to begin, Lee arrived in his small red car; it was an amusing sight to see this very tall man climbing out of such a tiny vehicle. Gregory and I walked out and met him in the driveway.

"Lee, this is Gregory."

"Hello, Father," Lee said warmly.

"Hi," Gregory responded dispassionately. This was not a good sign. He didn't even offer to shake Lee's hand.

The three of us were off to the movie. Lee and I conversed with each other, trying to include Gregory in the dialogue. Gregory wanted nothing to do with the conversation. He simply mumbled yes or no if asked a question. His disdain for Lee was apparent by his snubbing the both of us.

I was so embarrassed. I tried to ease the situation by talking incessantly. It didn't help. We entered the theater and watched the film. We left and drove back to the rectory.

Gregory remained silent the whole time. He made no effort to extend himself in friendship. Tonight, he was indignant. I'm sure he would have been pissed if the Pope himself called me, asking if we could be friends. Gregory was deliberately rude all evening, and he remembered that I had said that if he didn't care for Lee, I would end the friendship. Gregory had calculated this evening so that he could "win."

We arrived back at the rectory. He got out of the car, and without a word, he rushed inside. He slammed the door behind him, as if to say, "Fuck you!"

"That is how a priest acts?" Lee asked. "He should be ashamed of himself."

I could tell Lee's feelings were hurt. "I'm sorry. You don't deserve this."

"I'll never visit him again. What a rude priest...if one can call him that."

I again apologized for Gregory's uncivil behavior. Lee got in his car and drove off. I headed home. I was sad that I may have damaged my friendship with Lee because of Gregory's despicable behavior.

The following day Gregory blasted me on the phone. "Listen and listen closely; he's no good for you. People out there want one thing, to use you. I forbid you to see him again."

"You were rude. You never gave him a chance."

"I can't understand why you want this so-called friendship. Is our friendship not enough? You just don't appreciate all I do for you. I buy you clothes, find you a job, take you out for dinners. I buy you gifts. This is how you repay me. You know you're going to be a priest soon enough, whether you like it or not. Get used to it."

"I never said I wanted to be a priest. You convinced yourself of that fantasy."

"I'm done with this conversation." He hung up.

I continued to see Lee, despite Gregory's opposition. But my introducing him to Lee came with a price. Gregory penalized me for several weeks after the movie night implosion. At the dinner table with my parents, he ignored me completely. When I asked him to pass the salad, he refused to do so, changing the subject of conversation. When it was time for him to leave, he left without saying a word to me. His rudeness was so obvious that, as soon as he had driven off, my parents began asking questions.

"What did you do now to make him upset?" my mother asked.

"I didn't do anything."

"You must have done something for him to act like that," my father replied.

"He can be an asshole sometimes," I said with a little anger in my voice.

My mother snapped back: "Watch your language. You don't talk like that about a priest!"

"Well, he is. I can't deal with his attitude. He's so controlling. He tells me that any friend I make will use me and steer me away from the course he has in mind for my becoming a priest."

"Well, I'm sure the two of you will work it out," was my mother's optimistic reply.

17

August 1986. My parents invited Gregory and me to join them for a visit to my sister Donna in Washington, D.C. I was happy about seeing her again. I only got to see her about once a year at Christmas. The trip also meant I would get to see the sights. Gregory was especially excited to visit the Washington National Cathedral with its English, neo-gothic style and stained-glass windows. Historical records indicated that it took eighty-three years to complete building the cathedral.

We arrived at my sister's apartment in Virginia just over the bridge from Georgetown and Washington. Gregory worked his charm on Donna. In no time, they were acting like old friends.

We spent the entire next day touring the city. That evening, we headed to the hotel my parents had booked for the night. They had reserved one room with two double beds. I was none too thrilled that my parents didn't book a separate room for Gregory and me to share. We were all sleeping in the same room. We all watched a bit of television before the four of us retired. I climbed into bed, followed by Gregory next to me. My dad turned off the lights.

I could hardly believe it, when, with within minutes, he was groping me. I was stunned and frightened. My God man, my parents are within an arm's length. I had an idea. I begin to chuckle out loud.

"Gregory, stop trying to tickle me," I said, hoping that my demand would deter him from touching me. But, no. It wouldn't. Gregory continued touching me. I laughed again, while savagely pinching his arm.

Michael Roberts

"Would you both stop fooling around!" my mother said, admonishing us as if we were children. If only she knew her words were more accurate than she would ever suspect. He withdrew his hand, and I rolled over and went to sleep. Thanks, mom, for helping me dodge the bullet. What a son of a bitch! The stress he was placing on me was debilitating. I was already an extremely anxious, paranoid young man. Now, he was pulling stunts like fondling me while my parents were in the room! He seemed to relish in his sexual play at any time and, apparently, any place.

The next morning, we left D.C. and arrived back home late in the day.

Fall 1986. I snuck out of my parents' house and went to the bar. I longed to have what I believed others were having…a normal life. I was desperate to find some semblance of myself because Gregory's control was slowly destroying me. Still, I knew that, in order to placate him, I would have to continue lying to keep him happy.

Upon arriving at the bar, I recognized a few older men who always said hello. I gravitated to them in an effort to overcome my shyness, which was often mistaken for being anti-social. After an hour of chatting, I entered the big room with the dance floor. Hiding in my usual spot by the disc jockey's booth, I watched the uninhibited, dancing mass of men. Moments later, a young man approached me.

"Hello, how are you?" he said with a cheerful smile.

"Good, yourself?"

"Great! Matt, by the way."

"Michael. Nice to meet you, Matt," I said, shaking his hand.

"Care to dance, Michael?"

I paused. "I was just about to leave, have to be up early," I said wanting to avoid any attention or being noticed on the dance floor.

"No problem," he replied.

"You come to the club often, Matt?"

"Once in a while. Would you like to get together some time?" he asked.

189

"Sure, that would be nice," I replied.

We exchanged numbers. I left and headed home.

I was excited with the prospect of a new friend. Unfortunately, it would also further drain my energy as I kept another secret from Gregory. This was apparently the new normal for me. All of the lying seemed to bring disorder to my life. I was out of my comfort zone. Still, I was determined to keep friendships compartmentalized: Lee. Matt. Gregory. I had to!

When Lee and I were not together, I visited Matt. I enjoyed my friendship with him, but on a different level. I was learning that with all friendships, I would be getting to know different personality types. It gave me different perspectives of the human condition. As I learned more from others' unique life experiences, I expanded my own knowledge. Despite the mill stone around my neck, I was growing. At last, my life was expanding. I loved it!

There was one slight issue emerging from my time spent with Matt. He was growing very fond of me, but I, on the other hand, was attracted to his friend Jay, whom I had seen a few times at the bar when he was with Matt. The first time I went to visit Matt at his apartment that he shared with two other guys, I was shocked when Matt introduced me to his roommates, Brandon and Eddie. Brandon was the bartender with whom I'd had my first intimate encounter at Peter's house. It was rather awkward when Brandon pretended to be a stranger. My assumption was that he and Eddie were a couple, and he didn't want his partner to know that we had hooked up a few weeks earlier. I was quick to catch on. I acted as if I were meeting Brandon for the first time.

I was always pleased when Matt's friend Jay would show up at his apartment when I was visiting. I was becoming quite taken with Jay. I couldn't help but stare at him. This may sound bizarre, but I was strangely captivated by the slight gap in his front teeth. His masculine attire was always the same—tight jeans, plain T-shirt, and sneakers. I was infatuated with this sexy stallion. The only complication was that I believed he thought Matt and I were an item. But, I had an open window of opportunity one night when Matt went into the kitchen, leaving me alone with Jay.

"You live nearby?" I asked.

"Yes, about twenty minutes away, in Winchester."

"I've been to that area several times. I love skiing."

"I'm a skier as well. The mountain is only nine miles away from my home."

"How do you know Matt?" I asked curiously.

"I met him though his roommate."

I never asked which roommate.

"Matt's a great guy. We're only friends."

I did it. I sent the message to Jay that I was available. Now, I could allow myself to fantasize. Let's get naked, have sex, get married, and have children. At least that was what I envisioned in my fantasy. Without becoming too lewd or lascivious, let me just say, I desperately wanted to get to know him better, and by better, I mean: intimately. I couldn't get him out of my head.

Over the next few weeks, I would fantasize about Jay, although I knew it was virtually impossible to get to know him, given Gregory's domination over me. I daydreamed that it was feasible for Jay and me to have a love affair that lasted, even if we had to run away together. Even if my parents were to shun and to disown me after learning about my sexual orientation, I'd still have Jay by my side.

Saturday night, Gregory, unaware of the fact that I had two new friends, decided to take me to the gay bar where Reggie was "performing." The bar was hosting a talent show that Gregory was asked to judge. One of the acts of course, was the drag queens, staring Reggie.

I watched the show from the side lines. Plus, I wanted to keep an eye out to see whether Lee, Matt, or Jay were there. I knew Gregory was asked to be the judge. I wasn't surprised when Reggie's group, The Hollywood Harlots, won. As the night progressed, several drag queens lip synced for the crowd. Songs such "I Am What I Am", from the Broadway musical *La Cage aux Folles* and "I Will Survive" by Gloria Gaynor.

Actually, I was relieved that that my new friends weren't visiting the club that night; therefore, they weren't witness to Gregory's attempt to fondle me.

The following week, while cleaning the sacristy, the secretary called me in to her office. She worked only a few hours a week for the church.

"Hello, Michael," she shouted down the hall.

"Yes. I'll be right there."

"Michael, you had a phone call. I wrote the information down."

"Thank you."

She handed me the note. As I read it, I smiled. I could not believe what I was seeing. Please call Jay at this number. He had sent me his phone number. I was stunned that he wanted to talk with me. Was I living in a universe where one's heart's desires do come true? Was my Prince Charming coming to rescue me on his noble white steed? I walked back toward the sacristy, smiling and dancing around the room like Gene Kelly in *Singing in the Rain,* minus the water and umbrella, of course.

When my shift finished, my first priority was to call Jay, before heading to the gym. The church secretary had gone for the day, so I figured I could use the telephone in the office. I first tried to control my nerves. Then, as I pressed each number, I tensed, knowing I was that much closer to hearing Jay's voice on the other end of the line. The phone rang twice. Then he answered.

"Hello."

"Hello, Jay. It's Michael."

"Hi. How are you?"

"Great, and you?"

"Better now," Jay said.

With that amazing response, I was temporarily dumbstruck. It took me a moment to regain my composure, as I attempted not to say anything foolish.

"The secretary gave me your message. I was surprised but happy you called."

"I liked you the moment I saw you at the club," Jay said. Then he continued, "I thought maybe you and Matt were an item, until you mentioned that you were just friends."

"I was hoping you'd pick up on that," I said somewhat sheepishly. "I'm glad you called me back, Jay. I think you're one good-looking guy. I was actually trying not to gawk at you when I saw you. I couldn't help but find you attractive."

"I think the same about you, Michael. Would you like to get together some time?"

"I would love to," I relied.

"Let's talk more on Friday."

"Awesome, I look forward to it."

I hung up the phone. Holy crap! I was ecstatic, unable to contain myself. I wasn't even sure how I got home or what my name was. For the remainder of the week, the only thing I thought about was Jay.

On Friday, Jay called and invited me to meet him at the club the next evening. I told him I'd arrive between ten and eleven o'clock. My rationale for choosing that time was that I could safely escape Gregory, telling him, "I'm tired. I'm going home." I would throw in a few yawns for good measure.

Saturday night, my strategy worked. After leaving the rectory, I went straight to the bar, which had become my safe haven, my place of acceptance. I headed to the dance floor where I spotted Jay talking with Brandon, the bartender. I was jealous. I stood off to the side, not looking in their direction, hoping Jay would notice me. It worked. As soon as he saw me, he excused himself from Brandon and approached me.

"Hello, handsome."

"Look who's talking," I replied.

"I hoped you would come tonight."

"Of course, I wanted to meet you."

"Can I buy you a drink?" he asked.

"Sure, what are you drinking?" I asked.

"My favorite, a Cape Codder."

"That's my favorite too."

That was the only drink I was familiar with, so it had to be my beverage of choice. I just hoped he didn't think I was an unimaginative buffoon.

"Wow! Who knew?" he remarked.

He walked to the bar and returned with my drink. He explained that he felt he may have hurt Matt's feelings. He told me that Matt really liked me and was hoping something more would develop. I expressed my same concern about not wanting to hurt Matt's feelings. We each considered Matt a friend, and neither of us wanted to lose his friendship. We spent the next hour chatting. We even danced. I had to remind myself that too much fun was sinful. After a cute kiss good-night, I left for home.

Still living at home, it was essential I keep this new boyfriend a secret. I was scared that Gregory would learn about Jay and seek revenge by telling my parents I was gay. I was not always confident that I could keep Gregory isolated from Lee, Matt, and Jay. I was embroiled in my own, personal conundrum, the Separation of Church and State, my state of survival.

Over the course of the next two weeks, my relationship with Jay blossomed. Gregory never suspected anything. When Gregory called my parents and I wasn't home, I prepared myself for a slew of questions. Sometimes, I would rehearse various scenarios. I would tell Gregory stories such as: I walked around the mall looking for sales and gifts for you. I went looking for an extra job, I stayed at the gym longer to be in shape for you, I went to the abbey to pray. I went running or drove to the store looking for a gift for you. Unfortunately, I saw these lies as necessary to my survival.

Whatever I told him, I knew he wouldn't believe, but telling him a story was better than admitting the truth. I often became more radical in my lies, once telling him that I had talked for several hours to a Trappist Brother, John, from the Saint Leonard's Abbey. I figured the odds were high that somebody named John lived in the abbey. On another occasion, I came up with the lame excuse that I got lost coming back from the abbey; I said I had taken a wrong turn and ended up in a different town.

Gregory's busy schedule, at times, gave me the much-needed breathing room to build on my new connections. Unfortunately, when I started seeing Jay, my friendship with Matt faded, but fortunately, Lee and I remained close.

One weeknight, Jay called to invite me to his parent's home. I mentioned that I would call him back to let him know which night was best. After learning of Gregory's schedule, I told Jay that the following night would be perfect. Gregory would be away at a reception. I assumed that Jay believed my limited availability was a result of me living with strict parents. Arriving at his home, I was greeted warmly by Jay's parents. His mother and father seemed to be very open-minded, considering that Jay kissed me several times that night, with no comments or judgments from his mom and dad. It was an extraordinary experience for me—to feel free...to be myself. This was not a world I was used to. I felt that any kind of male-to-male displays of affection were frowned upon by virtually everyone.

Even in my family, fathers and sons never hugged one another or any other male members of the family. Holy shit. A public display of my own homosexual tendencies in my parent's home would be damning and an immediate cause for a novena—nine straight days of prayer. Ultimately my parents may have asked for an exorcism at my house. For me, the only other place that I could be myself was in the darkened corners of the night club.

Late one evening, I met Jay at the club. My secret, about my relationship with Jay, was about to become public. Reggie spotted Jay and me from across the room. I was panic-stricken. I knew this was the end for me. Not wanting to alert Jay to my plight, I stayed for another hour. With me trying to avoid Reggie's prying eyes, Jay and I made our way through the crowded dance floor and danced at the far end. Reggie, undoubtedly on a quest to find me, located us thirty minutes later in the middle bar area. With my head held high, I walked right past him, even as he gave me a cocky smirk.

I left that night, waiting for the shit to hit the fan. It would not take very long. Reggie, the glory-grabbing gossip queen, made sure to disclose all he knew to Gregory. The phone rang the next morning. My mother answered the call. She told me that Gregory seemed angry and wanted me at the rectory right away. I left, deciding to face the dragon with no sword. Entering his cave, he unleashed a barrage of violent expletives at me. I sat motionless, accepting his hostile, profanity-ridden assault.

"What the fuck were you doing at the gay bar? Is this how you repay me for all the Goddamned stuff I do for you? Do you want to live on the streets? Your parents would be devastated if they knew about you. Why do you always hurt me? You're a fucking heartless, selfish bastard."

Caught in his snare, I, the meek mouse, spoke before being incinerated by the dragon.

"Gregory, I promise to never go back. You were right; these lecherous gay men just wanted sex. They would all use me if they could. I learned a valuable lesson. You're the only one who cares about me. You would never use me like they would. All they want to do is dance, do drugs, and have sex. I promise with all my heart never to go again."

"Didn't I fucking warn you, stupid asshole? Let this be a warning. You are fucking up your family. They're already appalled with you, and finding yourself living on the streets would be all-the-more-likely with your current attitude. You'll be kicked out, as I've mentioned a thousand times before."

"You're right. I'm fucking stupid."

"Maybe this was a good lesson you needed to learn. I know you won't repeat the same mistake. I better never learn you were at the gay bar again, or else. Do I make myself loud and clear?"

"Yes."

My passionate plea for clemency eventually calmed him down. Neither of us spoke for a few minutes. I knew better. I waited, feeling totally dejected and chastised.

Glaring at me, Gregory delivered a final salvo, "I'll see you tomorrow. Now get the hell out of here."

I left feeling defeated. I wanted both Reggie and Gregory to die a slow, painful death, accompanied with a two-for-one special—an eternity spent in Hell.

Jay called the following day, asking if he could come over to my home to meet my family. I found the courage to say okay, afraid if I didn't say yes, it may push him away. I did, however, share with him that my parents had no idea I was gay and that he should not say anything to me about being gay. I also mentioned to him that I needed to tell them that you're just a good friend, whom I'd met during my one semester at college. Jay understood. He said he would support me by corroborating my story. I loved his reassuring comment, "When you're ready,

Michael, you should be the only one to reveal your true self to your family. No one else has that right."

I admired him even more.

Jay arrived at my home around seven that evening. I tried to be nonchalant as I introduced Jay to my parents. We chatted briefly then I stood up, indicating it was time to go. We were heading over to Matt's apartment.

Who knew the holy demon himself would be stopping by? Oh my! It was too late! Before we could get out the front door, Gregory's car pulled up to the front of the house. Really God? You have got to be fucking kidding me! The timing of Gregory's arrival was outrageous. Did Gregory have a camera installed in the front of our house? Gregory opened the front door, seeing me standing with Jay and my mother. My father had gone downstairs to watch a game on TV.

"Hello Gregory," my mother said from the kitchen.

Standing motionless in the doorway, Gregory glared at me. He said nothing. My mother, Jay, and I stared back at him.

Without a word, he turned and stormed out of the house. Jay, now uncomfortable with this bizarre display, mentioned that he thought it would be best if he went home. He thanked my mother for her hospitality and said good-bye to both of us. Ten minutes later the phone rang. I knew it would be Gregory, so I answered it before my mother could. Heaven only knows what he might say to her or tell her.

"You fucking slut! Tramp! Whore!"

I tried to act calm. "Just a classmate visiting, nothing to worry about."

"You are going to pay for this."

He slammed down the phone.

My mother was upset, wondering what was going on with Gregory. Because I was not even sure what to say, I said nothing. I just knew they thought I had done something wrong, causing Gregory to be furious. I went to bed that evening worried more than ever that my days of living in my parent's home were numbered.

The following week, when Gregory was at our house for dinner, he completely ignored me again, often making snide remarks or pathetic facial expressions. At times he would whisper threats to me. One night when he was helping my mother set the table, he asked her where he could find the steak knives. He told her, "I can handle knives very well. I've had several imbedded in my back." If only that was true! Anytime he was next to me that evening, he would whisper, "You're going to pay for this, slut. Your parents will know the truth." As always, he knew just how to scare me. I was a nervous wreck the whole time he was there, and he knew it. Not only did he know it, he delighted in it.

The following night, I was working in the church, vacuuming around the altar. Gregory was still paying me forty dollars a week for these part-time chores. I turned off the vacuum, and headed to the front of the church, when I saw Jay walking up the aisle.

"Hello," he said cheerfully.

"Hello. You can't be here. Gregory will be furious," I said.

"Why? What's wrong?"

"Let's get together in a few days. I'll explain."

"Okay, I'll call you on Thursday. I just wanted to say I miss you," Jay whispered.

"I miss you too. Thank you for understanding," I said as he left the church.

I met Jay a few days later on Thursday. I disclosed only a part of what had been transpiring between Gregory and me. I mentioned he was controlling me, threatening to tell my parents that I am gay. Jay replied that he would support me in whatever decision I chose to make. I continued to see Jay secretly whenever possible. I was becoming adept at switching personas, depending on who I was around.

18

February 1987. Jay asked me to spend the weekend with him at a friend's cabin on an island for a few days. I had stayed with Jay at his friend's cabin once before, when Jay was watching over the place while the owner was gone. It was there that we had our first intimate experience. I really cared for him. We also had a lot of fun that weekend. I remember him playfully smacking my ass with a frying pan he'd had just taken out of the cabinet. We both laughed when he teased me about the stunned expression on my face.

My only reservation with the upcoming trip was with Gregory. He assumed I had no more outside connections with anyone. I worked diligently to convince him that my only desire was to be with him.

That night, after Jay asked me to go to the island cabin, I spent the evening seated with Gregory in his room, telling him my new, highly imaginative, totally untrue, story.

"Gregory, as you have guided and mentored me many times about becoming a priest, I have finally considered pursuing a vocation, becoming a priest."

"I knew it! I knew you would smarten up."

"I guess you were right all along," I said.

"I have been telling you this for some time now. This is your calling. We can now be together," he said.

"I would like that."

"I'll show you the way."

"I have decided to spend this upcoming weekend at the St. Leonard's retreat house. I called. They had only one available space for this upcoming retreat. I will be gone Friday to Sunday. It might be possible for me to leave early Saturday or Sunday, so I can spend some time with you."

"I think it's best if you stay there the entire weekend," Gregory said. "The silent praying in that peaceful setting would be a rewarding, spiritual event for you. I only wish I could go with you."

With my best poker face, I replied to Gregory, "I think you're right—I should stay the whole time. Maybe you could come," I said, knowing full well that he couldn't.

"I wish I could as well, but I can't. I will, however, drive you."

Oh shit! Wrong response! Danger Will Robinson!

With some fast thinking, I said, "I think I should take my car in case I want to leave after the first day."

"I'm glad you are making better choices for yourself," Gregory offered.

It worked. I'd convinced the troll at the bridge to let me cross. I had succeeded with my acting skill, along with my saying that I might leave early. I had told my parents the same story, the same "retreat story."

Early Friday morning, I parked my car at Jay's house. We spent the weekend at Jay's friend's cabin. We had a lot of food, fun, and relaxation. I admired Jay for being "out" about his sexual orientation. It seemed like being out would make life so much easier. My affection for Jay grew stronger. Was I experiencing the feeling of being "in love" for the first time? I arrived back home late Sunday, with no one the wiser about my island adventure.

I had many doubts prior to leaving for the cabin, because it would not be unlike Gregory to drive to St. Leonard's to see if my car was there. I devised a backup plan in case he decided to check on me. I would simply say that I parked the car in a lot across the street in case the abbey needed the parking space. If asked, I would just say that a brother of the abbey told me where to park so that my car wouldn't be towed.

A few weeks later, I heard that the owners of the Brass Rail were opening up a new bar, Club 482. The announcement also stated that the old location would remain open for an undetermined period of time before closing permanently. It was an emotional day for me. The old Brass Rail was the

Michael Roberts

symbol of my coming out of the closet, my coming of age, my accepting that I was gay. It was the first and only place in my life that made me feel welcomed and accepted for being authentically me. It was my citadel, a place where there was no judgment, criticism, or castigation from the bigoted world, in which I lived.

April 1987. About a month after our trip to the island cabin, Jay abruptly severed all communication with me. I had been dating him since the previous November, so this made no sense to me. I was crushed. My attempts to contact him were futile. Not only was I hurt, I was baffled when I heard that he was dating a guy who was into drugs and that Jay was getting into drugs. Hearing that made it a little easier to let him go.

A couple of weeks later, I decided to sneak out of the house and go to the bar. The old Brass Rail was still open. My mission was two-fold. First, I simply wanted to ask some of Jay's friends about why he had disappeared. Secondly, and perhaps more importantly, I wanted to see if Jay was there. I arrived and went straight to the dance floor. There he was, dancing with another guy. My heart started to race. I proceeded to my usual dark corner near the DJ's booth, where I could watch Jay dancing with his date without being seen. Within minutes, they were kissing and hugging.

I was emotionally devastated. This guy, whom I trusted, now appeared to be nothing more than a charlatan. I was a wreck, standing in the shadows holding back my tears. After a few minutes, I'd had enough of torturing myself, so I left the bar. I was not even able to respond to either the doorman or the bartender, both of whom bid me goodnight. I drove home, went to my room, and cried.

That week, I was miserable trying to work through the emotional pain of having been dumped by someone I cared about. Nothing seemed to improve my despair. Only my best friend, Lee, was able to soothe my raw feelings. He suggested that I get out of the house. The thought of a change of scenery and a little distraction might help ease my depression.

Two days later, Lee called and told me we were going out, regardless of whether I felt like it or not. Of course, this left me with having to concoct another lie for Gregory, so I told him I would love to spend the next evening, Saturday, with him; he would have my complete and undivided attention. I even promised we could fool around, even though I hoped I didn't really have to deliver. Gregory was fine with my story. He said Saturday was perfect because he needed to catch up on paperwork.

Friday evening, Lee picked me up and we were heading toward his favorite club, about an hour away. I was still feeling depressed, but I mustered the emotional strength to force myself out of the doldrums. Lee parked the car, and we walked up a side street to the Mine Shaft gay bar. The club was located on the third floor of what looked like an office building. As we entered, we heard Walk Like an Egyptian, by the Bangles, blaring from the speakers. The place was not crowded.

"Lee, it's rather dead here tonight."

"Yes, I expected more people," Lee replied.

We took a seat on some bleachers, the kind you'd see in a high school gymnasium. Fewer than a dozen people were dancing. I found myself occasionally staring back at the waiter who was, quite obviously, staring at me. Our little game of peek-a-boo continued for about ten minutes until he walked over to us.

"Hello, can I get you a drink?"

"Sure," I said. "We'll both have a Cape Codder."

I found it rather odd that when the waiter spoke to us, he covered his mouth with his hand. I assumed he was either concerned he might have bad breath or was rather shy. He was quite handsome, about 5'9" with jet black hair and cocoa-brown skin. He was wearing a white tank top with blue and yellow striped pajama shorts, tight enough to show off his svelte body. He reminded me of the character Mowgli from *Walt Disney's Jungle Book*. When he returned with our drinks, he, once again, tried to conceal his mouth; however, at one point, he lowered his hand, revealing a mouth full of braces on his teeth. Mystery solved. As he walked away, I thought about how cute he was and how captivating his shyness made him.

Lee and I decided to leave after about an hour. As Lee and I walked down the stairs, a loud voice echoed from the top landing of the staircase.

"Do you need any directions to the highway?"

I looked up to the top of the stairs, to find the handsome waiter looking back at us.

"We know the way home but thank you."

"You're welcome, take care," he replied with a big smile. This time he did not try to hide his braces.

I was actually pleased to find myself thinking about the waiter. It detracted me from my all-consuming thoughts of Jay. In fact, my thoughts of Jay were starting to diminish.

About a week later on Friday night, I got in my car and drove alone to the club, hoping to meet the sexy waiter. I was eager to learn more about him. At this point, I didn't even know his name, but I felt compelled to return to the bar and find him. I was exploring a whole new world. I arrived and raced up the stairs to the club. I was on a recon mission to get to know more about the man behind that adorable face. But, he was not there that night. My mission was a failure. I left after a couple of hours, sad that my foray had been totally unproductive.

When I arrived back home, I found a note from my mom saying Gregory had called. I went to bed, but sleep eluded me. I knew I would be interrogated again as to my whereabouts the previous night.

Early the following morning, Gregory arrived at our home. He walked in, offering a brief hello to my parents, and then, barged into my room, as usual.

"Where the hell were you last night?"

"I went to the Abbey by myself then drove around. I had lots on my mind."

"I don't believe it, you Goddamned lying slut. You were probably cruising the gay areas around the library."

He stormed out of my room, ignored the social amenities with my parents, slammed the front door, and again sped up the street. My mother walked into my room wondering what was going on. She was getting annoyed by these spats;

furthermore, she stated that she would no longer tolerate his temper tantrums or his door slamming. I lied and told her that he got mad because he thinks I was spending time with Peter, whom he despises.

"Why is he so angry at Peter?"

"They got into some kind of an argument. I have no clue what it was about."

She looked directly into my eyes, then turned and left the room without another word. I'm pretty sure she sensed that I wasn't telling her the whole story.

How could my mother still love me if she had to cope with the thought of me being attracted to men? My mother subscribed to a strict, Catholic doctrine that considered homosexuality an abomination. Perhaps equally devastating, how could she be truly accepting of Gregory if she knew who he really was? A man whose life included sexual assault, verbal and physical abuse, theft, lying through his teeth, not to mention his domination over my life?

Despite her age, my mother was less than worldly in her knowledge of the world outside her church; she was a courageous, self-sacrificing matriarch who said her rosary daily, prayed for us nightly, and took care of all the household chores. And she never missed church. I just couldn't find it in myself to tell her the truth. I knew it would hurt her, and I would risk losing her. As always, it was easier for me to tolerate the abuse and control, than it would have been for my parents to learn how I suffered.

The next night, I embarked for the Mine Shaft club, again hoping that the waiter would be working. This was my third time going to the club, so I hoped luck would be on my side. As I stepped in inside the club, I immediately saw him standing at the bar talking to the bartender. Oh God. Now what should I do? I took a seat at a table, acting as though I just stopped in for a drink. He spotted me and walked over.

"I saw you here last week," I said. "I was hoping you would be working tonight."

"I saw you here as well. Where is your boyfriend?" he asked.

"He is not a boyfriend. He is just a good friend. I'm Michael, nice to meet you."

"Karl. Can I get you a drink?"

"Sure, I'll have a Cape Codder."

When he returned with my drink, I reached for my wallet.

"This one is on me," he said with a smile.

"Thank you. That was really nice of you."

"You're welcome. Well, back to work," Karl said.

"How long have you been a waiter here?" I asked.

"About a year," Karl said. "I'm also a dancer here on the weekends."

That was interesting to me—a church boy. I was talking to a go-go dancer. We spent the next hour stealing glances at each other. I decided it was time to leave, but as I started putting on my jacket, he rushed over to me.

"Would you like to go to a movie some night?" he asked?

"Yes, I would like that."

"How is Tuesday night?" He gave me a strip of paper with his phone number on it. "Give me a call Monday night. I'll be home."

"That would be great," I replied. "Have a good night."

"You too, Michael. Drive carefully. Don't forget to call me."

Driving home, I chuckled to myself. There was no chance in hell I'd forget to call him.

On Tuesday night, May 17, I went on my first date with Karl. The movie that evening was *Mosquito Coast,* starring Harrison Ford and River Phoenix. After the movie, we went back to his apartment. He had a roommate, so his bedroom seemed like the most private place to visit. We chatted about our lives, without revealing the parts that seemed too personal or uncomfortable. Our time together that night was all-too brief, but we parted ways, planning to get together again soon.

Over the course of the next few weeks, Gregory, the anaconda, became more constricting. Now, he was calling me three to four times a day. When I wasn't working at the cemetery, he would stop over unexpectedly and demand more of my time. I knew his behavior was partly due to the realization that he was losing his grip on me. I also knew, it was going to become even more difficult for me to start living my life while still placating Gregory. In hindsight, I realize how sad it was that I didn't know I had the power to tell Gregory to go straight to hell...or better yet, to go pound sand up his ass.

On Saturday night, I arrived at the rectory for an evening of the *Golden Girls,* a show that Gregory and I both enjoyed. It was one of the few shows that made me laugh and feel good inside. I followed him up the stairs to his bedroom, wondering if this would be the night that I would broach the subject of me having more freedom...to live my own life. I was scared to ask him for any independence because he had been taking over control of my life. He always talked for me. He was choosing my career, planning my days, ordering my food, even selecting the clothes he thought were appropriate for me.

"Gregory, I want you to understand that you are my number one friend. My true loyalty is only to you. I do, however, need to build some other acquaintances."

"You'll be used. I'm telling you right now."

"I think it helps us minister to others if we have a broader understanding of human nature."

"I'll teach you all you'll need to know."

"I think having interactions with other people will help me expand socially. Give me a different perspective on life."

I did my best to convince him, but he was a hard nut to crack. I wanted desperately to know life beyond this town, his parish. I needed to allow others to help shape my life.

"Lee's a good guy. More importantly, he's no threat to our friendship, Gregory."

"I'm sure Lee wants your friendship. He's out to use you, period. You'll come back, crying when you get burned. I'll just say I told you so."

"If I'm going to be a priest with you in the same Diocese, maybe even spend our lives together, I need to know how to work with people and understand them." I couldn't believe the words that were coming out of my mouth. I thought, where the hell did I get the courage to blurt them out? I was into this lie so deep; how could I ever get out of it?

He said nothing.

"You have friends, Reggie, Sandra, Kelly, Father Colin, and others," I replied. "You're worried about Lee? The only acquaintance I have? That's really unfair. I plan on getting together with Lee once or twice a month regardless of your insecurities."

"I am warning you. I don't get mad. I get even."

We returned our attention to the television, although we watched the *Golden Girls* in complete silence. I left the rectory that night, feeling disappointed in Gregory's attitude about me having other friends, but I was also proud of myself for expressing how I really felt about wanting other friends. Back in my bedroom, I wrote another poem.

Sanctimonious chains you placed upon my anatomy.
Cold iron of heavy repressive restraints.
I frantically gnaw on this alloy of domination.
Your auditory canal is impervious to my lamenting cries.
I must no more acquiesce to my beastly captor
Remaining cells must fight, never to surrender, lest I will die.

19

Remember that all through history, there have been
tyrants and murderers, and for a time, they seem invincible.
But in the end, they always fall. Always.

—Mahatma Gandhi
Peace Activist

Karl and I grew closer throughout the summer. At that point, we had been dating for about five months. We made an effort to take our relationship at a slow pace, and we kept it a secret from my family and Gregory. Whenever our schedules aligned, Karl and I would go to movies, dine out, or stop in at a local gay bar. Fortunately, I had a car, but Karl lived about an hour away from me, making it harder for us to get together. Also, getting out of town was always dependent upon Gregory's opening the proverbial cage door so that I could make an exit.

I resisted taking Karl to my parents' house, not only because of the gay issue, but more importantly, I was afraid Gregory would discover our relationship. It was imperative that I kept Gregory in the dark at all costs. I never forgot his admonitions, "You'll be on the street, once others learn that you're a homosexual." He continued to exert a powerful, controlling influence on my life.

Michael Roberts

Even though Jay had virtually disappeared from my life, I heard from him once at the beginning of summer. I explained that I had met someone who I was serious about. I could tell by his voice that this news was painful to hear. He insisted we get back together, but I told him I had already moved on emotionally. The phone call ended with us wishing each other well. I later learned that he took the news hard and had moved to California. I was never sure if it was my relationship with Karl that prompted his leaving.

Early Fall 1987. I started to notice a few warning signs emerging in my relationship with Karl. I began to suspect that his ex-partner, Steven, was more than just his roommate. When I asked Karl about Steven, he would only say that they were once a couple, but that the relationship had ended. Now, they were only roommates. I asked only because whenever I would visit Karl's at his apartment, Steven was cold, sometimes even rude to me.

Right before Christmas. I decided to surprise Karl with a quick, unexpected visit. I arrived with a small decorated Christmas tree and a few gifts under my arm. I wanted to make his holiday extra special because he seemed to struggle financially. When I knocked at his door, he opened it, looking as though he'd seen a ghost. I handed him the small bundle of gifts and wished him a Merry Christmas. He seemed happy to see me, but he seemed slightly paranoid. He looked out the window every few minutes.

"Are you okay?" I asked.

"No, I don't want Steven to find you here."

"Why?"

Without any explanation, Karl turned away from the window then told me to hide in the bathroom and lock the door. Not fully grasping the situation, I did exactly as he instructed. I went into the bathroom and locked the door. I heard the apartment door slam violently. Then it sounded as if objects were being either thrown or knocked to the floor.

"Where the hell is he?" Steven shouted.

"Steven, stop. It's over."

As the yelling continued, I tried to decipher what was being said. I felt like sobbing. Did this former boyfriend have a gun, a knife? I didn't know. The fact that Karl told me to lock myself in the bathroom suggested that I could be in physical danger. Suddenly, there was a knock at the bathroom door. I remained silent. The knocks grew louder. Steven was becoming more violent with every bang of his fist. I looked around the bathroom, trying to decide if I should escape through the window.

"I know you're in there. Get the fuck out here!"

"Stop now!" Karl yelled.

Steven raged on. "Come out of there. I'm going to beat the shit out of you. I'm going to fucking kill you."

Panicked, I wondered what I might have done that would make Steven want to kill me. Was he still involved with Karl? Was Karl lying to me? The obvious answer was yes—Steven was still in love with Karl. Too bad that Karl hadn't told me. A few minutes later, the banging of the door had stopped. Karl told me that Steven had left, and that it was safe to come out. I stepped out of the bathroom and headed straight for the door. I was getting the hell out of there. I didn't know if I'd see Karl again. In fact, I wasn't sure I wanted to.

On my way out the door, Karl said, "I'm sorry, Michael."

I said nothing as I hurried out the door. I hopped into my car and sped off.

All in all, I was okay emotionally. I was frightened and a little angry with myself for ever getting involved with him. Trust was extremely important, and Karl had lied to me. And of course, in the back of my mind I remembered Gregory's warning that men would only use me.

Arriving home, I was relieved that Gregory had not performed his Sherlock Holmes act, investigating my whereabouts. I was always on alert, hoping I wouldn't get caught. I retreated to my bedroom. I was safe. I vowed I would never again deal with Karl or with the chaos that had just ensued at his apartment. For me, it had been anything but a Silent Night.

The following day I went to the town mall; it was a mental distraction for me. Upon returning home, I found a Post-It note on my bedroom wall, next to where my three-tier shelf had hung. The note simply read: I need this! Gregory had taken the shelves off my wall!

"What the fuck?" I mumbled. I was livid that, in my absence, Gregory would take another one of my possessions without asking. He had done this several times before, but I always overlooked his thievery, or as he would call it: redistributing the wealth. I had overlooked such behavior in the past because he was, after all, a priest.

However, this time was different. I was pissed. I climbed into my car and drove to the rectory. This was new for me—I'd never had the courage to confront him in the manner I was about to. When I arrived at the rectory, I found the kitchen door ajar, so I walked right in. Hoping Pastor Gabriel was not around, I stormed into Gregory's room. He seemed unfazed at my abrupt intrusion.

"Why the hell did you take my shelf?"

"I needed it," he said with a cocky smile.

"How dare you?"

"You'll get over it."

"That was lousy of you."

"You're young; you'll get over it."

"You're an asshole."

He repeated, "You're young; you'll get over it."

He then explained that he had just purchased the *Wizard of Oz* collectable statue collection, twelve figurines in all. He needed a shelf and thought that mine worked perfectly. Still angry, I ignored his command to stay. This time, I was the one storming out. I should have ripped the shelves off the wall, but I didn't. That week, I did think about smashing all of his cheap, made-in-China figures. If he were one of those Oz characters, he would definitely have needed to ask the Wizard for a soul.

In spite of the ugly events at Karl's apartment, he was still very much on my mind. After several weeks passed without a word from him, the phone rang one evening.

"Hello, Michael. It's Karl. I'm sorry for Steven's behavior."

"It's okay," I replied.

I fell for Karl's apology hook, line, and sinker. I believed he wasn't in love with Steven; although, it was obvious that

Steven was either very possessive or still in love with Karl, or both. But, Karl and I never spoke of Steven again.

I continued to see Karl throughout the summer. It was a bit easier for me to spend time with him, because Gregory would now leave periodically to spend time in a vacation trailer my parents had purchased one state away. The trailer was parked at a campsite; it was nice. It had an attached, screened-in porch my father built to keep out the mosquitoes. Gregory loved spending time around the firepit.

I had gone to the trailer with Gregory only once. I found myself bored out of my mind. I'll admit to being judgmental, but I abhorred being surrounded by beer-drinking, uncultured, people at the campground. Even though I found it rather peculiar that Gregory would travel to my parents' vacation retreat without me, I enjoyed the freedom his absence afforded me.

After his return the following week, I spent an evening at the rectory with him, watching TV. Later, at about ten o'clock, Gregory surprised me by saying that he wasn't up to being playful. He was going to bed and instructed me to leave. I was thrilled that I was freed for the rest of the evening. As I was leaving, I heard his phone ring. I stopped at the top of the staircase. It was Reggie calling. I found it odd that the phone call rang exactly at 10:00 P.M., just after he had asked me to leave.

"Perfect timing, Reggie," Gregory said. Thinking I had left, he continued his conversation with Reggie. He had no idea I was listening.

Reggie said something.

Gregory replied, "Yes, Michael just left. Stop saying Michael is no good for me. I know he's not the brightest, but the sex is good."

Wow! What a ringing endorsement from Gregory! I stood at the top of the stairs, listening. Even though I hated the way Gregory treated me, I was both hurt and angry at what he was saying about me.

Gregory continued, "No, he does everything I tell him. I'm in control, and he knows this is a bimonarchy. Michael's opinion is inconsequential."

Michael Roberts

Reggie said something and Gregory snaped back, "Reggie, you're jealous because I take Michael out to nice dinners and treat him to nice things. I had listened to enough of this bullshit. I moved quietly down the stairs. What I had just heard was enough for me to finally realize I was just being used by Gregory. The prick had sexually enslaved me, and even though Reggie didn't want a relationship with Gregory, Reggie was jealous.

I remembered the story that Peter told me about how Reggie met Father Gregory. Peter said that Sandra had taken Reggie to Father Gregory because Reggie was struggling with his homosexuality. He needed help understanding his sexuality and the role religion played in his sexual orientation. I later learned that Gregory's help consisted of getting Reggie in bed with him. I would never know any more of the details, but the pattern seemed similar to what had transpired first with Peter and then with me.

I slipped out the back door of the rectory and drove off. Yes, my feelings were hurt, but if only Reggie would return to his relationship with Gregory, I would be free of him.

Eventually, I introduced Karl to my friend Lee. The three of us hit it off. We were the new Golden Girls, or more aptly, should I say: the gay *Three Musketeers*—all for one and one for all.

May 1988. Karl and I discussed moving in together. When time allowed, we searched for a place in the suburbs. Karl had friends in the area who offered to help us find a place. With their help, they reported back to us with a few leads. We took a break from apartment hunting, while Karl went back east to visit his parents.

Meanwhile, Lee and I began to plan a surprise party for my parents, who would soon be celebrating their twenty-fifth wedding anniversary. I spent several days coming up with ideas, mapping out a seating arrangement, and making phone calls to invite friends and family. Upon hearing of my plan, Gregory immediately insisted that he would perform the readings.

About that same time, I started to hear rumors from a few gossipy parishioners who appeared to be irritated with

Gregory. Their level of admiration appeared to be waning at an alarming rate. Among the women in the parish, there were whispers about Gregory's parties with men only, his keeping company with Reggie, who was very effeminate, and the locked doors and drawn curtains at the church hall. The churchgoers weren't saying that Gregory was gay, but they were concerned that he was consorting with gay men and drinking a lot. I often wondered what they thought of me.

I always saw these women as pain-in-the ass parishioners who had nothing better to do than be part of their own soap operas: *As the Church Turns, General Rectory,* and *Another Religious World.* Maybe if these devout, rumor mongering women got laid once in awhile by their beer-bellied husbands, they may be less inclined to stick their noses into other people's business. I always found it funny that, without much effort, one could trace the source of the rumors back to a handful of meddlesome parishioners.

The gossip within this small circle of parishioners seemed to leak like water through a sieve. This began the season of discontent for Gregory. Parishioners were taking note of his often-harsh tone and rude behavior. Parishioners also complained about his insistence on controlling all aspects of the church.

Gregory's attitude was: it's my way or the highway. This once-admired, young priest was now slowly becoming beleaguered, disliked for his domineering personality. I would later learn that the members of the parish Women's Club, as well as choir members, were also upset with him, but I was never privy as to why.

I did learn that Gregory had been benefiting from the generosity of a wealthy woman in the parish. She had been giving him money, gifts, and spoiling him with fancy dinners at upscale restaurants, even spending hundreds of dollars to have a custom-designed vestment made for him. He gravitated shamelessly to anyone who lavished him with praise or gifts. The satisfaction I found in all of this was that a small group of parishioners had started to see who Gregory really was. If only they knew the whole story.

20

June 24, 1988. The night before my parent's anniversary party, Lee and I spent many hours decorating the local hall, where we were having the party. The hall wasn't the fanciest venue in town, but I was working on a budget. Lee and I hung streamers and balloons. We arranged chairs and tables and set out plates and silverware. Working into the evening, Lee surprised me with a bag of silver stars he had made by covering cardboard with aluminum foil. We hung them with the attached strings from the ceiling. It was perfect for a silver anniversary.

The night of the party, the DJ started setting up one hour before my parents arrived. I set out all the food on the tables. We had a cold cuts tray, a pasta salad, a tossed salad, veggies, dips, various cheeses, and, of course, a decorated twenty-fifth anniversary cake.

I hoped my parents would be pleased with the event. Lee assured me that I had done a beautiful job. He stressed how proud he was of me for the party I was throwing. Forty-five minutes before my parents arrived, friends started to arrive, as did Gregory who was accompanied by his priest-friend, Father Colin, who was visiting from Pennsylvania.

When my parents arrived, they were totally surprised. Gregory immediately began the wedding ceremony. My parents were repeating their wedding vows. When his role in the nuptials was over, Gregory told me he was leaving with Father Colin. He said his quick good-byes then disappeared into the night. I knew why he left—the gay bars were calling him.

The party was a hit. My parents were so appreciative of my efforts and were delighted to celebrate their anniversary with so many of their friends and relatives. I was relieved, but my next major hurdle was about to come.

No one in the family knew that I was moving into an apartment with Karl. This was a huge step for me. I was about to embark on what I hoped would be my emancipation from Gregory. Karl's friends had found an apartment for us that was close to them. This was really going to happen. I knew my next move was to prepare Gregory for my move out of my parents' house.

A couple of days later, I went to the rectory to tell Gregory that I was moving out of town. On my way there, I thought: Oh, what the fuck! Here I go. I walked into the rectory without mincing words. "Gregory, I'm moving out of town." I did it. I stood up to the devil.

He began to laugh. "Oh my God. That's hilarious!" He placed his finger in his glass of scotch, swirled the ice cubes, took a huge gulp, and laughed again.

"I'm serious," I said.

"Yeah right. You couldn't survive on your own if your life depended on it."

"I have been thinking about modeling in larger cities here in the United States while I go to school to build up enough class credit hours, so I can transfer to seminary school." I added the comment about the seminary only to enhance my story.

"You, a model? Whoop dee fucking doo! You're not that good-looking."

"I would still like to try."

"You will live here, enter the seminary, and Goddamn it, become a priest."

"I want to see if I can model. I could make lots of money, and surprise you with gifts."

The creative line of bullshit kept escaping my mouth. I used everything in my "bag of lies" that I could think of.

"I've heard enough. You're not going anywhere."

"I found an apartment."

Michael Roberts

"Do you think your parents would like to learn about their son, the one who sneaks downtown to gay bars, acts like a slut, and sleeps around like a whore? You lie and use others. You're disrespectful and self-absorbed. Do you think God would approve of your behavior?" That son-of-a-fucking devil was resorting to his old playbook, trying to intimidate me with threats. He had played this manipulative game so many times before, that I had to believe he wasn't about to tell my parents anything. Surely, he had to know that by exposing me, he would also be exposing himself.

"I need to learn how to be on my own. I have an apartment. I've paid the deposit and will share the apartment with a roommate. I can't afford to rent the place by myself. I need to do this for me. I promise I will visit every week. If I fail at modeling, I swear I will become a priest. Let me go to school, earn college credit that's transferable." I realized I was pleading with him.

"You're pathetic. I will give you a few months. You will be back on your knees crying to all of us for help. I hope your parents aren't furious with you."

"What do you mean? I just told them I was moving. They said they would support my decision. They're concerned about me, but they understand that I need to find my path."

"I'm not talking about that," he smirked.

"Really?" I said. "Are you planning on hurting me by telling them I'm gay? I'll do the same, tell them you're gay."

"You'll see who has the upper hand. They would never believe your wretched lies. Others can testify to that."

"Who? Reggie, that fucking, flaming fairy, or Sandra that Titanic, tacky cunt and her pathetic sons?"

I hated Gregory with every cell in my body, and I meant every word I was saying to him. I had saved some money and had stored away household items in my Aunt Wilma's basement. I was ready to move. My growing feelings for Karl were my impetus for believing that this was my chance to escape. I got up from my chair in Gregory's room, and without saying another word, I walked out and slammed the door.

217

July 1988. It was moving day, I explained to my parents that my roommate was going to help me haul my items. I gave them a few more details, telling them that Karl was a nice guy and an ideal roommate. I added a white lie—that I had found Karl in the newspaper. I told them he was looking to share a room as well, and I felt he was trustworthy.

The next day, Karl helped me load all my possessions into a U-Haul truck. I was going to follow behind him in my car. When it was time to leave, my mom walked to the car with me. My dad had not uttered a word to me since early that morning when I told them it was moving day. Was he just being his usual, stoic self. He didn't say good-bye or good luck. Nothing. I wasn't surprised that he didn't say good-bye, but it still hurt.

My mother only said, "Take care Michael."

In my head, I wondered if they sensed the real truth about my relationship with Karl. Were they happy to get rid of their homo son? Was my father staying away purposely, afraid to see affection between two men? Did they think that Karl was the gay man corrupting their son with this disgusting homosexual lifestyle? If they did suspect that I was gay, I prayed they would stay in denial and pretend that I was their normal, healthy son who might someday become a priest.

I gave my mother a hug. "Bye, Mom. I'll miss you."

I drove my car closely behind Karl, who drove the U-Haul. We were off to our new apartment. We arrived about an hour later at the small apartment located on a busy street, with almost no parking. We had to park wherever we could find a spot, even if it was a few minutes away. The apartment was a renovated attic on the third floor. There was a small kitchen that opened to a small living room. The only other space was a tiny bathroom and a single bedroom. We would also be sharing the apartment with Karl's cat Meshu. I loved our feline roommate—he was black with a white chest. He looked like he was wearing a tuxedo. He had a little white around his mouth and he wore "white socks" on all four paws.

We carried all our belongings up the stairs, took a few minutes to rest, and then returned the truck to a local U-Haul store. We unpacked and went to the grocery store before we finally flung ourselves on the sofa; we were exhausted.

We just sat there, holding hands. We were finally together, building a future.

It took a few days to get settled in. The phone company connected the phone. We organized the kitchen. Even Meshu seemed content in his new home. I knew I loved Karl, and I wanted to live with him, but I was starting to feel a bit homesick. I missed my parents. I wasn't surprised that I missed them. I knew it would take some time to break away emotionally from my family and develop a life of my own. As soon as the phone was installed, I dutifully informed the family of my new phone number. And still influenced by the tentacles of Gregory's control, I also gave him my new number. By the end of the week, Gregory called me. I answered the phone. His tone was none too friendly. What a surprise!

I covered the mouthpiece, so Gregory wouldn't hear me, and said to Karl, "I'll go in the bedroom, so I don't disturb you."

"You're not disturbing me."

I pretended I didn't hear him. I stretched the long phone cord into the bedroom.

"Hello Gregory," I said softly.

"Why are you whispering?"

"My roommate is napping."

"You sleeping with this guy? I don't fucking trust you. You have been a slut in the past. It wouldn't surprise me," Gregory growled.

"Gregory, stop. I have no interest in him. He is an unattractive, straight, immigrant—not my type. I only share an apartment with him. He has his own room. Actually, I seldom ever see him."

"Good. When will you be back in town?"

"Maybe Sunday."

"I'm horny."

"I have to go. I have something cooking on the stove."

"Love you."

"Yeah, love you, too," I said. Why the hell did I say that? In fact, I was deeply disappointed with myself for telling Gregory I loved him. I didn't love him, and I didn't like the thought of lying to Karl. I was ashamed of myself. Yes, I had moved away from Gregory, but I still saw no way out of my emotional trap. I was being controlled even from afar. I knew Gregory would use any of the weapons in his arsenal. I had been brainwashed by a master scholar who appeared to be a Catholic priest. I was his victim, entombed within my mind.

"Who was that?" Karl asked, as I came back into living room.

"Father Gregory."

"Your priest friend?"

"Yes. He's also a friend of my parents. He and I chat about once a week. He is the priest at my local church. Remember, I told you I often did odd jobs at the church. My parents invited him over once a long time ago, and we all hit it off. And, I was also an altar boy at the church."

I had begun lying to Karl.

"Does he know you're gay?"

"Yes."

"Is he gay?"

"I don't think so."

"Isn't being gay against the church doctrine?"

"I am sure it is, but Gregory never judges me. I don't talk much about this part of my life anyway. I think he's a bit more open-minded than many priests. I thought it would be odd for you to meet him, because I got the impression that you're not religious. Plus, the whole gay-boyfriend thing might be uncomfortable for all of us."

I continued receiving Gregory's phone calls in the bedroom. I always told Karl that I didn't want to disturb him.

21

August 1988. Big news! I was going to Paris to model! My sister's roommate had a close friend, named Serge, a French fashion consultant, who had seen a few of my photos. He thought I had modeling potential. With Serge's connections, he could get me into the Best One Modeling Agency, if I was interested. Of course, I was interested. I was over the moon and accepted the offer. Not only could I get a chance to model, I could also prove everyone wrong, especially Gregory, who had laughed at me for wanting to try modeling.

Karl was very supportive, but one of his close friends told me that Karl felt as if he were being abandoned. When I called Gregory to tell him I was going to Paris, he was diametrically opposed to this Paris trip.

"Gregory, I have a chance to go to Paris to model!" I told him. I hadn't been this happy in a long time.

"When are you going to come to your senses?" he asked.

"I came to my senses, and I'm going to Paris."

"You think you can survive in another country? You're going to struggle with the language and starve."

"What do you mean starve, I saved some money."

"How long do you think that'll last? Go. You'll see the hundreds and thousands of pretty faces trying to find work. You think you're anything special?"

"The worst-case scenario is that I'll get to see Paris. How many people can say they lived in Paris?"

"You're wasting your life. You know damn well that you're going to become a priest if I have anything to say about it. This foolishness has to stop. I'll have to have a talk with your parents on subjects I don't think they want to hear about. Move out of your apartment and let's be together. You're not getting any younger. It's a good time to begin seminary life."

"Look, Gregory, I'm going, and your threats aren't going to stop me."

"Don't say that I didn't warn you. When you come back crying, who will always be there to pick up the pieces?"

Without saying another word, I hung up the phone.

Over the next few days, he called me repeatedly, trying to persuade me not to leave. Of course, he'd always resort to his favorite weapon; he would tell my parents that I was gay. Pound sand up your ass, Gregory. I'm going to Paris. I had less than one month to get ready. I needed a passport and some clothes. I was a little apprehensive about leaving the country on such an adventure, but I saw it as a chance of a lifetime. Aside from visiting my relatives in Canada, I had never been outside of the United States.

The day came for me to leave. I said my tearful good-byes to Lee and Karl. And yes, I said good-bye to Gregory, without the tears. My mom and I hugged each other and said good-bye. Several days earlier, my dad had told me to be safe and to take care of myself. But, he wasn't there to say good-bye the day I left. His emotional abandonment always hurt, but at that point I was so used to his not appearing to care about me that I was filled with apathy for him. I was also getting to the point that I didn't care if he did suspect that I was gay. And, I think, deep down, I blamed my parents for not protecting me from the priest.

After a ten-hour flight, I arrived at the Charles de Gaulle Airport, in Paris, France. I was tired, but exhilarated. I had been instructed to take a taxi to an apartment that the modeling agency provided for models. It was a temporary living arrangement for their models while they were on assignment. I was told I would be sharing a room with another male model for several days.

As the taxi pulled out of the airport, I was immediately astonished at the world emerging before my eyes. I saw architecture dating from the Middle Ages to the twenty-first century—from Gothic to the French Renaissance. I had never seen such architecture—the building facades with intricate carvings, domes, and columns. Mesmerized, I rolled down my window, wanting to "soak in" more of the city. As my taxi entered the core of the city, I was amazed at the throngs of people on the streets. Some were clustered at outdoor cafes. Others walked briskly along streets of the business districts; others strolled leisurely as they window-shopped. One of the things that stood out to me was a woman in a white coat, carrying what appeared to be a dozen long loaves of bread in her arms. I was later told these were called baguettes and were usually about two feet long. Apparently, Parisians bought their bread fresh daily.

Then, the taxi driver pulled up in front of my apartment building. Not speaking any English, he just looked at me—a look that said: now it's time for you to pay me. I paid him and stepped out of the cab. My apartment building was among a string of buildings on a very narrow street.

Most of the buildings had retail shops and eateries on the first level; the upper levels were apartments. I found my apartment on the second floor. The apartment itself was small—a one bedroom with twin beds and a bathroom.

My roommate had already arrived. His name was Mark. He was another American, twenty-three, my age. He was quite handsome. Tall, quiet, and very nice. I was sure he was straight. During the few days that we shared the apartment, I had hoped to become friends, but he seemed to be a loner, and I respected that.

Shortly after I arrived, Mark left on an errand. Before I started to unpack, I sat on my bed, thinking. Here I was in Paris, France, on a modeling assignment. I was excited but was also a bit overwhelmed. Was I in over my head? Was I good-looking enough? My roommate was a bit standoffish. Did he dislike me because he sensed that I was gay? I didn't leave the apartment for the first few days.

I was not scheduled to meet Serge, the fashion consultant, for more than a week, and I had use of the agency's apartment for only a few days. However, friends of Serge's, a married couple, Paul and Claudine, offered me a room in their home at no charge, and I could have full access to their home until Serge returned; then, he'd help me make different living arrangements.

Paul was a well-known photographer, and he would be the one to take my photos so that I could build a portfolio. Both Paul and Claudine were gracious and welcoming; I adored them. I didn't see much of them—they both worked all day. By that time, I had begun to venture out to explore Paris. I learned the subway system and picked up a few French words.

I finally met Serge eight days later upon his return from a business trip abroad. He was a tall, thin man, about ten years older than me. He wore round, horn-rimmed glasses and always reminded me a bit of Woody Allen, except taller. He was also a freelance journalist—he wrote a lot for *Marie Claire* and other top fashion magazines. We hit it off immediately. I could tell that, like me, he was gay. In fact, he invited me to stay with him for the rest of my time in Paris.

Serge's apartment was near the famous Moulin Rouge dinner club and cabaret in downtown Paris, and even though it was small, the rent was exorbitant. His apartment was on the fifth floor. The building was old, but not without character. The lobby floors were covered in tile—old mosaic patterns. The apartment consisted of one room, with a bed and sofa, a kitchenette, and bathroom. I slept on the sofa.

The building had an old elevator. I'm guessing from the early 1900s, reminiscent of an old Agatha Christie movie. The elevator was so small that it carried only one person at a time. I never quite trusted that elevator and usually walked up the four flights of steps.

Serge and I hit it off. I trusted him. I knew that he would guide me. He knew all the ins and outs of the modeling profession. His best friend, who was a hair stylist, would cut my hair. Serge's friend Paul took my pictures.

I adored Serge's quick wit and quirky sense of humor. He always had me laughing. I always enjoyed being in his presence. However, over the next few weeks, I began to feel that he was developing an attraction to me. I thought the world of him but was not attracted to him romantically. I would notice him staring at me from a distance at parties or at an event. He seemed to want to be around me as much as he could.

He frequently took me out to dine in fine restaurants. We often went to dinner with his friends. I enjoyed those times, but always I felt I was out of my element. I was the American who

224

didn't speak French. When others laughed, I felt rather foolish, never understanding a joke or a comment. I was not educated in art, culture, or French films. I was perceived only as the cute American boy. It wasn't a pleasant feeling. At times I felt like I was only Serge's accessory, a male escort or eye candy.

As planned, I worked with Paul who developed my modeling portfolio, a presentation for the agency that had brought me to Paris. It was exciting to wear clothes from Jean-Paul Gaultier and from other well-known designers. It was all thanks to Serge. He knew a lot of people who could help me succeed. He told me it could be several weeks before I got any interviews for modeling jobs. These interviews were known as "go-sees." It wasn't too long before the agency was sending me out for interviews.

Often, at the end of his busy workday, Serge would ask me to accompany him to fancy restaurants, parties, fashion shows, and grand openings. He often supplemented my wardrobe, allowing me to borrow the most stylish attire. I was flabbergasted that I, a small-town kid, was mingling with designers, stylists, and some of the elites of the fashion world.

One evening we attended a private party with the crème de la crème of the Paris fashion world. I knew none of them. I tried to smile and to chat with people at the party, but felt out of place, like a moth among butterflies. I did my best to fit in; one evening I even smoked cigarettes because everyone else was smoking. Of course, I hated smoking. I'd inhale the smoke, keep it in my mouth for a moment, and then exhale as though I knew what I was doing, all the while trying not to gag.

I can't say I didn't see this coming, but after I'd been in Paris for a few weeks, Serge expressed his feelings for me. He wanted me to live with him and to start a life in Paris. As much as I cared for him, I was not in love with him.

When I was alone with my thoughts, I thought about the once-in-a-lifetime chance I was being given in Paris. I was at the early stages of a burgeoning career that held the promise of success. It appeared that I was close to becoming a well-paid model with the possibility of international fame and global travel.

In time, all things change. After approximately two months of being in Paris, I decided to leave. Why would I leave? I had dreamed of becoming a model, because I knew it would make me happy. Finally, I could be somebody who would be seen, acknowledged. But then came the rude awakening. Here I was in Paris, but the glitz and glamour of being a model, was not making me happy. Being a model did not change who I was inside. In spite of all the adulation, my dream had not brought me true happiness.

Furthermore, I was missing my partner Karl, with whom I was madly in love. I believed he was the man I would spend the rest of my life with. I had to decide whether I could live in Paris and become a model or lose the one person who I loved the most in the world. I chose Karl over a life in Paris. I assumed I could find modeling jobs on the East Coast.

It was difficult to leave Paris, and most of all, it was going to be painful to leave Serge behind. He was an incredible person and had been my mentor. He showed me a world of culture. He provided me with the old-world experience of living in Paris. I would ask him questions about Paris. In fact, I was always asking him questions about all sorts of things. He knew so much. I think that's part of why he fell for me. I was naive, uncultured, and not pretentious. He had worked with many models who displayed those unattractive qualities. Back at Serge's apartment, I told him that I wasn't going to further my modeling career in Paris.

"Serge, I am going home," I told him.

"What are you saying?"

"I miss Karl."

"You're just homesick. This happens to many models living here." He explained that we'd just finished putting together my portfolio. "Your career is about to take off! Now is not the time to leave!"

I could tell he was hurt. "I am so sorry I've hurt you. You have been the most amazing friend I have ever had. I will miss you. This was a painful decision for me, but I am leaving."

He tried to persuade me to stay. He told me that I would get lots of work in Paris. I would be taken all over the world to do photo shoots. He said that I could live with him while I was modeling.

226

"Serge, I've already purchased my ticket. I leave tomorrow."
I saw the hurt in his eyes. After he left the apartment,
he was apparently too upset to return that night. I think he
probably stayed overnight with a friend. I never saw him again.
I spent the last night alone, before leaving for the airport the
following day. However, he did call me the next morning to
say goodbye and that he loved me and that he would miss me.
I was heartbroken that I caused him sadness and pain.
He was so good to me. I felt ashamed that I had seemingly
taken advantage of his overwhelming kindness and generosity.
Certainly, that was not the case.

It was the end of September when I arrived home, after
spending almost two months in one of the world's most
fascinating cities. I was glad to see my family again. As for
Gregory, I got the speech that I expected, "I told you that you'd
be back," he said smugly.
Most of all, I was glad to be back with Karl, but I was
worried about what I would do next. Should I continue to
pursue a modeling career? Would I have been more successful
in Paris? Should I choose an alternative career path? If so, what
might it be? Within a few weeks of my return, I was accepted
into a modeling agency on the East Coast, but I also needed
another job until more modeling jobs came in. I still had bills
to pay.
I found a job within walking distance of our apartment.
The assignment involved caring for a quadriplegic man, Jack,
who was paralyzed from the upper chest down. He was
left with extremely limited strength in his arms. My primary
responsibility was to raise him off the bed with a large metal
hoist every two hours to lessen the risk of his developing bed
sores. I also cleaned his apartment and prepared his meals.
One task that I found rather difficult was removing fecal waste
from his rectum. He had no bowel function, so that chore was
important. I'd put on rubber gloves, insert my finger into his
rectum, and dig out any waste.
I worked rotating shifts with his other caregivers. The night
shifts were my least favorite because I would occasionally doze
off on the sofa, only to be awakened by Jack who needed help

with something. The upside of the job was that it provided me with some flexibility to travel to modeling calls within the area.

Eventually, I started getting hired for modeling jobs. These jobs were restoring my sense of self-worth. I was, once again, proving to myself that I could earn money and be independent. I would never have imagined that I would, over time, be booked for many modeling jobs, which included print commercials for companies such as American Tourister, Sony, Delta Airlines, Papa Razzi, Hewlett Packard, Polaroid, Armani, Renaissance Hotels, Bill Blass, Vanson Leather, and WearGuard. I did runway shows for Joseph Abboud, Harley Davidson, Alfred Dunhill, Barneys of New York, Cignal, and Aquascutum. I also did hand modeling for Buttoneer, Sensormatic, and Xyplex. I was hired to do outfit showings for the management teams of Swiss Hotels, Foxwood Resorts, and a uniforms company.

I loved the work. At times, the money was good, but it was not nearly steady enough for me to support myself. I was proud of my accomplishments, but still disheartened by the lack of encouragement I received from family members. Not surprisingly, Gregory had zero positive comments for me.

However, Gregory had no choice but to accept the fact that I was living outside the town I grew up in, pursuing my modeling career and learning to become self-reliant. In true Gregory fashion, his primary focus now was how he might benefit from the situation. He would send me notes, telling me about presents he wanted me to buy for him. He continued to expect me to stay loyal to him and to lavish him with gifts. He also believed I lived with a roommate in whom I had no romantic interest.

I was not about to tell him or my parents that, at times, finances were tight—so tight that when I visited my parents or Gregory at the rectory, a few cans of their tuna and soups quietly disappeared. I was ashamed to be pilfering their food, but I didn't want to totally give up on making it as a model. I especially wanted to prove Gregory wrong. I sure didn't want any of them to know that I was low on funds.

22

Late 1988. I was introduced a second time to Father Roger at a dinner party Gregory was hosting at the rectory. He was a friend of Gregory's, whom I'd met at the Halloween party thrown by Gregory's ex-boyfriend a couple of years earlier. Father Roger was one of the priests who had dressed as a nun. I remember thinking he was very humorous and friendly. Very likable.

Several weeks later, Father Roger called me to tell me that it had been a pleasure to meet me. We chatted for a few minutes about his life and mine. I avoided the topic of Karl, for the mere fact I didn't want Father Roger telling Gregory anything that would come back to haunt me. Father Roger continued calling every so often, apparently wanting to kindle some kind of friendship. I liked him as a friend. He was a good person, but I was never sure how he came to have my phone number. My only guess was that he got it from Gregory.

Over the next few months, he would call weekly. He gave me his private phone number. He told me to call whenever I wanted to chat. Many of our conversations were about his vacations, his parish, and his relationship with his partner, a Franciscan monk, who was working to become a priest. They were keeping their relationship a secret until the partner was ordained. They planned to work together in the same diocese. Father Roger seemed to value me as a person. He was a good listener and was always supportive. I recognized that I had never had an issue with two consenting adult priests having a relationship, regardless of what the church doctrine stated.

A few months into our telephone conversation, I had the confidence to tell him about my relationship with Karl, but I asked him not to share this information with Gregory. I knew he would never say anything simply for the fact he risked being exposed as well. He agreed. I knew my secrets were safe with him.

Over time, my so-called friendship with Father Roger became slightly uncomfortable. He was divulging more than I needed nor wanted to know. He started talking of his sexual indiscretions in hotels, back roads, and gay bath houses. He told me about his "happy ending" massages and about his trips to a porno shop. He'd checked out Montreal's gay scene, and enjoyed his nights out with two priest friends, who were also gay.

Like Gregory, he spoke about his taking a promise of chastity, but not celibacy. He shared with me details of the group sex he had with three men in a hotel room after meeting them at a popular gay bar in Maine. To avoid the risk of being caught by any local parishioners, he wisely always sought his pleasures somewhere distant from his church. Once he mailed me a pornographic video and magazine. It was in an envelope with no return address. I took his calls in the bedroom, where I would listen while he continued the salacious details of his homosexual adventures.

As time progressed, I grew less interested in receiving his calls, simply because he only wanted to talk graphically about his sexual escapades. He seemed uninterested in discussing anything but sex. Looking back, I'm at a loss to explain why I ever took his calls in the first place. Maybe I was living vicariously through his sexual experiences? Was I nervous Gregory may find out about my life with Karl if I didn't maintain communications with Father Roger? Was I permanently conditioned to being controlled by priests and by older men? Was it guilt? Was it the fear of God?

Christmas Eve 1989. The year ended with a bang—a bang in terms of Gregory making a fool of himself. I arrived at the church service about thirty minutes early to hear the choir perform their pre-Mass concert. Other parishioners were starting to arrive also. To Gregory's credit, he always put on spectacular Christmas Eve events each year. I was looking forward to an evening of holiday music.

All of a sudden, I heard a commotion. It was Gregory yelling as he came down one of the side aisles of the church. His yelling echoed through the sanctuary, as he threw his arms in the air—his trademark sign of anger.

"I can be out of this church in two months," he yelled. "There was nothing here when I arrived, and you can have nothing again if I leave. I'm the one in charge, Goddamn it. This is the last time I will put up with your attitude!"

What the hell was he talking about? From the looks on the faces of other parishioners, they were as dumbstruck as I was. Was this any way for a man of the cloth to act in church?

It turns out that he was angry with the choir director Priscilla, who was in the loft with the choir, preparing for the program. She had been a respected, active member of the parish for fifteen years. She, however, was the one who had to remind Reggie of the church rule: anyone who didn't show up for rehearsals would not be allowed to sing in the choir for the Christmas Eve program. Reggie had not been attending rehearsals, yet he had shown up that night, expecting to sing in the choir. The irony was that it had been Gregory's rule that if you didn't show up for rehearsals, you wouldn't be in the program.

Priscilla told Reggie, "I'm sorry, Reggie. You have not shown up for our practice sessions. You won't be singing in the program tonight."

Reggie left the choir loft and took a seat in a pew below. When Gregory learned that Reggie wouldn't be singing in the choir, that's the point at which he became livid and started yelling. Gregory walked Reggie back up the stairs to the choir loft.

When Gregory told Priscilla that Reggie would be singing in the choir, she told Gregory that if she were forced to allow Reggie to participate, she would resign her position as choir director on Monday morning. At that point, Reggie left the loft and took a seat in a pew below.

The next week, Gregory sent Priscilla a letter. It contained her final check and said that she would no longer be serving as the choir director. His letter said that she had picked the most important night of the year to show her true colors. He informed her that she had embarrassed one of the most important persons in his life, Reggie, and that no one does that and gets away with it. He closed out his letter, referring to her and several of the choir members as being small minded, backstabbing, and immature.

Sadly, not only was Gregory's behavior unbecoming of a priest, but he was also demonstrating his true character. The choir director, along with members of the choir, sent a letter to the Vicar, essentially a deputy to the bishop, describing Gregory's behavior on Christmas Eve in front of parishioners.

When no action was taken as a result of their letter, Priscilla and several members of the choir confronted Gregory in person, asking for a meeting with him.

"A meeting?" he asked. He turned his back to them and walked away, uttering, "When I'm good and ready."

January 1989. I reluctantly agreed to meet Father Roger at a nearby restaurant, where we were to be joined by several of his priest friends. Upon my arrival, I sat silently at the table, listening to gay men chat as though they were non-clerics of the Catholic Church. Most of the conversation involved sexual innuendos, gay humor, daily life with their partners, and a few feminine gestures thrown in for fun. I barely engaged in the conversation. I would answer questions when asked, converse a little, and smile when others laughed.

Maybe I could have enjoyed myself if I were not always worried about Gregory's wrath. I was relieved when the lunch was over. At his insistence, I met Father Roger several more times. Ironically, Gregory was unaware of the connection between Father Roger and me. It was just one more secret life I was keeping hidden from Gregory.

My final encounter with Father Roger was in late 1989. Karl and I had a serious conflict that caused him to leave the apartment and to stay at his mom's for over a week. Father Roger, in the meantime, knew what was happening with my relationship based on our conversation. Interestingly, Father Roger, knowing that Karl wasn't at the apartment, asked if he could stay over at my apartment the following night; he was planning to visit a priest-friend in the area. In fact, he asked me to join them. He made it clear that he was on a tight budget, so staying at my apartment would help him with his budget. I agreed to his staying overnight but felt slightly apprehensive about his staying with me while Karl was gone.

That evening Father Roger arrived, we headed to the heart of the city, to an Italian restaurant Roger loved. Roger's friend Father Thomas, whom I'd never met, was already waiting for us. I was disappointed that throughout the evening, I was the target of their sexual objectification. Through their comments and facial expressions, they treated me as nothing more than an unfeeling sexual boy toy. I vowed never to meet with Father Roger or his friends again. Unfortunately, I had committed to allowing him to spend the night at my apartment; however, I decided that upon his departure the following morning, I would avoid taking any more of his calls.

Father Roger and I arrived back at the apartment around eleven. I pulled out the roll-away bed that Karl and I had purchased for guests and set it up in the living room. Like a well-trained nurse's aide, I put the sheets on his bed, with hospital corners, no less. We said goodnight. I climbed into my bed, and he climbed into his. Several hours later, I awoke to Father Roger climbing into the bed with me. He began rubbing my back and buttocks. In keeping with my common reaction to such an assault, I simply froze. He continued, extending his hand toward my inner thighs. He then knelt next to me while sliding my underwear down.

I asked him to stop. He ignored me. Again, I told him to stop, but by that time, he had his tongue down my throat. Once again, my pleas went ignored from yet another clerical predator. I forced myself to drift off, allowing him to pleasure me, his toy. After he was finished performing oral sex on me, he went back to bed, but not before insisting that it would be best if we said nothing to Gregory about what had just happened. He knew what he was doing; he was silencing me by using my fear of Gregory's finding out. His behavior mimicked Gregory's in so many ways.

The next morning, I awoke, only to find a note on the bed stating that he had left early. His note also thanked me for last night and concluded with, "Have a nice day." After the encounter the night before, I wouldn't be having a nice day.

23

As the months of the new year passed, I was gradually getting better-paying modeling jobs. Among them were TV commercials for Maxwell House coffee, Gillette, Toyota, and Chevy Lumina. I modeled clothes for the TV show *People are Talking,* I was always happy to receive my residual checks.

Karl began working for an assistant to a chiropractor. I knew the chiropractor might be gay, and I always suspected Karl may have had an affair with him, but I had no proof, so I tried to let that go. And, here I was, still emotionally tethered to Gregory. I traveled back and forth to my hometown to meet with Gregory. I was intensely paranoid of Karl learning that I was not being monogamous as a result of my being controlled and emotionally blackmailed by a priest.

Keeping my dual lives from colliding was taking an immense toll on me. I became noticeably more manic in my behavior. My energy level soared, at times, to outrageous heights. I felt like my brain had been rewired. At times I felt frenzied. I had anxiety, too. I constantly felt as if I were tottering on the edge of a precipice.

Although the strength of my religious faith was seriously weakening, I still believed the foolish thoughts that God was angry with me for being a sinner. After all, I'd had many signs from God that I was being punished: the house fire, the backyard pool collapse, our beloved dog Charlie being killed right before my eyes, my molestation in the pet cemetery, being bullied in school, and Gregory's abuse. For many years, I was convinced that these events were signs that God was punishing me for being a faithless, bad person.

May 1990. Gregory called me to tell me what he considered important news. "Michael, I need your help moving."

"Moving where?" I questioned.

"I am being transferred to Sacred Heart of Jesus. I need your help with moving."

After six years at my church, he had received a new assignment. "I'm surprised to hear this news," I said, "But I'll come down to help you." I just wanted him to get off the phone. The following weekend we hauled his belongings to the rectory of his new parish. Was this a miracle or what? He was moving forty-five minutes away from my parents' home and an hour from my apartment. I was thrilled. Quite selfishly, I felt such relief; although I was worried about him finding other families to manipulate and to conquer. I hated the thought of his hurting someone else.

About a month later, Karl and I moved to a larger apartment a few streets away from our former address. Our new home had two bedrooms, a better kitchen, a screened-in porch, a dining room, and a larger living room. It would only take us only about a week to unpack and to make it livable. Suddenly, during the move, we noticed Karl's cat Meshu was missing. We were frantic. We assumed the cat had escaped when we were carrying boxes in through the front door. We spent hours searching, both inside and out, with no luck. Karl retreated to the bedroom. He was distraught that he had lost his faithful, lovable, feline friend—a friend gone, never to return.

"I'm going to find your cat," I said adamantly.

"Michael, he's lost. You won't find him," he said trying to hold back tears.

As I left the apartment, I said to Karl, "I'm not coming back until I find him."

I searched for two hours and finally found him outside at our old apartment. I was stunned that he found his way back there. Apparently, he wanted to find his old home. Meshu immediately responded to my calls and ran to greet me. Purring as I picked him up, he seemed almost as happy to see me as I was to see him. With the cat in my arms, I rushed back to our apartment.

"Oh my God! You found him. I can't believe it," Karl said as the cat jumped into his arms.

Believe it or not, I had become the kind of person who never gave up. I was a fighter with tough skin, hardened by the experiences thrust upon me. These qualities would serve me later on down the road, when I would battle the behemoth that is the Catholic Church and its good-old-boy network.

We spent the night hugging our cat and each other.

Later that month, Karl and I adopted a kitty named Evey. I was unaware how this feline would have such a profound beneficial effect on my psychological survival over the next seventeen years. She, and the other cats I eventually adopted, would play an important role in my life during times of struggle. Their unconditional love was always soothing.

Eventually, I resigned my position as caregiver for Jack, the disabled man. Over the next few years, I worked at a number of different occupations. In one job, I was a fish monger at a shoreline fish market. I came home smelling like the muddy low tide, but the cats were eager to greet me. One of the benefits was savoring the freshly caught bounty of the local fishermen.

For a short while, I worked as an aide in a home with special-need teenagers. The job was stressful, to say the least. Two other employees and I were in charge of six teenagers who, without any apparent provocation, could become physically aggressively, sometimes violent. At any moment, one of them might scream, kick, or bite their caregivers. What had I been thinking when I took this job? I didn't need any additional stress in my life. I was already struggling to survive emotionally.

Karl was working as a waiter in a bar when I met him. He also continued to perform as a stripper at the local bars and a go-go dancer at another bar near the city. I never was comfortable with his stripping for money. The religious teachings that bounced around in my head made me, in part, judgmental. What he was doing was sinful. Lust was one of the seven deadly sins. But another side of me was extremely envious. He seemed so free, not worried about what anyone else thought about his sexuality.

By the fall of 1990, my relationship with Karl was deteriorating. By March of the next year, Karl had decided to move out. I wrote in my journal: God, Please Help Me! I traced the letters over and over. I think part of his wanting to leave was because of the way I had behaved. Unfortunately, I had been in a destructive relationship so long that I had unknowingly picked up some of my abuser's behaviors. Like Gregory wanted to control me, I wanted to control Karl. I was jealous and had exaggerated expectations of him. He grew weary of it. I couldn't bear the thought of losing Karl, but somewhere, deep down inside, I knew I probably would because I believed I was psychologically damaged. I had probably been the cause of the breakup. Karl had many issues of his own, and he was unwilling to work on the relationship. The two of us couldn't make it work. I blamed myself, even though it was both our faults. I feared I had been so indoctrinated by my unscrupulous cult leader that I would never know how to behave lovingly in a relationship.

The day Karl moved was a heart-wrenching experience. The U-Haul arrived. Karl and a friend begin to load his possessions. I was in deep pain, but for some reason, Karl acted cocky and insensitive. In my attempt to act indifferent, I went into my bedroom and closed the door. I wanted to hide how totally distraught I had become. The pain consumed me like a lava flow careening down the side of a mountain leaving nothing but destruction in its wake.

When Karl and his friend took a break, I walked across the street to my friend Amy's house. She was oblivious to what was happening as I wailed while trying to explain why I was there. Finally, I was able to tell her that Karl was leaving me. Shaking uncontrollably, I walked over to her window and watched as the striped sofa was being loaded into the U-Haul.

I still cared very deeply for Karl, and knowing him as well as I did, I knew he wouldn't have considered many of the basics he would need to start life in his new apartment. I wanted him to be okay. Believe it or not, that morning, I went to a local department store and purchased towels, sheets, and dishes for him. I watched from Amy's window as they loaded the boxes I had packed for him. This was proof to me that deep down, I had always been a compassionate person, but sometimes my years of indoctrination by Gregory rose to the surface; in those times, I wasn't a pleasant person to be around.

I watched then as Karl, with his cat under his arm, closed the U-Haul door. I cried hysterically.

"Amy, I want to die. I can't live without him."

She wasn't sure what to say, so she just placed her hand on my shoulder.

I ran down the stairs, out the door, toward him. "Karl, please come back. Please don't leave."

He stood looking at me with no emotion. He just wanted to escape.

"I have to leave, or you're going to kill me. You're smothering me." He got in the U-Haul and drove away.

Trying not to blame Karl, I focused only on my issues—things I needed to change. I went to bed and left the room only to feed my cats, who seemed to be my only reason for living. The next day, I found a note from Karl that said: Michael, I hope you will be happy. I'll always think of you.

I cried and grieved for weeks over the end of my relationship.

The day after Karl left, Gregory called. He knew Karl, my so-called roommate, was leaving; I had told him earlier. He didn't know that we were lovers, but he assumed I was hurting because Karl and I were good friends. I gave him the impression that Karl lied and used me.

"I warned you that others will hurt you," Gregory said, all but bragging. "Was I not right?"

I didn't answer him.

"I'm the only one who knows you. I'm the only one who will love you. You know I do so much for you and ask for very little. I love you."

I stayed silent.

"You don't need to talk, I understand. I love you. Bye."

As the next few days passed, the only calls I received were from Lee and Amy, and, of course, from Gregory; I did my best to hide my pain from him. My mother called after not hearing from me for several weeks. She told me she received an envelope containing a sealed letter from Gregory. She also said he had called and sounded furious.

On my next trip home, I read the letter. Gregory was becoming angrier by the way I was giving him less and less attention. In the letter, he told me that he was Goddamned fucking pissed with me for not attending the christening of my brother's baby. He insisted that I was a messed-up person, who was hurting myself and my family. He told me I needed help. He closed by telling me that if I didn't get my fucking act together, I would face heavy consequences.

I was getting close to a breaking point. My relationship with Karl had ended, my parents were, I assumed, hurt, and I had Gregory on my ass. I knew I had to get out of bed and pick up the broken pieces of my life and put them back together.

I was still grieving the loss of my relationship with Karl, but with all of the outward composure of a veil-shrouded widow, I decided it was time to find another roommate. I knew I wouldn't be able to manage the rent alone, even with my landlady allowing me to use my deposit as one month's rent.

I ended up having several roommates over a short period of time. One was a professional clown. I often joked with my friends about the pros and cons of having a clown as a house mate. Her shoes were impossible to fit in any of the closets, but she needed only a tiny portion of the driveway for her parking space.

I remember one early morning there was a knock at my bedroom door. "Come in," I said half asleep. The door opened, and a fully dressed clown appeared. Talk about anyone's worst nightmare coming true. I was momentarily scared shitless.

"Michael, I'm headed out for a job. I'm sorry I left a mess in the bathroom; I'll clean it up when I get back. I'm running late."

"No problem," I told her. This early morning, rogue clown was not a comforting sight no matter how you sliced it.

I got out of bed and walked into the bathroom, only to discover white powder everywhere. Had this been a convention of cocaine addicts? I was not happy, to say the least. I spent forty-five minutes wiping down every object in the room. Even though I was displeased, I didn't want to jeopardize the status quo. I needed her rent money, and, in her defense, she did apologize for the mess in the bathroom. At one point, she also shared with me that she had been molested by her uncle, so I was rather sympathetic. Somehow, it made her a kindred spirit. As time passed, I learned how to cope with each of my roommate's idiosyncrasies.

At one point, I had an older couple who shared half the apartment with me. John was a chiropractor and his partner George, was a depressed alcoholic. I was concerned because I only discovered the fact that George was an alcoholic after the fact.

The day they moved in, I had no words to describe the challenging situations in which I was about to be entangled. Yes, situations—plural. First, they parked an eighteen-wheeler in front of the house. The truck was filled with the accumulation of years of collecting and hoarding. I was shocked; my landlord was furious. It was clear that even two apartments could never hold all they had collected. I told them I thought their only option was to store everything in the basement, even though the area was supposed to be used only for the washer and dryer. I informed my new roommates that their "cargo" was going to cause a major complaint from the owners of the building. We, therefore, devised a plan for having a massive yard sale that weekend in order to reduce the amount of shit. Whoops. I mean their treasures. The sale worked. They made several thousand dollars, and my landlord was satisfied.

I also discovered, much to my chagrin, that they owned several vintage rifles, some of which were loaded. Why did I let them bring loaded guns into the apartment? Knowing George suffered from depression, I was worried about his accessibility of such weapons. They stayed for several months then eventually moved into their own apartment down the street. But the saga continued when I received a phone call from John, who was out of town attending a business seminar.

"Hello," I said.

"Michael, it's John. I need a favor."

"Yes, John, of course."

"I'm very worried. I haven't been able to reach George for two days now. I'm afraid he may have harmed himself. He has threatened to kill himself in the past."

I assured John that I would check into it and report back to him. I was deathly afraid to go into their apartment for fear of finding a horrific scene, so I mentioned to John that I might ask my downstairs neighbor Dennis, to go with me. John thanked me and gave his phone number.

I knocked on Dennis's door, explained the situation, and told him I was freaking out about going to check on George. Fortunately, he offered to go check on George. Apparently, he sensed my fear and recommended that I stay behind and wait for him. After about fifteen minutes I became more worried when Dennis hadn't returned. Then, Dennis returned. He looked ashen white. The worst had happened. George had shot himself. Dennis said he saw the rifle on the floor and George's brains splattered on the wall. He had apparently placed the gun in his mouth and pulled the trigger.

Dennis had called the police from George's apartment and waited for them to arrive. He explained the circumstances to them and then returned to give me the news. I was horrified, especially after he had described the gory details. I dreaded making the phone call to John. Obviously, John was devastated, but the news didn't come as a total surprise, given that George had been quite depressed. I was always fond of John and George. I did my best to comfort John through the grieving process. I helped him plan the funeral.

Summer of 1991. The following week, I finally mustered the courage to tell my parents I was gay. I was twenty-six years old and had feared this moment for the past decade. Even though I was terrified of telling them, I was determined to become my authentic self. I had become so very weary of the stress-filled life of lies and subterfuge not only because I was hiding the fact that I was gay, but also because I was still hiding Gregory's abuse and control over me. Starting to free myself of these burdens was my only hope of regaining a modicum of sanity.

I had prepared myself mentally in case religion became a focal point of the conversation with my parents. My strategy was simply to list some of the absurdities the Bible mentions such as eating not meat on Fridays, never getting divorced, never getting tattoos or trimming one's beard. Not to mention never losing one's virginity before marriage. In my research, I found more than one hundred acts forbidden by the Bible. And worse, a person could be put to death for some things that are now a normal part of people's everyday lives.

When the time came to talk to my parents, I approached my mother, who was in her bedroom putting away laundered clothes. "Mom, can I talk with you for a moment?"

"Sure. What's going on?"

I felt as if my knees were about to buckle beneath me, but I didn't mince words. I got straight to the point. "Mom, I'm gay."

I stood frozen, hoping she would say something positive. Instead, she began to cry.

"I'm sorry, but I want to be honest with you, Mom. Why are you crying?"

"It saddens me that you are going to have an unhappy life."

I assumed she meant that life would be difficult for me in such a judgmental and bigoted world. "Mom, listen, anyone can have an unhappy life whether they are straight or gay."

"I suspected you were gay," she said. "When I was in your room, I found a love letter from Jay, but I didn't want to believe it." She paused. "Maybe you're better off not telling anyone. No one needs to know."

"Mom, I am telling everyone. I have nothing to be ashamed about. This is how I was born. It has nothing to do with you and Dad. Plus, my sister already knows."

"Well, I don't know what your dad's reaction will be."

She tried again to convince me to keep this a secret from our relatives, but I was not going to acquiesce. I didn't care if they found out. In my mind, they could either accept me, or they could fuck off. I owed nothing but love and respect to my friends and relatives, and that's what I expected in return.

I left her bedroom and headed for the kitchen to speak with my father. I braced for his rage as I walked out onto the enclosed porch where he was watching TV.

"Hi Dad."

"Hello," he said, not dropping his gaze from the TV screen.

I began making small talk. "What are you watching?" "How was work today?"

Finally, after a few minutes, I literally positioned myself toward the door in case I needed to flee his rage.

"Dad, I just spoke with mom. I told her I was gay." Again, I had the courage to blurt it out.

He said nothing. He continued watching TV, then he turned his head and looked just over my shoulder, seemingly not wanting to make eye contact with me.

To my complete surprise, he said, "I love you no matter what. It's your life, and I just want you to be happy. This doesn't change anything."

I was holding back the tears. I had always worried about this "coming out" day for years and always believed my mom would be okay with it, but my dad would be angry. I never expected such loving acceptance from him. In fact, in that moment, I don't think I had ever felt so loved by him.

"Thanks, Dad. I love you, too." I left him on the porch and drove home. I wanted to give them time to digest the news. It was as if a huge weight had been lifted off my shoulders.

Now, more than ever before, I was determined to bring more stability in my life. I wanted to build my financial reserves, get my body in shape, and find some emotional peace. In an effort to make some quick cash, which I desperately needed, I decided to enter a strip contest advertised in a local gay newspaper. I knew Karl had made quick money when he had performed as a dancer. I wasn't really confident with my body, but because my skill sets were limited, I could try making some money with something besides my brain. I'd try using my body. I was a decent dancer, so I entered the contest.

My next-door neighbor Amy, who was a skilled seamstress, helped me make a police uniform with Velcro, tear-away pant legs. During my dance routine, I could grasp the pants, give a quick tug, and the pants would easily tear away. I would be left dancing in nothing but my gold G-string.

I entered the contest and won! The prize was two hundred dollars. Subsequently, I was hired as a go-go dancer at the Palisades Bar. This was not another contest. I was actually getting paid for performing as a professional entertainer—a go-go dancer. A few weeks later, I got a job with Menz Production. It was an organization that sent dancers to gay bars across the region. I performed at more than a dozen bars. I created my stage name Christian, as my own inside joke. My subconscious mind-chatter was always present, judging me for sinning. But, because I was already on God's shit list, I disregarded the religious voices in my head.

Since Gregory had moved to a different parish, time and distance meant I had to spend less time with him. He was still a force to be reckoned with. I had to make sure he never learned of my new, part-time job—dancing. I did, however, mention that I once won a stripping contest. He was rather upset with me, but at the same time mentioned that he would like to see me dance. I told him I would be performing in a strip contest in a few weeks at the Brass Rail. He said he wanted to be there, that he would be proud to show me off to his friends.

Again, I entered the strip contest mostly for the chance of winning some extra cash. I also assumed with the help of Reggie, Gregory, and their friends, I might stand a better chance of winning, considering the crowd decided who won. The winner was chosen based upon the highest level of decibels reached on the club's applause meter.

I arrived at the club, cocky in my belief that I'd be winning some easy money. Unfortunately, it wasn't my night. An hour before the contest started, a bus load of lesbians invaded the club. All the women were there to support their female friend, who also entered the contest. I lost that night to a butch woman, supported by the shrieking and clapping of the lesbians. How could that be? It was a lesson in humility for me. Alas, Gregory wasn't able to laud it over his friends that his male ingénue had won. Later, I left the club with my pride wounded. I continued working in different gay bars around the area, saving money and paying off debts.

November 1991. I was booked to perform at another gay club. On my arrival, I walked around the club to see how many customers were present, calculating the number of tips that were possible. Then, I walked downstairs to the dance club. I was abruptly taken aback when I saw Karl, in his G-string, dancing on a small stage. The thought of the two of us being booked into the same club on the same night had never entered my mind.

It was uncomfortable for the both of us, but I was happy to see him. Yet, part of me wanted to prove to myself and to him that I was his equal on the entertainment stage. I worked the upstairs crowd while Karl worked downstairs. The dancers, scheduled on any given night, were supposed to dance upstairs part of night and then spend the other half of the night dancing downstairs. However, when I went downstairs to trade places with Karl, he was gone. I was told by a staff member that he left crying. I can only guess that seeing me had made him cry. My heart was broken. I still loved him and found it exceedingly difficult to accept that we were no longer together. I had built protective walls around myself, trying to compartmentalize the many hurts in my life, but seeing him made me realize how much I still missed him.

March 1992. I was given a chance for another modeling assignment in Europe! This time it was in Rome, Italy. My modeling agency booked me for a two-week assignment. I would be working with a female model Isabella; we would be doing shoots all over the city for stock film. We traveled with a makeup artist, photographer, and assistant.

We traveled the area around Rome. When we finished the assignment, we had posed for more than five thousand pictures. We posed for the photographers in various locations, and we had tons of wardrobe changes. Among the scenes were me and Isabella: dressed as parents pushing a baby stroller in the city streets, sitting in a café having coffee, dressed in formal attire outside the opera house, riding motor bikes, shopping, and eating ice cream while cuddling.

What made this trip especially interesting was that I was going to have a chance to visit my childhood friend Peter, whom I hadn't spoken with for several years. Of all the cities in the world, Rome was where Peter was taking theology classes. He was attending his last two years of seminary near the Vatican. Before leaving for Italy, I called Peter's mother to tell her that I was going to be in Rome. She gave me Peter's number and told me to contact him when I arrived. She also told me that she would inform him of the dates I would be visiting.

Soon after I arrived in Rome, I left a telephone message for Peter, giving him my contact information and the name of my hotel. We met a few days later at the Piazza Venezia near the Balcones Mussolini Roma Capitale. He was wearing a black suit and a long coat, looking like a businessperson. We shook hands. I think both of us were feeling a bit apprehensive about meeting, but I still felt he was sincere in his willingness to meet with me.

Peter suggested that we walk about ten minutes to a restaurant he liked, Ristorante Da Pancrazio, near the Campo di Fiori, built over the ruins of the first-century BC Theatre of Pompey. He mentioned that the restaurant was not only known for its delicious Roman fare, but it was also where Julius Caesar was murdered. When we entered the restaurant, I pondered the history of this part of the city. I was mesmerized. Peter asked the maître d' for Roberto, who I assumed Peter knew from dining here before. Roberto greeted the two of us with a friendly smile, and we followed him to our table, which was downstairs in a bistro.

Peter ordered for us. Two glasses of Negroni, a drink I'd never tasted. Peter told me it was a classic way to start an Italian meal. The drink was made with gin, sweet vermouth, and a fruity Italian liqueur. Fairly tasty. As an appetizer, Peter ordered cantaloupe wrapped in prosciutto. Our main course was veal saltimbocca, an iconic Roman dish, made with veal, prosciutto, and fresh sage leaves in a delicate white wine and butter sauce. It was a delightful continental dining experience. Avoiding the subject of Gregory, we spent the better part of the evening talking about his school, modeling, and things back home. But I was like a cork in a champagne bottle— ready to explode.

Finally, I blurted out, "Peter, I can't deal with Gregory's moods. I'm at the point in my life when I don't want to be his friend or have any contact with him anymore."

Peter, acting a bit pastoral, listened and nodded, but didn't reply. I assumed he wanted to avoid the conversation, because he just had no interest in talking about Gregory. Always the skeptic, Peter later told me the reason he said very little about Gregory that night—he felt he was being set up. He was fearful that I was fishing for information to report back to Gregory, whom we both feared.

As we left the restaurant, Peter invited me back to his room at the college. It was a twenty-minute walk from the Vatican. Peter escorted me to the student lounge, which had a bar, big screen TV, movie library, and a number of sofas and chairs. Several seminarians were seated watching a movie. We left the lounge and headed for Peter's room. On the way, Peter grabbed two glasses and a bottle of Asti Spumante.

"Peter, you're so classy."

He led me to the roof top, where I was awestruck by the most amazing view of the city. The view gave me a new perspective on such old cities—the lights, centuries-old buildings, and statues. It was truly a breathtaking panorama the likes of which I may never, in my life, experience again. Peter poured the sparkling wine into the glasses.

As he handed me a glass, he said: "Michael, to friendship. Right now, you're at the highest point in the city of Rome."

He moved his hand in different directions, first pointing to my hotel. Then with a sweep of his arm, he pointed out Castel Saint Angelo, the train station, the Vatican, and other sites of the city.

"I love it, Peter. I hope you're happy here. Don't you miss home?" I asked.

"Yes, home's wonderful. I look forward to visiting, but I love Rome."

"So, when are you going back home?"

"June! By the way, how's Father Gregory?"

I thought he'd never ask.

"I'm having problems with him. I'm sure you know how he is. You remember the nasty letter from Gregory—the one we both read that night we took a ride in your Camaro?"

"Michael, you have to do what I did. You just have to leave the situation; you have to get away from Gregory!"

"I don't know how. I'm trapped."

"He is a sick, sick man. He's always played us against each other. We have known each other for over twenty years. It's quite something that we are here in Rome trying to figure out what's going on after all this time."

"Peter, it's outrageous for him to say that you'll never be a priest. He continually says that you're a user and manipulator. When he saw you pulling in and out of your driveway, he'd say there goes or comes the slut."

"I simply don't care what he says about me," Peter said. "Who the hell does he think he is?"

"I won't even mention that I visited you. I'm pissed off that I have to go back home to that low-life, slime-bucket of a so-called priest, while you get to stay here pursuing your dream."

"You've got to get away from him," were Peter's last remarks.

When it was finally time to leave Rome, I had completed my modeling assignment. I ended up being in quite a few more ads, including those for travel brochures, Delta Air Lines, Sony, and large hotel chains.

I flew back home with indignation festering at my very core. I reflected on my visit with Peter, which was most enlightening for me. I realized that all of the derogatory things Gregory had said about Peter weren't true. I felt ashamed that I had wrongfully judged Peter's moral character over these many years.

24

Fall 1992. At last, it was the beginning of the end of my relationship with Gregory.

He called me. "Hello, Michael."

My anger, or should I say rage, was building even as I answered the phone. I felt like I wanted to inflict serious bodily harm on him.

"Hello," I snapped.

"What are you doing?"

"Sitting here talking to you."

"Don't be a wise ass. When am I going to see you?"

"Whenever."

"Sarcastic bitch, I see. How's work going?"

"Fine. I got to get going."

"I love you," he said.

Fortunately, I didn't respond with my robotic, I love you. Instead, the rage that had been carried for years exploded, and I began to scream at him. "You've ruined my life. You fucking ruined my Goddamn life. You never let me have a life. I fucking hate you. What did you want with me? You took me out of school and look at me. You've done nothing but control me. You know nothing about love, you fucking monster. Why? Tell me why? You son of a bitch, I want to know why you molested me? I've wasted eight years of my life being controlled by you. You're a fucking evil man. Why did you do this to me?" I began to cry.

He was silent for a few seconds. Then, he responded, "Why? Because you let me."

I slammed down the phone. I cried some more. I was beyond devastated, thinking about my life, time lost, and my lack of direction. I was a lost soul in the desert, searching for the "life-saving water" that I thought would never appear. I was dying a slow death.

"I want to kill myself," I shouted out loud in the apartment. For the first time, I realized the full extent of the evil to which this malevolent man had subjected me. I was reviled by the suffering I had endured at the whims of this ogre. I cursed the God who had failed me. I hated God! I knew I had to get myself to a hospital immediately. I was determined to survive, and I knew that I had to muster enough strength to bring retribution on this monster before he hurt another living soul. I left the apartment and drove to City Hospital, although I have no memory of how I got there.

Inside the hospital, I followed the maze of signs and hallways. I stopped to ask whoever was walking by if they could direct me to the psychiatric ward. One kind staff member pointed me to the right; another walked me to the sixth-floor department door of the psychiatric ward.

I entered the unit, desperately trying to explain to someone that I felt I might harm myself and that I needed help. I was asked to take a seat and was assured that a psychologist would be out to speak with me. I fell into the nearest chair. I held my head in my hands and waited for help. I was growing ever more unstable. Tears began to flow. My anger rose and my body began to tremble.

The torrent of memories was devouring me. I began to talk to myself as I wept. "God! Help me. God! Help me." I rocked back and forth as I held myself in a tight embrace. I felt I was falling to pieces. I heard people rushing around me. Were these other crazy people surrounding me? I was crazy as well. The chair underneath me was hard and uncomfortable. I was in physical pain. Maybe I should rest on the floor to relieve the pressure and pain of this metal chair on my buttocks. I felt empty, alone, and in my pain with no one around to save me. No one to throw me a lifeline.

"Michael?" I heard someone say. The sounds seemed muffled.

The kind voice repeated my name. I was unable to talk or move.

"Are you Michael?" a woman placed her hand on my shoulder. I woke up from the stupefied state I was in to answer her. "Yes."

"Michael, I'm Alison Lewis. Do you need help getting to my office?"

"No," I said, "I can walk." Like a zombie, I lifted myself from the chair and walked behind her down a hallway and into her office. I took a seat. I felt weak, tired, and drained. She was extraordinary in how compassionately she spoke to me. Was I being rescued from this deserted island in my head?

We spent over an hour talking. I told her about the abuse with Gregory, and we talked about my theologically screwed-up life. I stayed at the hospital for a few additional hours until I felt well enough to leave. I planned to see her again. Despite my pain, I knew I was a fighter who may have been knocked down, but I was determined to get back on my feet and fight hard for the win.

25

You may not control all the events that happen to you,
but you can decide not to be reduced by them.

—Maya Angelou
Civil Rights Activist

What the hell was I going to do now? I was dancing in gay bars, entering strip shows, getting a few modeling jobs, all in order to pay my bills. Daily, I was frightened that if my story ever became public, it would be a scandal, the likes of which I was sure the Catholic Church and its followers had ever seen. Would I receive death threats? Would my story be all over the news? I spent days, weeks trying to figure out my next step, no matter what path I might take.

December 1992. My anger was still eating away at me. I was unable to sleep. My depression persisted. I cried easily. I stared off into space for what seemed like hours at a time. I knew I was not emotionally well. The emotional pain was intolerable. I ignored Gregory's calls. I had to reach out to the church for help in exposing Gregory.

I called the chancery office and explained simply that I needed to talk with someone about my abuse by several priests. I was put on hold by a female receptionist. She came back on the line and asked for my name and phone number.

She told me I would receive a phone call. She ended the call with "Have a nice day." Have a nice day...really? You have got to be fucking kidding me? Stick the nice day up your ass. I would have expected to hear a receptionist say that she was sorry I was suffering. I wanted the church to know the torment I had been through. The hell I had been living with for years.

Speaking of Hell, I had figured out that it wasn't a world of flames below ground with a devil, holding a pitchfork, torturing all who entered. Hell was the most pathetic, crazy, idiotic crap I once believed. These pious clerics vomited this excrement from their pulpits for years in order to strike fear into the hearts and souls of their followers. If there was a Hell, I was living in it here on earth.

The next evening I visited my parents, only to discover that Gregory was their dinner guest that night. My mother was insistent that I join the three of them. So what else...I acquiesced. Gregory, on the other hand, had no clue as to the storm that was brewing for him, a tsunami that would engulf him.

It must have been most awkward for my mom and dad to witness the way I behaved around Gregory. I avoided him like the plague, even when he tried to talk to me. I was determined not to say one word to him. I simply pretended he didn't exist. My father frowned at me when Gregory spoke to me directly, and I completely ignored him. I could see my mother's discomfort. She knew something was wrong.

The moment that Gregory left, I decided I had to speak with her, to give her some idea about what was happening. I explained that I was trying to meet with the bishop to complain about Gregory's abusive behavior toward me. I continued to say that he has done things to me that have been hurtful. I spoke in generalities because I wasn't ready to shock her with the real facts. I mentioned only that I wanted him to see a therapist. He needed help, I said. She expressed concern, but just thought Gregory and I were having a disagreement. She had no idea about what had actually been happening.

One week passed since I had called the bishop's office. Finally, I received a call from a man who asked if I was available to meet with the assistant to the Bishop of the Diocese on Christmas Eve at 7:00 P.M. One rarely got an appointment with the bishop without first seeing his assistant. I agreed to meet him at the chancery. I didn't care what day or time it was. I needed to be heard. I was like a caged animal.

Christmas Eve, 1992. I arrived at the chancery parking lot and sat in the car, afraid about what was about to transpire. Trying to compose myself, I forced myself out of the car and entered the main door. A secretary at the front desk led me to a private room, where she told me the bishop would be with me soon.

I sat alone, waiting. At last, I am here, I thought. I was finally going to be heard and vindicated. God help me. I need some compassion. Furthermore, I hoped my story would cause Gregory to be removed from any clerical position where he might have the opportunity to victimize others. I even fantasized that he might be punished and ultimately defrocked. I never once considered asking the diocese for money—a settlement. No amount of money could ever repair the devastation inflicted upon me. Money could never replace all the years I spent in carnal servitude to an immoral son of a bitch.

After a few minutes, the bishop's assistant entered. He was dressed in a black cassock, purple sash, and a purple skullcap. He wore a large cross on a chain that extended down to his rather-portly abdomen. His large gold ring with a prominent amethyst stone was a symbol of his lofty office in the church's hierarchy. I was not going to kiss his ring, even if it was protocol. It was all part of a ludicrous, hypocritical pageantry, which I once cherished, but could no longer tolerate.

"Hello Michael. I'm Auxiliary Bishop Gideon. How can I help you?"

Oh my God! It was Liberace's look-alike. I glanced around for the piano and candelabra. I knew this bishop was gay as soon as he spoke. His voice was rather high and feminine. RuPaul, in full drag, was more masculine.

"Sorry, I'm a bit nervous," I said.

"Take your time."

"I want the bishop to know that I'm being abused by Father Gregory."

Father Gideon leaned back in his chair. As he placed his hand on the armrest of his chair, I once again noticed his big, fancy ring. Was this his not-so-subtle, calculated maneuver meant to impress me with his sanctity, power, and authority? Screw him and the pious cloud he floated in on.

"I'm sure it was a misunderstanding," he said somewhat pensively.

I was getting the impression that he was not going to be an ally. "He's controlling me. He's verbally abusive. He threatens me," I countered.

"Maybe it's best you keep a distance. Sounds to me like he's rather stubborn and a bit overbearing."

Was the bishop ignoring my complaint? Before this condescending jerk could dismiss me, I decided it was time to bring out the big guns. I spoke bluntly. "He has raped me for years. He forces himself on me sexually, using God and my parents as psychological weapons against me. He performs all kinds of lewd sexual acts, and then when I am forced to masturbate him, I am ordered to clean him up.

"He controls every aspect of my life. He spies on me, and he even conducted a mock trial charging me with contrived crimes against him. In addition, he goes to gay bars, and even worse, he lets his male friends perform female drag shows in the church hall. That's only the beginning. There's so much more to tell you—all facts that a bishop should be told about. I suffered a nervous breakdown, and I'm currently in therapy for all the harm that Father Gregory has done to me."

That got his attention. The auxiliary bishop looked stunned. He would not make eye contact. Clearly, he was uncomfortable. He covered his mouth with his right hand and looked up at the ceiling. I waited for him to say something. Then, like an anaconda with two large eyes staring directly at me, he took a deep breath and began to speak.

"Michael, you say that you're in therapy?"

That bastard fixated on only one part of my diatribe while editing out anything salacious, mortifying, or embarrassing that might bring shame upon either the church's or Father Gregory's "good name."

"Yes Father, I have gone to a few sessions at City Hospital and hope to be seeing a therapist soon on a regular basis."

"Well, I'm so glad you're in therapy; you should continue. In the meantime, I will be praying for you. I must get going to another meeting. Thank you for coming. You can let yourself out. I wish you a nice holiday." He got up from his chair and left the room.

I was now completely shocked. Completely disillusioned. I followed him out of his office and watched him disappear into another room. Feeling thoroughly betrayed, I got in my car and headed home. I was not at all sure that he would act on what I had told him. Was he trying to sweep this under the rug? Time would tell.

The following week, I received a phone call from the auxiliary bishop. Did he actually talk with the bishop? Were they finally going to do something? Anything? I was still hopeful.

"Hello, Michael?" the effeminate voice said.

"Yes Father, this is Michael."

"I'm just calling to make sure you're in therapy."

"Yes, I am."

What a stupid question. He just asked me that last week.

"That's great to hear."

"What are you going to do about Father Gregory?" I asked.

"We'll continue to pray for you. Be well." He hung up without even allowing me to speak another word.

They weren't going to do a damned thing. The bishop was ignoring all the heinous acts that Gregory had committed. I was simply being dismissed.

Now, I was irate. His cavalier attitude only heightened my anger. I'll be damned if I was going to stay silent. I needed a Goddamn lawyer!

26

After Christmas, I began to pursue justice, vindication, and the quest for my own self-worth. I searched in the telephone book for lawyers, in surrounding towns, who might take on my case or at least be amenable to speaking with me. I left messages with several law firms. No one returned my calls. My situation was unique for its time. This was before the nation had become aware that some, not all by any means, but some priests were sexually or emotionally abusing young people. Therefore, any such accusations must be without merit or credibility. Typically, most attorneys avoided such cases; they were concerned about priests being found not guilty.

January 1993. I received a phone call from a lawyer; her name was Linda Mathewson. She was willing to talk with me, so I agreed to meet with her that afternoon. I told her my whole story of how I had been sexually abused and controlled for years. She decided to take my case. She immediately sent a letter to the diocese outlining the depths of abuse I suffered at the hands of Father Gregory Burgess and Father Oliver Parker, the latter who had molested me when I first went to report Father Gregory's behavior. She also placed them on notice that she would be representing me should any litigation become necessary.

For days, we heard nothing in response to her letter. Then, about three weeks later, Linda called me tell me that we had a meeting later that month with Monsignor Terrence, from the diocese. Monsignor was a title for church members of high ecclesial rank such as bishop and cardinal.

Linda and I walked into the meeting together. I felt empowered having the legal support I needed to fight the church. We met Monsignor Terrence in a conference room. His demeanor was cold and unfriendly. We introduced ourselves, but there were no handshakes or a "pleased to meet you." He completely avoided any eye contact with me, and only spoke to my lawyer. His tone was curt.

"Linda, your client is accusing Father Gregory of misconduct. Is this correct?"

"This involves Father Oliver as well. This isn't a situation of misconduct as you mention, but a matter of sexual and emotional abuse, and in Father Gregory's case, rape."

The monsignor said nothing and looked down at his paperwork. What the hell could he be looking at? Perhaps his favorite recipe for humble pie? Then, he spoke directly to Linda.

"That's something we'll have to look into."

"I'll let my client tell you his story of abuse."

He looked at me disparagingly. He didn't want to be in that room. Too fucking bad! I wanted to punch him in his smug, sanctimonious, holier-than-thou face. I was nervous, but resolute in my pursuit of retribution. I took a deep breath and began chronicling some of the appalling details of my story.

"I was introduced to Father Gregory by my friend Peter, who's a seminarian with the diocese. I began a friendship with Father Gregory that turned into him emotionally controlling me and sexually abusing me. He twisted words of the Bible to fit his needs and to use as weapons against me. He dictated every aspect of my life. His span of control ranges from what I should wear, to what car I should purchase, to my career path. He even insists on what I should eat at a restaurant.

"He has emotionally insulted me, degraded me, and humiliated me. He ingratiated himself with my family, having dinners with them a few days a week to traveling on vacation with them. If I said no to his sexual advances, he would turn into a raging, adrenaline-filled monster. He emotionally blackmailed me. He threatened to tell my parents I was gay if I reported the abuse. When our family had a house fire, all of us dispersed to separate locations until our home was rebuilt. I was told emphatically by Father Gregory that I would

Michael Roberts

live in the rectory. My family agreed and I had no say in that choice. I lived there for many months. While living there, he would sometimes chase me around the rectory, or sneak into my room in order to force himself upon me sexually."

Monsignor Terrence grimaced. From his expression, I couldn't tell if his look was one of disbelief or anger at the audacity of my assertions.

I continued to speak. "I vigorously protested and said no to his sexual advances, but he didn't care. His enraged state made him quite physically strong, and my staunch Catholic upbringing would not allow me to inflict bodily harm upon a member of the priesthood. He would undress me, put his mouth on my penis, and orally stimulate me until I ejaculated in his mouth. I would then be required to masturbate him."

Monsignor, now rather shocked and embarrassed, leaned forward, and cut me off.

"Okay, I have heard enough."

"There is much more to this story," I said.

He ignored my comments and addressed Linda. "What are you looking for?" he asked.

"My client is looking for Father Gregory to be removed from the priesthood immediately and for compensation for the horrific abuse inflicted on him."

Monsignor Terrence stood, picked up his notebook, and said, "At this point you will have to contact the diocesan attorney, Jim Arnold."

The flustered priest handed Linda the diocesan attorney's contact information. Then, with a dismissive gesture, he apathetically told us to have a nice day, and left the room. Ironically, but predictably, as soon as compensation is mentioned, they flee like cockroaches. At least something got the smug bastard's attention.

Linda and I left with nothing tangible having been accomplished. Gregory would remain at his church; moreover, I would now have to consider going to court in front of a jury. As we departed the chancery, Linda told me she would contact me in a few days to discuss how her call went with the attorney.

At the end of January, I received a phone call from my mother.

"Michael, Gregory stopped by. He told me you hired a lawyer. What is going on?"

"I was expecting this to happen. First Mom, tell me everything that happened when he arrived at the house."

"I was in the kitchen. He walked right in. I was startled for a moment. He then sat in the living room chair by the window. I knew instantly, by his quiet demeanor, that something was not right. I sat on the opposite chair, facing him. He told me that you had hired a lawyer. He showed me the front of a letter he received, but he didn't let me read it."

"Mom, remember that time after dinner when I told you I wanted to meet with the bishop to complain about Gregory's emotionally abusive behavior?"

"Yes, you said that you only wanted him to seek therapy."

"I went to talk with the Auxiliary Bishop Gideon and then met with Monsignor Terrence, head of the Diocese's Human Services and Fiscal Affairs to tell them both that Father Gregory needed help. I am seeking some kind of restitution to help me rebuild my life as well. The bishop virtually ignored me and referred me to their lawyer. Things have changed now that I have a lawyer. Blame the diocese for this. What else did Gregory say?"

"He asked me how much you wanted. I told him that you only wanted him to go to therapy and to get help. I didn't know you wanted money. He told me that you were the one who needed help."

"Well Mom, he needs help. Was anything else said?"

"I asked him if he had sex with you. He said only a couple of times. That you were messed up and that he tried to help you."

I was shocked that he actually admitted to my mother that he had sex with me. How that must have shattered her view of him as a priest. Then I said, "Gregory said he tried to help me? That man has severely, maybe even permanently, injured me in so many ways."

What she said next completely shocked me.

"I asked him to leave the house and never to come back. He took off and that was the end of it. I'm glad your father wasn't home. He might have punched him. I'm angry with Gregory, but at this point, I'm not sure what else to say."

I told my mother not to say anything for now. She agreed, thinking it was best not to mention this to anyone. I told her I would discuss it with her in more detail later on. However, we never discussed the matter again. To my mother, silence meant peace, especially for something she didn't want to know about. Even my siblings knew very little about the abuse I had suffered.

Believe it or not, there was a side of me that was feeling a little guilty. Was I sad for the hurt I was causing Gregory? Eventually, I came to understand that it was normal for the abused to feel compassion for the abuser.

The first week of February, Linda contacted the attorney's office for a second time. He never returned her first call. It was unsettling to think that he either didn't care or simply considered our case groundless. Linda explained to me that their slow response wasn't surprising. In fact, she expected it. We're not a priority to them. They think we'll just go away and drop the case against the church. Apparently, the story of David and Goliath eluded them, so they perceived no immediate, credible threat to the giant called the Catholic Church.

Later that month, after Linda left a few more messages, Jim Arnold returned her call. He explained to her that a psychological evaluation of her client would need to be completed. I, of course, agreed. I was amenable to doing anything to corroborate my allegations. Linda told me that she'd find a licensed psychologist who would conduct an evaluation. In the meantime, she planned to send a letter to Alison Lewis, the psychologist with whom I'd met at City Hospital; Linda was requesting that she send a copy of her evaluation of me.

In mid-March, Linda received my evaluation from the psychologist. The letter read:

> I have completed a psychodiagnostics evaluation of Michael Roberts. He is a twenty-seven-year-old, single, white Catholic male who is seeking psychotherapy at this time to help sort out some troubling experiences and their effect on his well-being. It is my estimation that he struggles with tremendous uncertainty and low self-esteem which interfere with his ability to establish

satisfying relationships, a satisfying career, and a strong identify for himself.

Michael reports that these symptoms appeared around the age of seventeen; he started a confusing and unsettling relationship with Reverend Gregory Burgess. Michael reports that while at first, this relationship offered him all the warmth and acceptance he was lacking from his relationship with his real father, it soon became evident that Father Gregory's affections came with a price. Michael reports that he was coerced into performing sexual acts with Father Gregory. Michael complied but felt confused and uneasy by the priest's demands and behavior. Michael also reports that as the relationship progressed, he felt emotionally abused by Father Gregory, who would attack his already impoverished self-esteem whenever Michael made any steps towards independence from the priest. Thus, he felt controlled by, and unable to separate from Father Gregory.

Although it is unclear that no single event is ever fully responsible for the development of symptomatology, it is my professional estimation that Michael's relationship with Father Gregory was the single most traumatic event which has contributed to Michael's current struggles with identity, employment, and interpersonal relationships. I have recommended that Michael begin weekly individual psychotherapy to address the above issues. It seems justified that the church bears the financial responsibility for these sessions as compensation for Michael's hardship.

Alison Lewis,
Ph.D. Psychologist

Toward the end of March, my therapy sessions with the psychologist had ended. And, I had heard nothing from my attorney. I was growing impatient with her. I was also frustrated that the diocese was just stalling, maybe long enough for me to wave the white flag and to surrender. That wasn't about to happen. I knew things were moving slowly because I assumed that both parties needed to gather information to substantiate what happened, but I felt abandoned by the church's hierarchy that seemed only to care about the potential, financial loss.

Michael Roberts

So far, it seemed that they had no intention of removing or even reprimanding Gregory. Three months had elapsed since my initial meeting with Auxiliary Bishop Gideon. No one from the church seemed compelled to seek the truth. I left unanswered messages for Linda over the course of the next three weeks.

Finally in early April, Linda called me to tell me that she had found another therapist who would also perform a diagnostic evaluation the diocese required. Linda said that, with this psychiatrist's assessment and with the assessment from the therapist at City Hospital, the strength and validity of our case against both priests should be assured. My appointment with the psychologist, Dr. David Yates, was scheduled for May 4, 1993.

Later that month, I received a phone call from Peter. It was nearly midnight. I was surprised to hear his voice. "Are you okay?" I asked. "You sound awful. What's wrong?" I could tell that he was holding back tears. I waited patiently, letting him tell me the reason why he had reached out to me.

"Michael, I had a mental breakdown. I decided to come back home. I've been home since mid-February."

"Oh, Peter, I'm so sorry. What happened? If you don't mind me asking"

"Have you ever thought about what Father Gregory did to us?"

Oh my God! If he only knew. Peter had no idea of the hurt I had been experiencing for years. I summarized what had happened between Gregory and me.

"Peter, yes I have thought about it. In fact, I was in the City Hospital psychiatric department dealing with the pain he caused me.

"I also met with Auxiliary Bishop Gideon, and he seemed to want to pray the issue with Gregory away and to sweep the whole thing under the rug. I hired an attorney, and I'm pursuing a lawsuit against Father Gregory, Father Oliver, and the diocese. If you want to talk to my lawyer, you could join us with the lawsuit."

"Thank you! I'm living at my grandmother's right now. We should try and get together. I'm still trying to process everything."

"Peter, I am here for you if you need me. Give yourself some time to think things through, and let's talk whenever you feel you're ready."

"Yes, let's do that. Have a good night. Thank you," Peter said.

I invited Peter to join me in my lawsuit against the church; however, he said he was not ready to do so. Instead, he said he hoped to settle matters for himself with the help of his priest friends. Peter was asking that Father Gregory seek therapy; he was also asking for a cash settlement with the church, the details of which he did not share with me. Peter told me he would consider joining with me in my legal case if the church was not forthcoming on his case. Peter was reassured by church priests that he would be taken care of, and that money was not an issue. Peter also told me that he had been told when church officials confronted Gregory, he denied everything related to the abuse of both Peter and me.

Meanwhile, I continued to earn money by go-go dancing in clubs. One of the places I worked was a club called Caesars. It was a great way to make tips from the enthusiastic audiences. I performed a strip routine, which I began by coming on stage wearing the same police uniform my neighbor had made for me. After I was down to my G-string, I danced around and socialized with the audience. Many gave me generous tips, but never touched me inappropriately. Club rules strictly prohibited body contact with the dancers.

One evening, I noticed an older man with a gray beard, seated alone at a table. It occurred to me that I had seen him before at this club. I remembered gravitating toward him when I had danced there before. He always handed me a tip, never trying to touch me or to stuff dollars bills into my G-string. He seemed to respect every dancer, and he had a gentle demeanor about him.

When I finally had a few minutes to chat, I approached his table. I learned that he was a Catholic priest, Father Bob. Initially, I found myself being judgmental. What was a priest doing in a strip club? Then, I reminded myself, I was at the same club, taking off my clothes. This man, like all human beings, had inherent sexual desires. It wasn't my place to deny him that natural inclination when he was hurting no one. It was my job to entertain the audience, regardless of their occupation or eccentricities. In fact, Father Bob became a friend.

I continued dancing as much as I could to pay my bills, but I also dreamed about going to college. I wanted to better myself, but I was unsure of the career path I should take. I also said nothing more to my family about my pending litigation. Gregory was now stationed at another parish. In fact, not only did the local diocese seem to ignore my suffering, but Bishop Marcus had promoted Gregory to pastor of two churches on his fourth assignment.

I was glad he was further away from my parents. I knew my mother harbored resentment toward him, but she knew very little about what had really happened. I feared hurting her by revealing any more facts.

27

May 1993. I met with a psychologist Dr. David Yates, who performed a psychological evaluation of me for my attorney. I held nothing back. I told him my entire story. I met with him three more times that month.

During the time, I was dancing at Caesars, where I saw Father Bob. I asked if I could talk to him privately sometime to discuss a sexual abuse issue. He seemed concerned and was happy to oblige. Two days later, we met in his office at his parish church. I told him everything that had happened to me. He was not only shocked, he was saddened.

Furthermore, he was deeply distressed at the church's lack of response. We spoke several more times over the course of the next two weeks. Father Bob promised me that he would send a letter to the bishop, calling attention to the problem with Father Gregory. For the first time, I felt validated by a priest. Finally, a priest listened to me without trying to take advantage of me sexually. I felt respected by a priest for the first time in years.

In his letter to the bishop, Father Bob wrote that he was convinced that my account of what had happened with Father Gregory was truthful. He also told the bishop that I had been deeply and negatively affected by this prolonged experience, and that I needed competent, professional intervention to recover and to get on with my life.

About a week later, Father Bob received a letter from Bishop Marcus, who said that he shared Father Bob's fervent prayer that I would find healing peace and joy. The bishop ended his letter saying that he would also be praying for Father Gregory and the community of the faithful, who must bear the devasting weight of sexual abuse complaints against priests and others in the roles of sacred trust. From what I was hearing, the church's position was crystal clear. They had no interest in working with me. Any form of disciplinary action against Father Gregory wasn't even a consideration. The diocese just ignored my plea for restitution, help, and closure. Their negligence, avoidance, and cover-up were emblematic of these sanctimonious, deceitful, hypocritical, bastards who piously considered themselves Christ's Vicars on earth. I despised them. There was no way in Hell or Heaven that I was going to give up my pursuit of some kind of justice and vindication.

Throughout the month of May, Peter and I, as friends, continued to see each other every week. I tried not to push Peter into joining forces with me and with my attorney. We spent time just talking about all that had happened. Peter shared with me strange and sordid stories that took place among religious leaders in Rome. He told me about seminarians hooking up with each other and about senior priests' involvement with boys. Abuse of children by priests wasn't unique to America.

Late May 1993. Dr. Yates sent Linda, my attorney, my diagnostic evaluation. It was a detailed, six-page report. The report was divided into sections that explained our initial meeting, the problems discussed, family history, and my romantic and sexual history. In part, Dr. Yates's report read:

> There is no doubt in this examiner's mind that Michael's psychological adjustment and life functioning has been significantly compromised as a result of his long-term sexual exploitation by Father Gregory. Michael's difficulty in his relationships with his father as well as growing up in an environment where his homosexual interests were ridiculed and or he felt ostracized have clearly had an impact on his adjustment.
>
> It is as clear, however, that his having been seduced by Father Gregory and existing in a relationship for many years, in which he felt emotionally dependent and significantly controlled by Father Gregory, had a substantial detrimental effect on his psychological functioning.

267

A number of areas have been identified in Michael's psychological adjustment that have been exacerbated or in some cases even caused by the sexual exploitation by Father Gregory. Specifically, he struggles with considerable vulnerability around trust in relationships and as a result intimacy is easily disrupted and his intimate relationships are tenuous.

In addition, a connection has been established between sexuality on one hand and power, force, and aggression on the other. This is a commonly noted difficulty in the experience of victims of sexual abuse and exploitation and it is this examiner's opinion that this difficulty of Michael's adjustment stems quite directly from his emotional and sexual abuse by Father Gregory. There is considerable repressed anger as a result of his exploitation. Just as palpable is the sense of grief he has over the loss of his longed-for mentor. Michael clearly experienced a sense of Father Gregory's caring about him and wanting him as someone who would receive guidance.

Michael was almost desperate for this kind of relationship in his life. Although he felt some benefit of this kind of relationship, his understanding that the relationship existed in large measure as a vehicle to allow sexual exploitation creates a tremendous sense of betrayal in Michael that has deeply affected his capacity to trust others especially those in authority and most deeply those in the priesthood. He experiences considerable fear of loss and violation in intimate relationships.

His development of work and career on the one hand and love relationships and intimacy on the other have been interrupted and delayed as he spent many years responding to Father Gregory's needs and apparently feeling quite controlled by Father Gregory's psychological and sexual agenda. Michael has also experienced a considerable intensification on his felt need for secrecy and deception in relationships in order to meet his needs as a result of the experiences with Father Gregory.

Michael can clearly benefit from an extended course of psychotherapy that would optimally be at twice per

Michael Roberts

week. In the context of an intensive psychotherapeutic process, he would be able to experience and work through the emotional concomitance of his betrayal and exploitation by Father Gregory. Other issues to be addressed in psychotherapy concern the alienated relationship from his father and his need to resume interrupted development in the area of work and love.

David Yates, Psy.D.
Licensed Clinical Psychologist

June 1993. Peter told one of the dioceses priests that he was considering dropping out—he no longer thought he wanted to be a priest. He was only about a year away from being ordained as a priest. He said that taking a break might enable him to think more clearly.

Soon after that, Peter received an envelope in the mail. When he opened it, he was shocked. He was staring at his own resignation letter. Peter had never written such a letter. He had not resigned. He had only contemplated resigning. It was becoming painfully clear that the church officials wanted him out of the picture. Peter told me, "This smells like a cover up."

His friend Father Amos agreed. Peter didn't know who had written the letter.

Peter confided in me that he believed the reason the diocese sent him to Rome was to get him away from the local diocese because of what he knew about Father Gregory. He also told me that he had acquired documented proof that a psychologist had strongly recommended that Peter should not be sent to Rome. Peter substantiated this by showing me an evaluation that was completed by a clinical psychologist. The psychologist had written that she strongly advised not sending Peter to Rome, explaining that the competitive environment could be detrimental to Peter's growth. Now, it seemed to Peter that he was sent to Rome to keep him quiet about Father Gregory's behavior, most likely because of what he reported to the diocese in the two meetings with priests in 1986.

A few days later, Peter did send the bishop a letter, saying he was resigning from the priesthood. I can only imagine the emotional turmoil he must have gone through. He had given

269

close to seven years of his life to his religious studies. Peter received a letter from Bishop Marcus, accepting his resignation. The bishop ended his letter saying he hoped Peter would find peace and joy. Now, it appeared that his religious institution had turned its back on him.

Later that summer, Peter decided to join me by signing with Linda as his attorney. We immediately began strategizing as a team on our case. Peter and I met twice a week. During our time together, Peter explained how Gregory was emotionally abusive and controlling. He was always asking Peter where he had been or where he was going. He called Peter a slut and a whore and told Peter that no one would ever love him like he did. However, Peter managed to escape the sexual molestation that I endured, but we both had been emotionally abused by the same manipulative, shameless priest.

Peter had even shared with me notes he'd taken about Gregory's physical anatomy, hoping to someday substantiate his claims of sexual abuse. He described Gregory as overweight and hairy head to toe. He also stated that Gregory had a small male appendage. How did Peter know this? On more than one occasion, when Peter had been visiting the rectory, Gregory would strip naked, turn the lights off, and tell Peter to get into bed with him. Peter would just leave the rectory. Peter also mentioned how Gregory would grope and grab him.

Listening to what Peter was telling me about Gregory was disturbing, but not surprising. Peter's experience, though not as prolonged, was identical to mine. Gregory even used the same lines with each of us. "I'm the only one who will love you. Everyone else will hurt you. God would like you to please a priest. I took a promise of chastity not celibacy." The list went on and on.

Another concern of mine was that, given Gregory's proclivities, I began to wonder if he had put me at risk of becoming infected with any number of sexually transmitted diseases. Later, I was tested and learned that I had not been exposed to any STDs.

28

August 1993. The diocese announced that Father Gregory Burgess, age forty-two, was being put on administrative leave. By now, Father Gregory had been gone from my parish nearly four years and had served as a priest at two additional parishes since the time he had moved. Parishioners at his current parish were surprised and angry. One parishioner said, "We are shocked and surprised at the actions of the diocese for not telling us what happened." Another one said, "The announcement took us by surprise, because there were no indications that Father Gregory was having any problems. To the contrary, he was one of the best, most hard-working priests we've ever had." A spokesperson for the diocese said, "All the reasons are confidential. It is not policy to discuss why a priest is put on administrative leave."

The gossip was that Father Gregory was being placed on leave because he wouldn't approve the diocese's plan to close one of the two churches where he was the priest. There was talk that a few parishioners where he was last stationed had seen a tearful Father Gregory moving out of the rectory. Little else was known about why he was leaving. All that was known was that he wasn't given another assignment and was living with his mother in a nearby town.

A month later, I received a phone call from Linda. She told me that when she was discussing our case with the diocesan lawyer, he accused me of being a male prostitute.

"Michael, the diocesan attorney Jim Arnold, says you were seen entering a gay bar, then seen dancing on stage in a skimpy outfit. He says that you're a prostitute."

"They can go to Hell, Linda. I was dancing in a club to earn money."

"You accepted money for sex, he said."

"Those are tips I earned for dancing. There was no nudity and no propositions for sex, let alone sex acts themselves."

"Arnold said this won't look good for you if we go to trial. He recommended that you think about ending this suit with the church."

"This is blackmail, Linda. I'm pissed."

She told me not to worry—to ignore his tactics—and that she would be in touch.

I was fucking furious, ready to punch every religious leader in the face, even the bishop and his shyster lawyer. Apparently, they would allege that my professional dance bookings in gay clubs was a clear indication of my low moral character. The allegation was completely false. They had the unmitigated gall to have me followed and spied upon, all in an effort to compile a damaging dossier against me. If I'd been followed to a club, how many other times was I being followed? It was clear that Jim Arnold wanted to play hardball. They were low-life scum as far as I was concerned. Unfortunately, for them, this turn of events only strengthened my resolve to wage war against them. I would let them experience a new meaning to the fear of retribution.

Peter and I grew ever more frustrated with the diocese members who appeared to ignore all that had happened. Clearly, they were evading our plea for justice and for validation. Linda, who communicated with us every few weeks, seemed completely unable to navigate these legal waters and to force matters to their rightful conclusions.

September 1993. I listened to a telephone message. An unrecognizable voice spoke in a whisper, "I'm going to kill you!" Then the caller hung up.

From my caller ID, I could not tell where the call came from. The number had been blocked. I received another death threat the following day. Also, I had a few hang ups when I answered the phone.

The calls were frightening. Whoever it was knew exactly what they were doing. They needed only to threaten my physical safety to make me feel shaken to the core. From that day forward, I began making sure all of my windows and doors were locked. I even propped wooden two-by-four planks against the inside doorknobs for added security. I made sure the front porch light and two inside lights were always on at night.

As an additional precaution, I hid all evidence and documents for my legal case on the wooden slats that supported the box springs under my bed. I spent many sleepless nights, wondering whether someone would break into my apartment.

Were the death threats from an angry parishioner who stood in righteous support of the Catholic Church? Could it be one of the priests or members of the hierarchy themselves using scare tactics? My suspicion was that it was one of Gregory's friends who always supported him in his abhorrent, totalitarian behavior.

29

I had received no other threatening calls. However, I was disheartened to learn that Peter, my attorney Linda, and church officials were meeting without me. Linda, Peter, and the diocese attorney were discussing the possibility of dividing our cases.

I was furious with Peter's and Linda's betrayal for even considering separate routes. I still believed that our cases were stronger together. I felt I was being pushed aside, left to fend for myself. When I confronted Peter on the phone, he said that he told Linda: "Get me out. I don't care how you do it. Just get me out of the whole thing." Peter didn't want to go to trial. He wanted out. He would take any settlement they offered. I think he felt beaten down, and he was mentally drained.

Without another word, I slammed down the phone.

Still deeply hurt, I held on to the hope that Linda would again focus her attention on my case as well. I knew Peter wanted to end this long battle, but nothing appeared to be happening with my case.

Seeing us as inconsequential, the church officials seemed to be wasting our time. It appeared to me their seeming lack of interest was odd, considering that we had so much damaging information. Did they assume we would eventually give up? I had no answers, and the attorney, whom I hoped would be a strong advocate for me, seemed clueless. With this nagging doubt in mind, I began to think about finding another attorney.

By late November my would-be assassin had made no further threats against me, but I remained concerned by the earlier threats. I met with Peter, who'd had a change of mind. He said that he was ready to go to court and let the truth be

known before a jury. That idea scared me. I was not ready to
face the long, drawn-out pandemonium that was sure to ensue.

Peter then told me that he was going to New York City,
with Father Amos, his ally, to meet with Father Benedict
Joseph Groeschel, whom he hoped would be an advocate
for us. Father Groeschel was a nationally known figure in the
Catholic Church. He was an author, psychologist, television
host, and activist who was known to be sympathetic toward
young people who had been abused by priests. Peter thought
such a popular religious figure might have an influence over
our diocese. I had no idea what Father Groeschel might do to
help us, but anything at this point would be an improvement
over what I considered Linda's incompetence.

Early in December 1993, Peter and his ally Father Amos
met with Father Groeschel in New York. Father Groeschel
greeted them cordially and asked why they had come to see
him. Peter laid out the whole story of abuse by Gregory. Father
Groeschel said he was appalled. After he listened to Peter's
story, he offered to get in touch with Bishop Marcus.

A couple of months later, the diocese flew Father Groeschel into town to meet with the bishop and with the diocesan
attorney Jim Arnold. They met at a local hotel to discuss the
matter of Father Gregory. Peter was not part of the meeting,
but he said Father Groeschel later told him he had never felt
so accosted by an attorney like he was in the discussion with
the bishop and Arnold. Father Groeschel said he'd never heard
such foul language and never felt so attacked. Father Groeschel
said Arnold accused him of being dishonest about Peter's story.
Why was Arnold being so aggressive? To protect the bishop
and the parish.

The upshot of the meeting was, Father Groeschel saying,
"I think you should settle this matter out of court." At the end of
the first week in December, Linda decided officially to separate
our cases. I was pissed, feeling I'd been abandoned. My rage
got the better of me, which prompted me to telephone Father
Groeschel myself. I told him everything that had happened to
me at the hands of Father Gregory. I was hoping he would take
some action on my behalf.

Father Groeschel was most supportive. He was dismayed
with what had happened to me. He said, "You make me realize

how important this is." He told me that when he talked with Bishop Marcus again, my case would take on an even greater importance. I never heard any more from Father Groeschel.

Later that month, in April, Linda had a second meeting with diocesan officials. Peter mentioned to me that the attorney asked him about my relationship with Father Gregory. The topic of the meeting was about compensation and what might happen with Father Gregory.

January 1994. Needing a new start in life, I started taking college classes. I had met with an admissions counselor several months earlier. I remember walking into her office, where I began to cry. I explained some details of my ordeal and the fear I had about starting school. I explained that I was suffering from low self-esteem that left me unsure if I had the intelligence to succeed in college. The counselor was wonderful. With the help of some computerized tests, we were able to focus on a career path for me to explore. I began taking classes toward a bachelor's degree in biological science. I took out loans, applied for grants and scholarships, and continued to work. College was not cheap.

Meanwhile, nothing was happening with our legal case. The walls this religious institution placed in front of Peter and me grew higher, seemingly unscalable. It was one of the many reasons why I left the church completely. Ultimately, I made the decision never to step foot in a church again. I came to see the Catholic Church and its leaders as egotistical, callous, and hypocritical.

I learned that Peter, Father Amos, and his priest friends had met with Bishop Marcus at the bishop's residence. At that meeting, a settlement of $30,000 was offered to the both of us. There was, however, no mention of the fate or a reprimand of Father Gregory and others.

I received a call a few days later from Linda who told me that Peter settled his case for the amount offered. I was saddened that he settled for such a paltry sum. I told her, "This is ridiculous. That amount is an insult."

"Michael, I believe this is the best we'll do; otherwise, we'll have to pursue going to trial. That will mean your story will become public."

"This isn't fair! It's not enough for all of the damage they caused me." I was hysterical.

"Take the amount. I'll help you move on."

"I'm not taking this amount, Linda."

"I don't think that's a wise decision," she said.

On the contrary, I thought it was very wise for me, and I replied. "Linda, you're fired!" I hung up the phone.

I was irate. She had failed me. Now the war begins, I said to myself. To me, it was clear that Linda seemed inept at fighting the way a competent, clever lawyer should have. She was weak, short-sighted, and manipulated by these corrupt leaders of the less-than-holy Catholic Church. I reluctantly admitted that getting her name from the yellow pages was probably my biggest mistake. (Interestingly, a few years later, Linda's license to practice law was suspended indefinitely, when she withheld monies that should have gone to one of her clients.)

"What the fuck am I going to do now?"

I spent the next three months making calls, searching again for a lawyer who would represent me. This proved to be a daunting task; nevertheless, it was a road I had to travel. I became so determined to find a lawyer that I had begun just walking into any law firm, regardless of their areas of expertise, and telling them of my desperation. Each lawyer or secretary would simply tell me that they were either not interested or would get back to me. When I did receive return calls, they all rejected my case, due to their inexperience with this type of case. They considered the subject taboo.

I was feeling completely dejected, when I remembered that my ex-partner, Karl, knew an attorney named Brad Patterson. In utter desperation, I reached out to Brad who remembered me, and he agreed to meet with me. I told him my story and he expressed his complete and utter disgust. Thankfully, he said he would see what he could do for me.

A few days later, I heard back from Brad. He told me that he would co-counsel with another firm that was willing to take my case. The new, high-powered lawyers, Norman Palmer and John Whitman, would be my contacts. Our first meeting was scheduled for later that month. I was elated. They had not wasted any time in deciding to take my case. I had these attorneys in my corner. I loved it.

May 1994. I arrived with Brad at the new attorneys' office. John and Norman took me to a conference room, where we exchanged introductions. They also told me that they had heard of Jim Arnold, the diocesan attorney, and that he had a reputation for being a son of a bitch.

Then, John and Norman asked me to explain everything that had happened to me over the past few years. After listening to my story, they explained that they would immediately draft letters to Linda, my former attorney, to the diocese attorney, and to Father Gregory.

I did it! I hadn't caved to the diocese. I was excited that this high-powered law firm was on my side. It felt as if I was being represented by my own, private, well-trained army. I would love to have seen the expression on the arrogant diocesan lawyer's face when he read the letter from my new attorneys. My fantasy was that the lawyer from the diocese might have soiled his underwear.

Late May 1994. My attorney Brad sent two letters, one to my former attorney Linda, and the other to the attorney Jim Arnold at the diocese. The letter to Linda was brief; the new attorney told her that he was taking over my case and that he would like copies of all of the files she had on my case.

In the letter to the diocesan attorney, Arnold, Brad wrote, "After reviewing the case carefully, it is clear to us that Mr. Roberts has been very severely harmed by the sexual abuse inflicted upon him by Father Gregory Burgess as well as by Father Oliver. Further, it is clear that officials of the Diocese were told of Father Burgess's misconduct as early as 1986. These officials, for their own reasons, protected Father Gregory Burgess."

Brad's letter said that his office had considerable evidence to corroborate my claims. He closed his letter saying that Father

Gregory took little care to be discrete about his activities, and my attorneys believed that he would be hard pressed to deny the facts. Brad's firm was seeking $250,000 in damages.

It had been in August of 1985 when I first went to Father Oliver's office to report the abuse by Father Gregory. Father Oliver listened. Then he responded by performing oral sex on me and then walked out of the office.

Then, it was the summer of 1986 when Peter had the first of two meetings with church officials to discuss Gregory's behavior. In his first meeting, he met with Father Amos and Father Pedro from the diocese. Father Gregory was also asked to attend that meeting. He had been told that the meeting involved a vocational issue; however, when he arrived in the parking lot and saw Peter's car, Gregory drove off.

"Now what are we going to do?" Peter asked as he watched from the window as Gregory drove away.

"We'll deal with it," Father Pedro said.

Peter produced Gregory's hateful letter, in which he had told Peter that he would never become a priest in this diocese or in any other. After he read the letter, Father Pedro sighed and shook his head. "Well, it's true that Father Gregory is developing a rather bad reputation in the diocese."

"What are we going to do about this?" Peter asked.

We'll take care of this. I assure you that you have nothing to worry about," Father Pedro said. With that, the meeting came to an end.

Two months later in the fall of 1986, in a second meeting, Peter and Father Amos met with Monsignor Rayburn. The monsignor had already read the letter to Peter from Gregory. Peter spoke of his fear of Father Gregory and also repeated the accounts of Gregory's attempts to sexually seduce him.

The monsignor asked, "Can you tell me what he has done to you?"

"He's very physical—he puts his hands all over me," Peter replied. "He's always trying to kiss me and to get into my pants. He tried to undress me. He tells me that no one will ever love me like he does. He's totally inappropriate." Peter explained. Peter, who wasn't fully aware of the abuse I was going through, never mentioned how I was abused by Father Gregory.

"This is very serious," Monsignor Rayburn said. "We need to take this a step higher. We need to meet with Bishop Marcus." Marcus was in charge of the entire diocese.

Monsignor Rayburn listened carefully and said, "I assure you that nothing like this will ever happen again. Everything will be okay. This letter will not bring any harm to your priestly ambitions. In the meantime, I suggest you avoid Father Gregory."

"I'm already avoiding him," Peter responded. Peter left the brief meeting, having no reason to doubt what he'd been told.

Peter also told me that not long after his meeting, he spoke about my abuse to Father Amos. However, no action was taken against Father Gregory.

Sadly, Father Gregory was never publicly held accountable for his actions. He remained a priest for the next seven years. In fact, he was now a pastor in another parish.

June 1994. Having had no response from the diocese, my attorneys told me they had given the diocese a deadline by which to reply to their letter. They were getting more accomplished in one month than Linda had done in eight months. I was aware that the diocese knew we had knowledge of their settlement with Peter. I was also sure they must be nervous about the evidence I had in my possession—such as facts that the bishops knew about Father Gregory's behavior in 1986, when Peter first reported his abuse. The bishop also had a letter on my behalf from Father Bob, the polite priest whom I'd met while dancing at the club. The other information I could use in court was the cover-up by the diocese when they sent Peter to Rome after his psychological evaluation strongly recommended that he not be sent abroad.

A few days before the deadline my attorneys had given the diocese, a settlement was proposed by the church. They offered me $75,000 as the church's portion. Father Gregory was assessed $15,000, and Father Oliver was also assessed $15,000. The total offer was $105,000. After deducting legal fees, my personal proceeds from the settlement would come to around $75,000. There was also a verbal agreement from the bishop that they would seek to remove Father Gregory as well.

Michael Roberts

After a few hours of soul searching, I reluctantly decided to accept their offer. I was emotionally drained, so I chose to take the path of least resistance. Not only was I emotionally depleted, but I was also in debt, struggling to pay for school, to pay off credit cards, and to reduce the debt I owed to my therapist. I signed the settlement document, not really sure what I was signing.

Most of all, I needed to put this chapter of my life behind me for the sake of my own sanity. I was painfully aware that the church would be getting away with a crime. They protected a predator who molested two teenagers. Gregory should have gone to jail for his offense, but the church was protecting him and their image. These same religious leaders also knew that if this case would have been adjudicated in front of a judge or jury, it would have made for a huge media story that would have hurt the image of the church in the eyes of the public.

August 1994. The church should be pleased that the media never got wind of my story. I spent years being abused sexually and spiritually by a Catholic priest. I was also molested by a second priest. Finally, I had lost what little was left of my sense of self-worth by allowing myself to feel objectified as I earned a living as a go-go dancer in bars.

That week, I received a letter from my attorney. My case was closed. Totally closed. I realized that the mayhem was behind me. No more lawyers. No church. No priests. I would soon be receiving a check, which I could use to rebuild my life. I was free to live. Or, so I thought. I was still filled with animosity toward the Roman Catholic Church. They were simply paying me hush money.

How was I to live with the knowledge that their settling the case was strictly to protect their image? No justice was being served—no culpability. No punishment for an assailant. How does one simply erase all thoughts of the crime of rape by a priest? Can years of molestation magically be forgotten? In my psyche, how was I to bury the church's lies, deception, and cover-up? This religion's culture of insulating itself from any responsibility was unconscionable. But it was a typical ploy of the church. The playbook was successfully executed, once again, without public notice, scandal, or retribution.

October 1994. I opened an envelope from my lawyer. Right in front of me was a check in the amount of $75,000. As I sat on the edge of my bed, looking at the check, I began to cry. This is the amount it cost them to keep me from going to the police. I let them get away with these heinous acts, this scandalous cover-up. In that moment, I regretted my decision to settle out of court.

During my next conversation with Peter, he expressed his discontent that the church lied to us about removing Father Gregory. They had breached their verbal agreement to persue defrocking him.

The bishop wasn't honest with us by giving us his word that he would begin Father Gregory's removal process. The only way to defrock Gregory was for the bishop to work with the Vatican. Only the Pope can officially defrock a priest.

30

Years after my ordeal with Gregory, I discovered a most shocking revelation about an old religious doctrine. It was the concept that came out of the Middle Ages, but it appeared to hold true for some religions to this day. The doctrine, known as "mental reservation," is a form of deception, which is an outright lie, but is used in moral theology to both tell the truth and to keep secrets from those not entitled to know them.

The Spanish sixteenth-century theologian Martin de Azpilcueta believed that God heard what one says in one's own mind while humans heard only what one speaks. Therefore, a Christian's moral duty was to tell the truth to God, reserving some of that truth from human ears if it served a greater good. The doctrine was embraced by Jesuits, an order of Roman Catholics. So, according to the doctrine, one could reply, "I don't know," aloud to another human while telling the truth silently to God, believing that he was morally being honest. Any church leader could use this form of deception to save the image of the church.

I don't know if priests were relying on this doctrine in the 1980s and 1990s, but it seemed to fit my situation—the way the church lied, concealed information, and ignored me and Peter. As I continued my research over the years, in 2009, I came across a blog, Will and Testament, by William Crowley, of the BBC. He wrote:

"This idea [of mental reservation] is said to have been deployed by church leaders in order to withhold significant information, or to give an inaccurate impression. In other words, priests and bishops, it is alleged, used the category to hide behind half-truths or formulations of words which were deliberately constructed in order to give a false impression when responding to reports of clerical child abuse."

November 1994. My mother called me to say she had received a letter from Gregory. I was eager to read what Gregory had to say, so I left for my parents' house within the hour. When I arrived, I ran in, said hello, and grabbed the letter.

In his letter to my parents, Gregory stated that he'd been on administrative leave for fifteen months as a result of the unfounded, insulting allegations by me. He said that he'd been in psychotherapy for twenty-two months, and after two sessions, he and his psychiatrist came to the conclusion that I was the one with the problem. He further explained that after also seeing a neuro-psychiatrist and other mental health professionals, they had written an eleven-page evaluation that said he, was a fit priest and a normal human being. Gregory claimed that I was screwed-up when I met him, and he lamented the fact that all he'd ever done was try to help me and to be a friend. Still, he said I had become a traitor like Judas.

An eleven-page report saying that Gregory was a normal human being? Normal? He sexually assaulted me when I was seventeen. He ignored my desperate pleas to stop. He had physically hurt me when he was enraged. He gave me, an underage teenager, alcohol. He conducted a mock trial to humiliate me. He insulted, shamed, and controlled me over many years.

Fueled by his anger over my not wanting to have sex with him, he had put my life in danger with his reckless driving. He could have inflicted physical harm by hurling projectiles at me. He locked me out of the rectory on a cold frigid night without my coat. He spied on me when I showered. He listened to me when I was on the phone. He hid in my bedroom when I was trying to sleep. He stole personal possessions. He withheld food until I had sex with him.

But the section of Gregory's letter that most infuriated me was his saying that all he ever wanted to do was to help me, to be a friend. So, I must ask: did that mean that Father Gregory knew I was screwed-up when he met me, but yet he admitted to having sex with me? His letter said he wanted to help and support me. In reality, he abused and controlled me for years. His letter was pure bullshit from an accomplished bullshit artist!

A few weeks after my case was legally closed, I received a phone call from the chancery office that Bishop Marcus would like to meet with me at his residence. Reluctantly, I decided to go. I couldn't be sure what they wanted from me. I made a call to my friend Lee, the puppeteer, telling him that I would like it if he could go with me to meet the bishop. Lee was happy to go with me.

When we arrived for the meeting that evening at the bishop's private residence, we were greeted by Monsignor Terrence, whom I saw as an asshole dressed in black. The black seemed to represent the blackness of his soul; the slight trace of white showing in his collar was all that was left of his purity. My first attorney and I had met with him once before, in 1993, when he referred us to the diocesan lawyer. Monsignor Terrence had all but ignored me at that meeting and spoke only to my attorney. He showed no compassion, and basically gave us the impression that our coming to his office was a pain in his ass.

He led us to the kitchen where the bishop was seated at a table. This was the same bishop who I once saw as a religious celebrity. Now, I saw him as an arrogant man, parading as a religious figure. I had little respect for his ethics but managed to be courteous.

"Take a seat," the bishop said.

As we sat, Lee whispered in my ear, "I think it's best if we talk in the other room." Lee was concerned that this meeting might be some sort of a setup, that I was being recorded. I trusted none of these religious parasites.

"I would like to talk in the other room," I said firmly.

"The kitchen is fine," the bishop responded.

"I prefer another room."

He nodded in agreement and led us to the next room. "Michael, I would like to apologize to you for what happened."

Now, he's sorry? Was he trying to clear his guilt? I hoped this haunted him the rest of his life. He had shown no compassion for me and for other victims of abuse. I wasn't sure why I had even come to see him. Both Lee and I were uncomfortable. I didn't believe his apology was sincere—his responses seemed robotic. I wanted to leave. Fortunately, it turned out to be a surprisingly brief conversation. When I looked at Monsignor Terrence, he turned his head, not wanting to make eye contact with me.

"Thank you. It hasn't been easy for me," I responded.

"I understand. Well, I hope you'll be able to move on with your life," the bishop said.

He understands? Why didn't I tell him about the horrific details I lived with? Why didn't I get angry? Why didn't I mention that he knew about issues with Father Gregory going back to 1986? I had so many questions as to why Gregory's abuse was allowed to continue.

"I'll do my best," I replied. "Peter and I have been through hell."

The name, Peter, seemed to have struck a nerve. He seemed uncomfortable. Why might this be? First, it was my belief that Peter had a lot of "dirt" on priests in the diocese. And secondly, the bishop was likely the one who sent Peter a letter, accepting Peter's resignation from the seminary, when Peter had never resigned. I can understand why I'd struck a nerve.

"May God bless you, Michael."

I wasn't finished. I looked him straight in the eye. "You know my life was taken away from me," I said. "I spent years being abused by this man, Father Gregory, who controlled every aspect of my existence. Living in that rectory was horrific."

The bishop interrupted me. "Michael, may you grow stronger in Christ's love. I'll pray for you. God wants us to forgive those who have trespassed against us."

I was ready to trespass all over his face.

"Michael, thank you for coming over to meet with me. We'll pray for you."

The meeting was over.

The bishop and Monsignor Terrence both left the room. I knew they wanted nothing more to do with this matter. I wish I'd had the courage to tell them to sit their pious asses back down in those fucking chairs. God, I wish I had! Instead, we followed behind the bishop as he saw us to his front door.

"Michael, may you follow in Christ's love. I will be praying that you to find peace in your heart," the bishop said.

"Thank you." I replied, holding in my anger.

Lee and I drove off, amazed at their lack of real interest in what had happened to me. Obviously, they both must have been absent the day Christian charity and compassion was taught at the seminary. Lee and I felt our meeting with the holy men had been pointless.

31

Over the next few months, I still struggled with my anger at the Catholic Church. At that point, I also had come to the realization that the effects of my years of emotional trauma were not going to go away any time soon. But I did think of one thing that might help me heal. I asked my attorney to send a letter to every priest who I had met during those years, letting them know they would face punitive action if they violated young people or knew of others who did and did not report it. I provided my lawyer names and addresses.

The letters went out to those priests. Even though I was of legal age during part of the time I was being abused or was subjected to inappropriate behaviors, I felt strongly that the bishop in each diocese should be informed of the behavior of the priests within their purview. The letters accomplished my goal. I never learned whether any priests were reprimanded; however, I felt strangely vindicated when not one of the priests came forward to challenge my story. I felt empowered at knowing those priests had been made keenly aware that molestation was immoral. My hope was that the church's bishops would be more proactive in seeing that other innocents didn't become victimized.

With the Catholic Church ordeal behind me, I was free to move forward with my life. I just hoped that I would heal over time.

Over the next decade, I rekindled a relationship with Karl. I bought a dilapidated, fixer-upper, and spent a few years making renovations. Meanwhile, I chipped away at my college degree, driving one hour each way to classes.

Eventually, my relationship with Karl came to an end. The breakup, however, was less painful than the first time our partnership ended. I did, however, finish college with a bachelor of science degree in biological science. With my degree now in hand, I was able to secure a position working in biotech sales with a large company. My job afforded me the opportunity to travel to most of the major cities throughout the United States. I also still received calls for modeling jobs.

Early one evening in the latter part of 2005, I received a phone call from Bishop Reynolds, a new bishop of the diocese whom I knew little about. I was puzzled by why he was calling me more than eleven years since my case was settled. It turned out he wanted my opinion about whether Father Gregory should be defrocked.

"Michael, this is Bishop Reynolds from the diocese. I've spoken with Peter. He has adamantly petitioned me to pursue laicization against Father Gregory. I wanted to know what you thought of it."

I took a deep breath. I didn't expect this call. I was a bit shocked, to say the least.

"Well, I have tried to move on with my life as best I could. I was told by Bishop Marcus that Father Gregory was going to be defrocked back in 1994. That was eleven years ago. Why didn't this happen?"

"What do you think about Peter's position?"

Like a politician, the bishop maneuvered away from answering my question. What was he doing, using mental reservation?

I replied, "What do I think? Of course, I want him gone. At one time, I even thought I could forget about the abuse by Father Gregory, but I was lying to myself. I was in complete denial. Gregory totally decimated my late teenage years and ruined most of my twenties. I have suffered all these years, powerless to rid myself of the damaging effects of sexual and emotional abuse."

"I'm sorry to hear that."

"Can we meet at some point?"

"Yes. That would be fine."

"Thank you for your time. I'll be in touch with you very soon."

"Okay."

"Thank you again. Have a good day."

I never heard from him again. I wasn't surprised.

March 2006. Peter Sullivan, my childhood friend, went to the local newspaper, reporting to them that Father Gregory, who was removed from the diocese in 1993, had never been defrocked. The article said that, at age sixteen, Peter had been sexually abused by Father Gregory Burgess.

The article continued. "Sullivan, who settled his case out of court in 1994, claimed that part of the settlement was a verbal agreement that Father Gregory would be official defrocked. Sullivan said he was concerned when in 2005, he recently saw Father Gregory, dressed in clerical garb, signing the guest book at a funeral. Sullivan said it raised concerns in his mind as to whether Father Gregory was still functioning as a priest.

A spokesperson for the diocese said that if Father Gregory Burgess was still functioning as a priest somewhere, he would be defying a mandate from the ministry. The spokesperson went on to say that several priests had been referred to the Vatican for defrocking, but he didn't know whether Father Gregory was among them.

32

According to the Catholic Church, Father Gregory Burgess was laicized (defrocked) in 2015. He was dismissed by Pope Francis at the Vatican. The official announcement said the decision to defrock Gregory was based on the church's commitment to the Charter for the Protection of Young People. The announcement continued to say that because of the laicization, Gregory may never function in any capacity as a priest or be referred to as "Father" in writing. The Vatican's decision to defrock Gregory was made in 2014; however, a formal announcement was delayed until the period for any individual appeals had ended.

Father Gregory was defrocked at age sixty-three—nearly thirty years after I first reported the abuse to Father Oliver. The diocese removed Father Gregory in 1993. Peter and I settled our cases with the diocese in 1994. Father Gregory's case for defrocking was sent to the Vatican in Rome in 2005, and it sat there for ten years. Three priests, one monsignor, three bishops, and two Popes had taken no action for nearly three decades. Both Peter's case and mine had been overlooked, ignored, or considered irrelevant to the church for defrocking Gregory.

Tragically, my case was not unique. Years after my case was settled, I came across an article about a priest who had admitted to sexually molesting nearly 100 girls at his parish in the 1970s and 1980s. Some believed he may have abused as many as 200 little girls. The article also carried a photo of the offending priest crying. Several dozen priests, including three whom I knew, sent a letter to the publication, calling the photo "in poor taste." Their letter said the event was tragic enough without showing the priest crying.

Poor taste in showing the priest crying? What about the poor taste in molesting dozens of little girls? The priests' letter said nothing about the little girls! I couldn't fathom why dozens of priests would be upset about a photo of a priest crying who had been charged with molesting close to 100 little girls.

Reading the article made me angry. It made me realize that there would always be priests who will never understand their victims. It seems that some priests who have abused children never fully realize the innocence they destroyed.

Sadly, I have never heard of a priest who supported a victim of abuse. From the highest position in the Vatican, the Pope himself, to the small-town parish priest, secrecy triumphs over truth.

Summer 2021. Looking back over my life, I still deal with the occasional ghosts that whisper in my mind. Sometimes the flashbacks haunt me. I have various triggers—places, sounds, or smells—that can cause memories to come flooding back.

One such incident occurred a few years ago, when my friend Lee and I had finished a hike along some local trails. We decided to stop in for a sandwich at Jeremy's Kitchen. I hadn't been back there for more than thirty years. Father Gregory and I used to go there once a week for their sandwiches, made with artisan breads. I was sitting with Lee, enjoying a Reuben sandwich, when all of a sudden I was hit with a flashback of being there with Father Gregory. At first, the memories gave me a jolt, but I regained my composure.

On another day, I walked through the church where all the abuse began. I walked quietly down the aisles, and the thing that took me back in time was the smell—not an unpleasant smell, but it was just the smell I remembered from being in that church. I later learned from a psychologist that smell is the sense that will take us back in time more than any other sense. But most importantly, as I walked through the church, I didn't feel all the anger I once felt.

Similarly, one day I drove by the house, where my so-called trial was held in the basement. The memory didn't really anger me. I just felt disdain for Gregory and for his friends who gathered to humiliate me. Perhaps more than anything, I was reminded of how totally silly it was; although, at the time, it was insulting, if not traumatizing.

Once, I even drove by Father Gregory's mother's home without feeling much anguish. Another time, I saw Reggie, Father Gregory's former cohort, at a gay Pride event—he was in a booth, selling homemade crafts. As I passed his booth, I gave him a nod and walked on by with my head held high. Actually, it was at that moment that I realized that I had made progress in healing. Coming upon Reggie didn't make my heart race or send me into flashbacks. It was then that I said to myself: I fought the fight, and I won.

Some time ago, I came to realize that I will carry reminders of my emotional trauma my whole life. I can never totally erase the memories of the days when I was Father Gregory's mental prisoner. Some memories are painful. Others are less painful. I seemed to have overcome much of the pain from my past. I guess time does heal. At least, time helps. I've learned to make my past experience a part of me, but there is also a part of me that will never forget what I endured behind sacred walls.

EPILOGUE

Probably the most pressing question people have after they hear my story is: What became of Father Gregory Burgess? Information has been hard to come by, but I have been able to learn a few things. Apparently, he has kept a fairly low profile. As of 2021, Father Gregory turned seventy. Public records list him as retired. I've learned he lives with a man, in a small town, not far from where he once served as my parish priest. I don't know whether his housemate is a friend or a partner.

Father Gregory may not have had an urgent need for employment after he was put on administrative leave. Most likely, he was paid by the Catholic Church from the time he was put on leave in 1993 up until he was defrocked by the Pope of the Catholic Church in 2015.

According to Kelly E. O'Donnell, Doctor of Canon Law (JCD), "If a priest has been accused of sexual abuse but has not been defrocked and remains within the diocese obeying the bishop, canonically he should be cared for with a salary, health benefits, and retirement, depending on diocesan regulations for years of ministry. The priest may even receive a reduced salary. He may not be fully vested for full retirement if not in active ministry for the requisite amount of time."

Some people ask why Father Gregory was never charged with sex crimes and put in jail. The answer is simple: I did not go to the police. The diocese settled out of court with me. They paid me off quietly—it was a closed matter known only to me and the church officials. If I had gone to the police, criminal charges would have been filed and Father Gregory would likely have been charged with indecent assault and battery and possibly non-aggravated rape. He would probably have been convicted and sentenced to jail. He would have also had to register as a sex offender.

I settled out of court for a few reasons. One was that church officials wore me down emotionally. They took years in dealing with my case. I wanted to move on. Frankly, I was also concerned about confronting the diocesan lawyer, Jim Arnold, who played hardball every step of the way. He's the one who accused me of prostituting when I was only performing as a go-go dancer.

If my case had gone to trial, I also worried about the publicity, especially having my parents subjected to the probing questions of journalists. My parents had a good reputation and causing them shame and embarrassment was something I was not willing to do.

I also took the settlement because the money, $75,000, at the time seemed huge to me. I had never had anything close to that amount. Looking back, I have often regretted settling out of court. I took the money and protected a crime. If I had it to do over, I would go to court and teach all those bastards a lesson. I would say to them, "You fucked with the wrong person."

As for the other priests who molested me, Father Oliver has passed away. Father Roger has retired.

Another question I'm asked is: Did you not, at times, feel pleasure from the sex acts that Father Gregory performed on you? This matter is complex and somewhat difficult to explain. In short, I absolutely did not enjoy it. Yes, I would ejaculate, but felt absolutely no pleasure. To the contrary, I always felt horribly ashamed and dirty after each assault.

I remember reading an article by a trauma abuse expert. She mentioned that pleasure involves more than just a physiological response. It also must involve cognition and emotion, not just a sensory perception. She further explained that, at some point, a victim may feel hopeless and defeated. At that point, immobilization, the psyche's defense mechanism, may kick in, causing dissociation—meaning the victim essentially may not "feel present" during the traumatic event. This emotional "numbing" protects the victim psychologically and emotionally.

Michael Roberts

Further, experts explained, a victim may not have any sensory response. An abused person may be oblivious to an orgasm. If there is pleasure, or the victim perceives some excitation from the encounter, this may have a significant impact on the victim's perception of self—the victim may develop doubts about his/her participation in the assault and develop feelings of enduring shame and guilt.

Sadly, many victims of abuse carry these doubts internally for years without fully realizing what had happened to them, and it was not because they liked it. If these victims seek therapy, many of these subconscious memories will surface, and a therapist can help the abused person process the traumatic memories of the assault rationally. This allows the victim to let go of some of the guilt and, most importantly, the shame, which is probably the most destructive human emotion. Fortunately for me, I have healed some of my emotional scars through therapy.

Unfortunately, the number young people who have been victims of abuse by priests is not clear. As of May 31, 2019, information published by the United States Conference of Catholic Bishops (USCCB) indicates that the conference has counted 20,052 victims who were known to the bishops from 1950 through 2018. However, experts believe that number is markedly underestimated. Similarly, the conference had counted 7,002 clerics who have been credibly accused of sexually abusing minors during the period 1950 through June 2018. Out of the 118,184 priests during those years, 7,002 were accused of abusing children. That was just under 6 percent of priests, also considered an underestimation.

Why are these estimations thought be low? According to Mike McDonnell of Survivor's Network of those Abused by Priests (SNAP), "The church has always underreported the information about abuse by priests, and many dioceses have never reported any numbers." McDonnell is the communications manager of SNAP (www.snapnetwork.org). "In many ways, the church has valued the reputation of the priests and the church as being above that of the victims."

A survivor of priest abuse between the ages of eleven and thirteen, McDonnell says his way of coping was using alcohol. "I took my first drink of alcohol at twelve and my last at age thirty-five, when I got into recovery."

McDonnell says the average age of victims coming forward with claims of abuse is fifty-two. Why so late? Shame and guilt prevent people from sharing their stories. Signs of abuse that parents can watch for: acting out—lashing out at others, irritable moods, and depression. Other symptoms include shifts in attitudes—not caring or shutting down emotionally. Use of alcohol and or drugs is another sign. The SNAP website lists a number of resources that support victims of abuse.

Another website, bishop-accountability.org has maintained a list of priests credibly accused of abusing of young people. The website is the largest public library of information on the Catholic clergy abuse. In addition to listing priests who have been accused of abuse, the site also contains a digital collection of documents that include survivor accounts, investigative reports, and media coverage.

In 2002, nearly two decades after my ordeal, the nation's eyes were opened to the problem of priests abusing children. An investigative team of journalists from the *Boston Globe,* reported a decades-long cover up of child abuse within the Boston Archdiocese. The story shocked America. According to the journalist's findings, the Archdiocese of Boston went to extraordinary and expensive lengths to cover up the scandal.

This narrative was the premise of the movie, *Spotlight,* which chronicled the story of how, beginning in 1976, Father John Geoghan was accused of child molestation. (I later learned that approximately 130 children had been abused). Geoghan was re-assigned to several parish posts involving interaction with children, even after receiving treatment for pedophilia. The assistant district attorney told the police not to let the press get any information as to what happened. Subsequently, all evidence was suppressed, and the priest was released.

Michael Roberts

When the *Boston Globe* team was first assigned to the case, thought they were initially just investigating one priest who had been reassigned several times. Instead, they exposed a cover-up by the Boston Archdiocese which protected many priests guilty of abusing children. Cardinal Bernard Law knew about the abuses and simply chose to ignore them. Hundreds of victims suffered because of the strength and covert misdealing of the Boston Archdiocese. I mention this here, without risk of being personally liable, because it is now clearly a matter of public record.

Back in the late 90s, a number of years before the story broke about the Boston diocese, I had begun navigating uncharted territory concerning abuse by priests. I was scared, but I knew I could not stay quiet.

Since the Boston Globe piece came out, the nation has seen dozens of news stories about priests abusing children. A *Newsweek* article, from October 4, 2018, gave me additional insight about how the Catholic Church handles priests who have molested children. First, we need to understand that Canon law of the Catholic Church is the system of laws and legal principles made and enforced by the hierarchical authorities of the church.

The Newsweek article reads:

Canon law sees abuse through the lens of a priest violating his vow of celibacy, not from the perspective of harming a child. This has led bishops to interpret child sex abuse as a priest "really struggling with his sexuality" or as a "morals incident," not as a case of criminal behavior.

It requires that the bishop's first response be "pastoral," not punitive, to the priest. Punishment, which can include removing the priest's right to present himself as a priest in public and to perform the sacraments publicly, is only to be used as a last resort, when all other remedies have failed. That has led to the church failing to deal sternly and swiftly with suspected and confirmed cases of child sex abuse. Canon law encourages the bishop to wait and see if the priest will be a repeat offender. Bishops are also prevented from defrocking their own priests under Canon law.

In an article in the *Guardian* dated February 2016, reports the Catholic church is telling newly appointed bishops that it is "not necessarily" their duty to report accusations of clerical child abuse and that only victims or their families should make the decision to report abuse to police. The article continues: Tony Anatrella, who serves as a consultant to the Pontifical Council for the Family and is best known for championing views on "gender theory", the controversial belief that increasing acceptance of homosexuality in western countries is creating "serious problems" for children who are being exposed to "radical notions of sexual orientation".

I was also saddened to read a 2019 article on NBC news online mentioning that 1,700 priests and clergy from the Roman Catholic Church accused of sex abuse are unsupervised. An Associated Press investigation found that those credibly accused are now teachers, coaches, counselors and also live near playgrounds. And in their time since leaving the church, dozens have committed crimes, including sexual assault and possession of child pornography, the AP's analysis found.

The review found hundreds of priests held positions of trust, many with access to children. More than 160 continued working or volunteering in churches, including dozens in Catholic dioceses overseas and some in other denominations. Roughly 190 obtained professional licenses to work in education, medicine, social work and counseling—including seventy-six who, as of August, still had valid credentials in those fields. One person ends the story with "Tracking them is something they could have done as part of a general display of responsibility for the problem that they had helped contribute to."

I still believe however the Roman Catholic Church has thousands of files hidden away somewhere or have been destroyed. They have never been forthright or transparent with the public. This is something that goes back centuries.

The image of the church has always been the standing issue when it comes to the doctrine of mental reservation. Wikipedia defines: mental reservation (or mental equivocation) is an ethical theory and a doctrine in moral theology that recognizes the "lie of necessity." If a priest doesn't want to say the truth and doesn't want to make an

Michael Roberts

outright lie; in such circumstances, equivocal statements are generally preferred. This type of equivocation has been defined as "nonstraightforward communication...ambiguous, contradictory, tangential, obscure or even evasive." I believe the church still employs the old tactics of mental reservation and secrecy. I have seen some improvement in the last ten years to reach out to victims. But the church has a long way to go in implementing policies and outreach programs to help those abused. In my case they treated me like I was the perpetrator.

The only hope I have seen recently was in an article dated June of 2021.

Pope Francis issued the most extensive revision to Catholic Church law in four decades insisting that bishops take action against clerics who abuse minors and vulnerable adults, commit fraud or attempt to ordain women. The revision, which has been in the works since 2009, involves all of section six of the church's *Code of Canon Law,* a seven-book code of about 1,750 articles. It replaced the code approved by Pope John Paul II in 1983 and will take effect on Dec. 8. The revised section, involving about ninety articles concerning crime and punishment, incorporates many existing changes made to church law by Francis and his predecessor Benedict XVI. It introduces new categories and clearer, more specific language in an attempt to give bishops less wiggle room. In a separate accompanying document, the pope reminded bishops that they were responsible for following the letter of the law.

Looking back, I recognize that, somehow, I managed not to let my abuse destroy me. Too many victims of trauma abuse end up addicted to sex, alcohol, or drugs or even end up committing suicide. I broke the chains of shame years ago, living my life as a proud gay man. I believe that the church can be held somewhat accountable for the deaths of many gay men and women. From their lofty pulpits, many priests have promulgated the theory that the gay lifestyle is unnatural, against Christian beliefs, an abomination, and truly

301

evil. Their followers feel that they have the right to gay bash, harass and, in many cases, cause physical harm or even death to those who do not fit the moral or religious norm as the Church has defined it. These same followers reject the fact that science has proven that homosexuality is not a learned behavior; but is, in fact, an integral part of an infants' genetic markers at birth. Directly or indirectly, I believe the Church has blood on its hands.

People hold the Bible as the pillar of absolute truth. Should we stone woman in the streets for prostituting or continue to have slaves working for us? I would spend years finding contradiction and discrepancies. I struggled with the way the Bible describes nature, which is at odds with proven scientific evidence. I saw the Bible filled with violence, genocide and prejudice...a missive which, today, is often used as an excuse and permission to justify more violence and oppression. I saw the church as judgmental and irresponsible with a hierarchy more-than-willing to lie and distort the truth to protect the institution, using the doctrine of mental reservation. It became obvious to me that, in my case, it came down to two things...image and money. They concealed crimes to protect the reputation of the church. I recognized that God for me was a perception, invented by man. Perhaps the accepted concept of God was created to comfort us in our fear of mortality. My conclusion was that: if I believed in a God, He created evolution.

As a former devout Catholic, where am I today with my religious beliefs? As I mentioned earlier in the book, my faith had started to wane as the years of my abuse ticked by. Now, nearly three decades after my abuse by Father Gregory and the legal red tape I had to deal with, I consider myself spiritual, but have little respect for religion, especially the Catholic Church.

As a child, I was conditioned to fear religion. I was indoctrinated to believe what was written in the Bible. I don't blame my parents for their teachings—they were passing down only what they had been taught. I grew up hearing stories of a vengeful God who flooded the earth, drowning everyone. I heard stories about King Herod proclaiming that all male babies under the age of two should be killed. There

Michael Roberts

are scriptures about God turning people into stone. I heard sermons about the devil and his fiery hell. During communion, the priest would tell us we were drinking and eating the body of Christ. I came to believe that God could see me at all times. In my later years, I began to realize the absurdity of stories in the Bible. For example, take the story of Noah's ark. Am I to believe a 600-year-old man spent decades making the craft, built only of wood? With no steerage or propulsion, this craft was to have floated for months? Science tells us such a wooden craft would have fallen apart in shorter order. Yet, this craft was said to have carried Noah's family and thousands of animals, saving them from a global flood. What about a sufficient supply of food for the animals and a method for the disposal of animal waste?

Another contradiction: the Bible says if someone slaps you on one cheek, offer them the other. Doesn't that contradict the Bible's "eye for an eye, a tooth for a tooth"? Should we still have slaves working for us? Is God a vengeful God or a loving God? Where did God come from?

I spent years realizing that many Bible stories are at odds with proven scientific evidence. There are more than 4,000 religions on this planet. Which one, if any, is based on truth?

As for my personal life, I have been successful. As I mentioned earlier, I worked for some successful companies after graduating from college. One company became a four-million-dollar company within several years. I saved all bonuses, tax refunds, and portions of my pay, and I taught myself about investing. I made one of my biggest stock investments in the early 1990s, with a company that was not as well-known as it is today. That company was Apple Computer.

Having become financially independent, I retired in my late forties. As a result, I was able to spend a number of years traveling to places such as Australia, Brazil, Peru, and more than two dozen European countries. I traveled all over the Caribbean and had many other exciting adventures—taking a helicopter ride over a glacier in Alaska and snorkeling in the Great Barrier Reef off the coast of Australia.

I have gone hot air ballooning over Napa and Sonoma valleys in California and have meditated at Machu Picchu in Peru. One of my favorite adventures was taking a weeklong rafting trip with a group; we traveled 280 miles down the Colorado River through the Grand Canyon National Park.

Toward the end of writing this book, I was able to find my old friend Peter. This was not an easy task, but eventually we connected. He was rather shocked at seeing me the day I showed up on his doorstep, nearly thirty years later. He was happy to see me, and when I told him I was writing a book, he knew exactly what was resonating at my core: I needed to tell my story. Peter was glad to share his memories of his experience with Father Gregory.

Peter graduated from college and entered the seminary but chose to leave it after three years. He told me that, given his experience with Father Gregory and the Catholic Church, he no longer had the desire to become a priest. He worked many years for an airline, before retiring. He lives quietly with his adorable dog. He has been received into the Episcopal Church.

I also continue my friendship with Lee, the puppeteer. We have remained very close. He always encouraged me to write this book. We have traveled together, and we often spend time just watching television and laughing at nonsensical programs.

I have other wonderful friends, including Earl and Ed, whom I adore. They are a gay couple who has been together for forty-five years. Earl was always enthusiastic about me writing this book. He helped me structure and edit it. He also read many rough drafts. His help was invaluable.

Lastly, nearly eight years ago, I met a wonderful man who has taught me the real meaning of unconditional love— my partner and husband Johnathan. We were married five years ago. He also gave me the loving support and the push I needed to finish this book. And I would be remiss if I did not acknowledge the love and joy I receive daily from our three precious feline "family members."

I also want to say that I love my parents, who may not have understood the gay issue, but have loved me regardless. They have also been supportive of my marriage. I love you Mom and Dad.

Michael Roberts

Where does one begin to explain, the horrors
witnessed in a haunted house?
The bevy of ghouls, goblins and demons that lurk in
the dark shadows... these beasts and monsters
that await you around every corner, ready to create
terror and torment.
You beg and bargain with the universe for this
anguish to end. You gather all the strength you have
left to find your way to any open door to escape this
formidable place. You claw through the cobwebs of
discomfort and misery. You agonize over the voice of the
incubus that reverberates in your mind.
Your body is now tormented and molested by the
unthinkable antichrist.
You scarcely survive this ordeal, shattered in
pieces, a brokenness of oddly shaped puzzle pieces. You
maneuver through life anesthetized and paralyzed,
deeply imbedded with a surreptitious river of loathing, for
the Catholic Church.

—Michael Roberts

ABOUT THE AUTHOR

Michael Roberts graduated with a bachelor's degree in biological science. He has worked as an environmental technician, performing sampling, data collection, and monitoring of soil, vapor, and water in contaminated waste sites. This included injection of bio-enhancing, chemical products, for neutralizing contamination and increasing bacteria growth to break down petroleum.

Roberts also worked as a sales and marketing manager for a biotech company that makes custom antibodies and peptides for use in biotech and pharmaceutical research to develop drugs.

Roberts has also worked as a model in Paris, Rome, and the United States. He has appeared in television commercials and numerous print ads and catalogs. He has also done hand modeling and runway shows.

Roberts is married to his partner, Johnathan, with whom he enjoys traveling around the world. Roberts future plans include volunteer work in wildlife conservation to help save endangered species.